Loneliness and Time

By the same author

Richard Meinertzhagen: Soldier, Scientist, Spy

Loneliness and Time

The Story of British Travel Writing

Mark Cocker

Pantheon Books   New York

All rights reserved under International and Pan-American Copyright
Conventions. Published in the United States by Pantheon Books, a
division of Random House, Inc., New York. Originally published in
Great Britain as *Loneliness and Time: British Travel Writing in the Twentieth
Century* by Martin Secker & Warburg Limited, London, in 1992.

Library of Congress Cataloging-in-Publication Data

Cocker, Mark, 1959–
    Loneliness and time : the story of British travel writing / Mark
Cocker.
        p.   cm.
    Includes bibliographical references and index.
    ISBN 0-679-42242-0
    1. Travelers' writings, English—History and criticism.   2. English
prose literature—History and criticism.   3. Voyages and travels—
Historiography.   4. British—Travel—Historiography.   5. Travel in
literature.   I. Title.
PR788.T72C64   1993
828'.08—dc20   92-50775

Manufactured in the United States of America

First American Edition

Contents

List of Illustrations

The photographs are reproduced by kind permission of the following: 1, Bodleian Library, Oxford (Rhodes House Library, Meinertzhagen Diaries, vol. 40, page 160); 3 and 4, Curtis Brown Ltd, London, on behalf of Wilfred Thesiger; 5, Jane Taylor; 6, Terence Spencer; 7, C. H. Pelham-Burn; 8, Joan Eyres Monsell; 9, Curtis Brown Ltd, London, on behalf of the Estate of Lawrence Durrell. Copyright The Durrell Collection.

FOR RACHAEL ANNA

Acknowledgements

This book could not have been completed without the assistance of many people. One of my major debts of gratitude is to Douglas Botting, John Hatt, Elspeth Huxley, Norman Lewis, Geoffrey Moorhouse, Iris Portal and Wilfred Thesiger, who all kindly agreed to lengthy interviews. I also wish to thank Richard Frere, John Murray and Tim Radford for their time and willingness to speak with me.

There is also a number of friends and correspondents who provided essential information, helped secure references or generally push the project along. I especially wish to mention Alexandra Alexandri, Lesley Bryce, Dr Phillip Clancey, John Cryer, Dr Tony Hare, Mr and Mrs J. Hollis, Paul Lewis, Frank McLynn, Rodney Martins, Steve Snelling, Ann Suckling, and Jane Taylor; then the infinitely patient Dan Franklin and Andrew Lownie, my editor and agent respectively. I am also deeply grateful to the former and current literary editors of the *Daily Telegraph*, Nicholas Shakespeare and John Coldstream, who allowed me to keep abreast of many travel books appearing in the last three years.

The staff at the British Museum (Natural History), the India Office Library and the Public Records Office aided my researches into various collections of papers. I also wish to thank Miss E. Talbot-Rice of the National Army Museum and the ever courteous, ever efficient Michael Bott, Keeper of Archives at Reading University Library, for their assistance. Lastly, the excellent staff at Norwich Central Library have been invaluable to the project over a number of years.

Acknowledgements

Gerald and Rosy Crowson generously gave me accommodation and a place to write on several occasions. Gerald Crowson, with whom conversation is to travel the world, also discussed the project both in the initial stages and thoughout its development. For all of this I offer my warmest thanks.

Finally I come to the contribution of my partner Mary. She has been a tower of strength and good humour in many moments of uncertainty. One memorable occasion occurred on the banks of Loch Ness when the kind stranger, who had given us a lift on his way to a funeral, pulled away with those dark words of advice – 'Beware the clegs'. For braving the clegs and other innumerable difficulties I owe her my deepest gratitude.

We had become, with the approach of night,
once more aware of loneliness and time –
those two companions without whom no journey
can yield us anything.

Lawrence Durrell, *Bitter Lemons*

Chapter I
Stiffkey

Given the available statistics, it would seem difficult to dispute that international travel is now a fundamental experience in contemporary life, or that its social and economic importance grows almost annually. In the ten years from 1977 the number of international air passengers to and from the United Kingdom alone almost doubled. In 1987 the figure was an estimated 65,734,000. There were, in addition, 26 million sea passengers. For the British people, confined to a green and damp archipelago, abroad seems an especially significant place. Of the 7.2 million foreigners entering Greece in 1987, one in four of them had earlier crossed the English Channel. In the same year, the frontiers, harbours and airports of Spain admitted more than one in ten of the entire British nation. For the two recipient countries travel is equally critical and a cornerstone of the national economy. Their 1983 receipts from visiting foreigners were almost £700 million and over £4.6 billion respectively. The combined income from foreign visitors for the twenty-five countries of the Organization for Economic Co-operation and Development in that year exceeded $114 billion.

While the figures appear to indicate the irreducible fact of travel's international importance, the relevance of all these wandering millions to a study of travel writing is perhaps less certain. It might readily be argued that the statistics concern a phenomenon fundamentally different from and even antagonistic to what travel writers generally think of as 'travel' – the tourist industry. Though the two activities now merge imperceptibly, those considering themselves 'travellers' conventionally insist on a radical separation.

They would probably put forward the argument that, although both species are temporary migrants to foreign places, tourists seek a very specific type of habitat: an environment in which the characteristics that render a country distinct and even alien, are carefully controlled or totally eliminated. Paul Fussell in *Abroad: British Literary Travelling Between the Wars* calls this tourist habitat 'a pseudo-place'. 'Kermanshah in Iran', he adds, by way of illustration, 'is a place; the Costa del Sol' is not.[1] Only marginally less familiar than the domestic environment, pseudo-places are anonymous, uniform, comfortable, effortless and crowded. For the tourist is essentially a social animal, and the presence of fellow nationals helps increase the feelings of security and of home.

Travellers, by contrast, generally insist that their activity depends upon the absence of the familiar. It is the very otherness of the visited country that makes the journey valuable. While the tourist seeks only a more leisured version of what was left behind – according to Fussell, 'the security of pure cliché' – travellers thrive on the alien, the unexpected, even the uncomfortable and challenging.[2] In fact, the more difficult the journey and the more circumstances are stacked against them, generally the fuller the travel experience. This element of opposition, of having to react to the places and people encountered, is at the heart of travel. The constant need to refocus and recreate permits a sense of renewal and an almost endless impression of freedom.

The dialogue between the individual and her or his surroundings is part of the traveller's deep self-consciousness, which provides perhaps the litmus test in the question of tourist/traveller identities. For the former, self-recognition as one or the other would never seriously arise. The status of tourist brings with it no feeling of exclusivity. As Fussell remarks, 'Tourism is egalitarian or it is nothing'.[3] For travellers, however, a deep feeling of being set apart, and a jealous scrutiny of anyone that might claim kinship are virtually inseparable from their sense of identity. Each new member to the club must prove his or her credentials, and the history of exploration and travel is littered with their disputes.

English Arabists like Harry St John Philby, denounced as an elaborate fiction (possibly with some justification) the 1862–3 crossing of Arabia by William Gifford Palgrave.[4] When Henry

Morton Stanley returned from Central Africa in 1872 with news of his rendezvous with the missionary David Livingstone on the shores of Lake Tanganyika, fellow African explorer James Grant preferred to disbelieve him. So too did the president of the Royal Geographical Society, Sir Henry Rawlinson. John Hanning Speke, discoverer of the Nile source for Europeans, and his erstwhile friend and companion, Richard Burton, were involved in a six-year vendetta that only ended when the former shot himself – a death possibly precipitated by their bitter dispute. After the two intrepids, Eric Bailey and Henry Morshead, foot-slogged out of Tibet in 1913 with the solution to what one traveller had called 'for fifty years the great romance of geography', another RGS ex-president, Sir Thomas Holdich, took the same sceptical line as his predecessor had with Stanley.[5] 'I am just re-reading Gertrude Bell's *Syria*', wrote Freya Stark in her diary of 6 January 1929, 'and comparing her route with ours'.

> She however travelled with three baggage mules, two tents, and three servants: so I consider we were the more adventurous. She also says that the water in the Jebel Druse 'is undrinkable by European standards', so I suppose our standard cannot be European.[6]

Such remarks are a perfect example of the travel-class consciousness common amongst the British. So too are the denunciations of his co-religionists made by the scholar, aesthete and travel writer Robert Byron:

> these modern travellers, these overgrown prefects and pseudo-scientific bores despatched by congregations of extinguished officials to see if sand-dunes sing and snow is cold. Unlimited money, every kind of official influence support them; they penetrate the furthest recesses of the globe; and beyond ascertaining that sand dunes do sing and snow is cold, what do they observe to enlarge the human mind?
> Nothing.[7]

The issues which separate one traveller from another need not be the burning controversies of geography, nor fundamental differences of approach. For a travel journalist on the weekend supplement of a national newspaper, what allows her to feel a cut above her fellow Europeans visiting the kasbahs of Marrakesh is a simple matter of 120 hours.

> It is possible to 'do' Marrakesh in less than two days [writes the journalist]. Many tour groups do and I timed their sight-seeing. It's four-minutes per museum floor, half an hour in Djemaa el Fna (less for those scared of pickpockets and dirt), one hour round the city walls in a carriage at trotting pace and as much time in the souks as it takes to buy a rug, a leather coat, and some fake Berber jewellery.
>
> With a week to loaf around the town I had the luxury of time to get lost – not difficult in the souks . . . I drank mint tea in the carpet shops . . . I tried on buttersoft leather jackets and tried out 'designer bags' . . . I fingered heavy silver and amber necklaces with starting prices of £200 but I did not have the patience or the energy to haggle down the price.[8]

The moral of the piece is plain. The others (who are not travellers at all, but tourists) are impercipient fools who rush round seeing nothing, permitting themselves to be swindled by cheats, and entertaining groundless fears of robbery or disease. True travellers, by contrast, take their time (at least, they take seven rather than two days). They are carefree, adrift on serendipitous adventures. They get on terms with the locals. They know the genuine article and its value when they see it, and they eschew souvenir hunting as the mindless pursuit of the tourist.

It is characteristic of the vehement individualism of the travel constituency that its vehicle for literary expression is a work invariably narrated in the first person singular. The travel book, its most common generic title, is traditionally a non-fictional account of the author's journey, and has a mixed cultural pedigree. Marco Polo's *Il milione* and the *Rihlah* of Polo's Arab contemporary, Ibn Batuta, both had considerable impact on their respective medieval societies. More recent British works such as Robert Louis Stevenson's *Travels with a Donkey in the Cevennes* and T. E. Lawrence's *Seven Pillars of Wisdom* are considered literary classics and enjoy perennial popularity.. Many writers of the twentieth century, prominent for their achievements in other genres, have also thought the travel book a sufficiently challenging and valid literary form to attempt it themselves. These include W. H. Auden, Lawrence Durrell, William Golding, Graham Greene, Aldous Huxley, D. H. Lawrence, V. S. Naipaul, Paul Theroux and Evelyn Waugh. Other authors – Bruce Chatwin, Norman Douglas, Patrick Leigh Fermor, Norman Lewis, Geoffrey Moorhouse, Jan Morris, Dervla Murphy, Eric Newby, Jonathan Raban, Freya Stark, Colin Thubron, Laurens van der Post, Gavin Young – have achieved international reputations solely or largely as a result of their travel books. Major national newspapers, journals and magazines devote considerable space to reviewing travel literature. Many publishers also give it some priority and about fifty in Britain claim to publish the genre. Hundreds of new titles appear each year. In British bookshops these are often allocated more space than poetry.

Despite the travel book's longevity and its recurrent popularity, when measured by other criteria its cultural status is far less certain. Unlike drama, poetry or the novel, it is almost never if ever studied in a formal context. It is taught neither in schools nor in higher education. One can complete a further degree on the most obscure novelists or poets; academic institutions even have lecturers and tutors in the tourist industry, but the literature of foreign places is apparently a non-subject. In the *Encyclopaedia Britannica* it is tackled in an essay absorbing half a page, which opens with the sentence: 'The literature of travel has declined in quality in the age when travel has become most common – the present'.[9] According to the *Oxford Companion to English Literature* it is not even worth a single line entry.

The reasons for this anomalous status possibly lie in its history. The domain of the travel author up until the end of the nineteenth century was almost exclusively the events of real life. The standard plot was an actual journey through an authentic foreign setting. The idea that the travel book was a work dealing with real facts – an impression often confirmed by index, footnotes and bibliography

– rather than an imaginary world, has led to a perception of it as a literature closely associated with geography or history or some other scientific discipline. In the golden age of exploration that attitude was, of course, frequently quite justified. And what helped compound this traditional view of the genre were the dual, and often conflicting, loyalties of one who was both traveller and author. Frequently at pains to establish credentials in the first role rather than the second, the writer was often forced into the most restricted form of narrative. The only criterion to influence composition of the travel book was to recreate the exact temporal sequence of observations and experiences during the travels themselves. Complete fidelity to the facts was seen as the best way to confirm the discoveries, authenticity and often the rigours of the voyage, but it is a method that seldom resulted in anything resembling art.

The classic Victorian travel book was a brisk, uncomplicated stream of empirical data fixed in a semi-autobiographical matrix. Primarily it described, explained, mapped and illuminated an unknown terrain. Its purpose and value were educational, and authors like Richard Burton, David Livingstone and Henry Stanley carried it to its ultimate conclusion. Almost all of their works are rich in information, minutely detailed, extremely long and in parts remarkably dull. Of Burton's twenty-five travel narratives, few were less than 500 pages; half of them were 800 pages long. Stanley was equally prolix. His six works of travel amount to a remarkable 3,500 pages.

Livingstone's *Missionary Travels*, a popular and important work, was largely devoted to a four-year period wandering in southern Africa. The 145 years that separate us from Livingstone's time are an almost insurmountable barrier to a full understanding of his book. The 600 closely printed pages knit together a confusing skein of African chiefs, their relatives, medicine men and their people. In total the author drew in fifty-nine different tribes, whose remarkably similar names – the Bamangwato, the Balonda, Bamopela, Bambiri, the Bango, Banajoa, Banyai, Barolongo, Baroro and Barotse are a small sample – occur and recur to tax the memory to the limit. And amongst this catalogue, Livingstone introduced a stream of distances, measurements, geographical coordinates and features, ethnographic observations and biological data. To glean the contents of *Missionary Travels* completely would require weeks of additional research.

Another Scotsman, Eric Bailey, was an author of travel books in much the same Victorian mould. Like Livingstone, he was also celebrated for his major journeys of exploration. Even before he was thirty he had undertaken an expedition of sufficient merit to win one of the Royal Geographical Society's medals – the Gill Memorial. Within eight years the RGS and its Scottish counterpart had bestowed their highest honours upon him. Fellow traveller and botanist, Frank Kingdon Ward, considered Bailey 'the most notable pioneer explorer' of his century;[10] while an obituarist felt that 'In its diversity of adventure his career as soldier, explorer, linguist, secret agent and diplomatist can be compared with that of Sir Richard Burton'.[11] In the decade following Bailey's death, his biographer recalled the hushed tones in which he once murmured his subject's name. 'To me,' he wrote, 'Bailey was a legend, a hero from another age, a combination of John Speke, Alexander Burnes and Richard Hannay'.[12]

Although Livingstone and Bailey might each have produced books that contained the adventures of an intrepid explorer, and while these works were both of classically Victorian stamp, there was one fundamental difference between their writings. *Missionary Travels* was published in 1857, twenty years into Victoria's reign. Bailey's last and most popular work, however, *No Passport to Tibet*, did not appear until exactly a century later. That hundred-year interval between the two perhaps provides one clue to the travel book's currently ambiguous status.

While some authors like Bailey continued in the same vein as their nineteenth-century forebears, others broke free of these traditions – a change that had something to do with the Victorians' unsustainable use of the resources. They had so thoroughly completed their geographical surveys that the regions on which one might have reported entirely new information were simply running out. Sometimes, however, the focus ceased to be the novelty of the data, and became the manner of its presentation. Retaining its foreign setting, the travel book could become a polished work of scholarship or memoir, or both. Even its status as

7

non-fictional writing has come under review. Authors have felt at liberty to reorder the sequence of their travel experiences, or to interpret events in the loosest and most imaginative fashion, or to substitute a deeply personal enquiry for the conventionally random stream of external facts. At times they have even thought it more appropriate to move off into pure invention. In fact, some travel books in the second half of this century have exploited many of the devices and displayed all the artistry conventionally associated with the novel or poetry. An author like Patrick Leigh Fermor, for example, in the composition of a single work, could agonise for years over the *mot juste*.

This enormous extension of style, content and intention in travel books has tended to confuse. The very fact that in 1957, Eric Bailey could produce a book so closely resembling its Victorian predecessors, and publish it less than twelve months before the appearance of Fermor's poetic masterpiece *Mani*, demonstrates the enormous elasticity and imprecision of the 'travel book' label. People have not known how to treat the genre because it is difficult to say exactly what it is.

Eric Bailey's writings confirm that other principal reason for the anomalous status of the travel book today. An explorer of great ability and courage he might have been; he was, nevertheless, a writer of little merit – an order of achievement common amongst travel authors. The three published works on the most important of his travels – *China–Tibet–Assam* (1945), *Mission to Tashkent* (1946), and *No Passport to Tibet* (1957) – are now almost completely neglected. Although his agent wrote, on receipt of the manuscript for the first, that there was 'red-hot incident in every line',[13] Bailey's reviewers were not quite so enthusiastic. *The Observer* commented on his 'austere staccato style';[14] the *News Chronicle* noted the 'halting detailed pedestrian tempo of the Bailey narrative'.[15]

To make matters worse, the author was an 'invincibly modest' character.[16] Casual acquaintances, unfamiliar with his life story, would learn nothing of his past from the man himself. A desperate inability to communicate was noted by a close friend for many years; while a relative by marriage, when confronted by the great man of adventure, could only remark on what a colossal bore he seemed.[17] Even his admiring biographer was forced to concede that in conversation Bailey was sometimes slow to get going and given to wandering. Ironically, it was his modesty, his capacity to blend into the background and remain unnoticed that had enabled him to penetrate to foreign parts, where a more forthright figure would have failed. On the printed page, however, his personal reticence often made for a subdued narrative.

No matter how undistinguished Bailey's travel works might be, both they and their forgotten author are still worthy of consideration. Part of this interest derives from the fact that he represents, in many ways, the end of an era. Sir Olaf Caroe, the Governor of the North-West Frontier Province at the time of Indian independence, considered Bailey 'the greatest explorer and geographically the most distinguished officer of the Indian Political Service during the last half-century of its existence'. 'In some respects', Caroe suggested, his travels 'were even more daring and further from the beaten track' than those of Britain's great Asiatic explorer of the nineteenth century, Francis Younghusband.[18] A factor that tended to accentuate his status as the last member of a dying breed was the thirty-five-year interval which, on average, separated his books from the journeys they describe. That he had delayed publishing an account for such a long period, and that in his writings he had clung so tenaciously to the world he had enjoyed as a young soldier, make them virtually imperial relics in a period of colonial decline. Yet his story provides valuable insights into a full range of goals, preoccupations and assumptions that were the shared background for almost two centuries of British and European exploration. Moreover, Bailey is not truly just a figure from the past, 'a hero from another age', for he typifies both the travellers of the Victorian period, and also a type who has persisted even until today. One might say that he represents, therefore, almost an entire tradition of travel writing.

When starting to consider the man, his books and their relevance to the travel genre, perhaps the most important place to begin is not with an account of his great Asiatic journeys, but at the Norfolk village and the country home where he retired and died aged eighty-five. Warborough House, a large, Georgian building screened by its flint-faced perimeter wall and lines of mature beech and evergreen oak, stands at the heart of the small coastal village of Stiffkey. It was Bailey's home for his final fifteen years until April 1967 – a place in which he grew old, immobile and eventually senile. Yet, even during Bailey's decline his house would have conveyed the man of action and adventure. Its solid, comfortable and spacious interior – with its orientalist's collection of books, its mahogany cabinets of preserved butterflies, natural history specimens, mounted game trophies, its Asiatic textiles and souvenirs – would have exhaled the atmosphere of the Himalaya. Yet Warborough reveals something of more than just a single occupant.

The house's generous size and commanding position within an English village of about 400 souls suggest the solid middle-class wealth that lay behind the journeys not only of Eric Bailey but entire generations of British adventurers. Until the middle of this century, travel, both as an activity and a literature, was largely the preserve of the social stratum to which Bailey belonged. Those very men and women whose names adorned the book-covers in his own library would have once sat down to write them in studies and in houses exactly like Warborough itself. It was this social environment from which emerged such archetypal travel works as Burton's *The Personal Narrative of a Pilgrimage to El Medinah and Mecca* or Samuel Baker's *The Albert N'Yanza, Great Basin of the Nile*, or Speke's *Journal of the Discovery of the Source of the Nile*.

If Warborough offers clues to the kind of people who travelled, it also suggests the cultural background which allowed them to do so. Through Bailey's medals and awards, or the framed photographs of the great occasions in his life, even the carefully preserved ceremonial costumes he would then have worn, it would have been possible to map out the career history of its distinguished occupant – a career that was absolutely typical of the professional lives of his community. Elder son of Lieutenant-Colonel Frederick Bailey and Florence Marshman, Frederick Marshman Bailey – always known as Eric – was educated at Wellington and Sandhurst, before he became an Indian Army officer like his father. His final posts in the mid 1930s, as Resident in Kashmir then Nepal, were the apex of a life spent in the service of the British empire. Bailey's class status and automatically elevated position in an overseas administration would have given him entry into an entire society for which foreign travel was a fundamental experience. It was in this milieu that Bailey's own travel ambitions would have been aroused, and through these social relations that he would have obtained his first opportunities to fulfil them.

Warborough provides further measure of this type of travel experience. Set just beneath the hill-top on the northern slope of the River Stiffkey, the house towers above most of the other properties in the village. It is also one of Stiffkey's largest buildings. That raised position and comparative largeness confirmed the social hierarchy that existed in Bailey's Stiffkey. But more than this, Warborough's dimensions were a scale by which its famous occupant would have measured himself and those he encountered, both in the domestic environment and whenever he travelled abroad. The house conveys in the most visual manner something about the assumed superiorities on which an imperial agent like Bailey would have operated, and even on which an imperialist age is founded. In a sense, Warborough symbolises a whole gamut of attitudes that informed its owner's encounters with foreign places and their inhabitants, and which helped shape the way he would interpret those experiences. And when Bailey came to produce a written record of his travels, Warborough was a permanent reminder of the community with which he identified and then sought to communicate.

If one moves outside the rectangular brick columns that flank the driveway to Bailey's final home one encounters a landscape of wider significance to both travellers and the travel genre. Looking south from Warborough's gate one can see, across the pantiled roofs of Stiffkey's flint cottages, the steeply sloped fields on the other side of the narrow valley. The ridges of those hills opposite are no more than forty metres above sea-level. Yet they are crowned with narrow belts of oak woodland that create a skyline which at times is barely five hundred metres from the observer. Such a short distance is completely uncharacteristic in this county. For the quintessential Norfolk scene is a softly rolling ploughland, whose horizons often seem only a few degrees above the horizontal. In this typical setting one is made aware, not so much of the earth rising upwards, as of a vast skyscape descending outwards to meet it. Standing in the Norfolk countryside can seem, at times, like being on the deck of a ship. In Stiffkey, however, one has an unusual sensation of confinement, of being in intimate contact with the encircling landscape. While this can seem unrepresentative of the county, oddly, one could imagine the village in almost any other part of Britain – in Devon, for example, or Somerset, or Shropshire, Northumberland, or perhaps Dumfriesshire.

In summer, before the fields turn straw-coloured and dry, that view to the south of Warborough, with its deciduous woodland and its permanent grazing meadows, is dominated by a colour that is dark, full-blown and gravid. It is this life-bearing green which is one ingredient in Stiffkey's powerful atmosphere of harnessed fertility, of a landscape coaxed through centuries of husbandry into a mild generosity. Even in winter, when this entire north-facing coastline can be subjected to powerful Arctic winds, it appears tranquil. As one walks to the villages either side of Stiffkey the gales come ploughing across the bare, flint-strewn fields and batter at the hawthorn hedges, so that many of them have assumed a permanent southerly bow. Yet Stiffkey itself is contained in its own micro-climate and, ducked down in the shallow vale, it remains undisturbed. This physiographic and climatic moderation is deeply congenial to human residence. It's hardly surprising that a settlement on the site predates the Battle of Hastings, and that its entailment to William the Conqueror was enshrined in the Domesday Book. Stiffkey is in many ways an archetypal example of the British landscape – a landscape that is central to an understanding of travel and travel writing.

From the wader-probed silts at the lowest tide-edge to the highest point in the land – a mere 1,344 metres at the peak of Ben Nevis – almost every square centimetre of the country's 24.5 million hectares features on the title deeds of one landowner or another. Britain is one of the most humanised countries on earth, without any appreciable area of true wilderness, except perhaps its north-westernmost extremities. Its national parks do not preserve populations of dangerous animals or forbidding inhuman habitats, but styles of vernacular architecture and traditional methods of farming. Its medieval wildwood, until the late Middle Ages a metaphor for a Dionysiac preconscious realm, is now confined to fragments that are bounded by roads and expanses of ploughland. Britain is a country divided, sub-divided and rationalised by a geometry of hedges, walls and country lanes. Those elevations called mountains in this country would be mere foothills anywhere else. The United Kingdom has no impenetrable swamps, no deltas, no desert and no jungles; its most famous forest is a semi-wooded area roamed by feral ponies and day-trippers in cars. There are no glaciers, no permanent ice, no volcanoes, no earthquakes, epidemics, malaria, sudden incurable fevers, rabies, alligators, no encircling homicidal sharks, deadly spiders, scorpions or jiggers. Its single venomous snake is a creature that has accounted for fewer casualties than the honey bee. Its most fearsome carnivore is the wild cat – a creature weighing no more than a moderate bag of potatoes. The last potentially dangerous animal, the wolf, was exterminated more than 250 years ago and probably never caused a single human fatality.

The national climate is equable, without extremes of hot or cold; the summers are cool, the winters mild. Except for north-western districts, few areas know anything but moderate rainfall. There are no hurricanes, tornadoes, typhoons or sudden, violent rains. A drought is a time when the populace might temporarily refrain from using the lawn-sprinkler. A single night of strong winds would once have been a national disaster; now it is a national event, commemorated in books and films. A major surge tide almost half a century ago is a drama sufficient to animate a lifetime of anecdote.

The sheer domesticity of the national landscape lies behind a decision which all travellers have made. It is also perhaps the one issue on which such a litigious assembly has unanimously agreed: the need to depart. Whatever it is that lured them away, it was something they felt this country was unable to offer. Britain is virtually the antithesis of all that travel has meant to this wandering community. Certainly, their books have derived a good deal of their meaning in reaction to it. Yet, in a sense, the enduring, stable and comforting greenness of Britain is as necessary to the travel book as the exotic otherness of foreign parts. For without that implied background monotone, there could be little appreciation of the dramatic colours overseas. Without the very predictability of home, there could be no sense of the thrill and adventure of abroad.

There is an additional facet to this process of reaction that for some travellers has supplied the experience with a great deal of its importance, and which has informed many of the travel works discussed later in this book. It has less to do with the sanitised condition of the external physical landscape, than with the traveller's feeling of internal confinement. While it might not have been something that a man like Eric Bailey would have considered central to his own motives, it played its part even in his travels. Moreover, the small village of Stiffkey and the career of one if its inhabitants provide classic illustration of the issue in question.

Only a few metres away from the medieval church where Bailey's own funeral took place in April 1967 are the remains of Stiffkey's other famous resident. While the perimeter kerb encircling this man's grave carries a seventeen-word legend that appears as clear today as when first laid more than half a century ago, the flower vase it encloses is empty, and the white stone cross is coated in green and yellow lichens. The whole has an atmosphere of simplicity and of quiet neglect. At the peak of his celebrity, however, the man laid to rest here would have been familiar to virtually every household in the country. Even the nature of his untimely death – he had been mauled by a ferocious lion– seemed a classic melodrama worthy perhaps of the most famous and intrepid explorer.

The funeral too had about it that element of theatre which had characterised much of his later career. On the day of interment in August 1937, what had been intended as a simple parochial matter escalated into a public event. Local bus companies brought in coachloads of holidaymakers from surrounding towns. The assembled crowds were estimated at 2,000–3,000. Stiffkey's narrow lanes were so choked with cars that the police had to be drafted in to deal with the bottleneck, and there were so many people pressing into the small village church that the doors had to be locked to allow the service to continue. Afterwards, as the coffin was being lowered into the ground, an aeroplane circled overhead, presumably as a sort of final salute, while the crowds filed towards the graveside to pay their respects.[19] No doubt, for many of these, standing before that rectangle of freshly turned earth smothered in wreaths was a moment of curiously mixed emotions. For the man they had come to commemorate had not achieved fame for any deeds of foreign adventure, despite the tragic drama of his end, but as the butt of bawdy music-hall jokes and as the subject of titillating stories in newspapers like the *News of the World*. It was sexual scandal that had propelled Harold Davidson into five years of notoriety and which had eventually led to the extraordinary manner of his dying.

Although he had been the rector at Stiffkey for more than a quarter of a century, Davidson, a former stage entertainer, spent six days out of every seven amongst the lowlife of Soho and backstage in the theatres of London's West End. There he focused his efforts on the young females who had gravitated towards the capital and the hope of a successful stage career. The rector felt that, in an atmosphere of disillusionment and poverty, these vulnerable teenagers could slip into physical and moral decline. It was his self-appointed task to save them from such a fall. Davidson's missionary efforts included finding and paying for the girls' lodgings, or helping them into paid stage rôles through his numerous theatrical contacts. He even accompanied a number of them to France, with the intention of securing them domestic service in Parisian households.

After years of neglecting his parish duties, the vicar became the subject of complaints and was eventually accused of impropriety. The bishop of Norwich had him followed by private detectives, and in 1932 these eventually produced the evidence to bring Davidson before the Consistory Court in Westminster on five charges of moral misconduct. These hearings were a tragi-comic affair, at the centre of which was the sad, confused figure of Davidson himself. He attempted to liken his association with the prostitutes of Soho to that of Jesus with penitent sinners like Mary Magdalene. Most of the scores of young actresses, prostitutes, landladies and waitresses that passed before the court also wished to endorse this image of the rector. Unfortunately the chancellor of the diocese trying the case was more interested in the ambiguous photograph featuring Davidson and a scantily clad nymphette, and the testimony of the eighteen-year-old Barbara Harris, who accused him of persistent sexual harassment. After six weeks, the court found him guilty and Davidson was stripped of his ecclesiastical offices.

Thus began the vicar's five-year effort to clear his name and bring his case to public attention. One of his methods was to appear in a barrel on Blackpool's Golden Mile, where punters paid twopence to see and hear his lectures. Another of his attention-grabbing performances involved him lying down in a glass cage while an automated devil prodded him with a fork. Finally he was an attraction in an amusement park in Skegness, where he appeared as a modern Daniel in the lion's den. This continued until the fateful night in July 1937, when he tripped over in the cage and Freddie the lion mauled him and broke his neck.[20]

What is so interesting about Davidson's story is not the man's racy double life on the backstreets of London, which was largely a fiction, nor the circumstances of his demise, which now seems deeply pathetic, but the prurient fascination that it aroused amongst an entire nation. Fleet Street editors of the 1930s had a field day with the randy rector of Stiffkey. As one biographer noted, Davidson's tale had all the necessary ingredients to chase Adolf Hitler, the great slump and Britain's record unemployment from the headlines. Typical of the fantasies genuinely entertained was the belief that Davidson's trips to Paris to find each of his young wards a post cleaning French pots, were really secret missions on behalf of the white slave trade, the rector bringing fresh English supplies for Parisian bordellos.[21]

It is a measure of the extreme prudery then current in British society that the newspapers covering the case avoided all overtly sexual language. In reporting the testimony of one witness *The Times* even eliminated 'kisses and caresses'.[22] For many journalists, the word 'intimacy' served as a suitably innocuous blanket to cover up all grades of sexual relations, including rape. 'Connection' was another synonym that drained intercourse of all its sexual overtones, placing it on roughly the same level as pushing a plug into a socket. Condoms were disguised as 'preservatives'. To the delicate sensibilities of the chancellor of the diocese even this alternative seemed too much; he thus referred to them in his notes as 'French LL', neatly converting them into a kind of language doctorate.[23] However much the media felt obliged to change the language, they persisted in their coverage, and in doing so they performed a double function. As they followed the affairs of Stiffkey's naughty vicar

16

they could indulge society's appetite for sexual titillation. Yet, at the same time, it could be justified as the public exposure of corruption. Simultaneously, the nation could indulge its fantasies and condemn them all in one neat turn.

Harold Davidson was not a traveller (had he been, he might well have avoided the painful years of notoriety). Yet his story does contain much of relevance to the subject. Just as Stiffkey reveals a physical landscape central to an understanding of British travel, so does the experience of Stiffkey's fallen vicar disclose a social, moral and intellectual background against which travel, both as an activity and literature, has often taken place. It was in response to this kind of moral confinement that some travellers came to view abroad as an increasingly attractive alternative. In a sense, travel was a joyous flight from Davidson's life in a barrel or his hellish imprisonment with an automated devil.

Even if moral condemnation did not impel their excursions, it certainly made their travels seem all the richer, and it informed a number of their books. It was the perceived inhibitions in British society that go some way to explain the wanderings of figures like Sir Richard Burton, Norman Douglas, Harry St John Philby, Robert Byron or Gavin Maxwell, and even the literary exile of poets like D. H. Lawrence and Lawrence Durrell. One of the central dramas of Burton's later life, for example, was his urge, despite the constant risk of prosecution, to 'bring to the West the sexual wisdom of the East', through his translation and private publication of Oriental erotica.[24] To a man like Maxwell the more open acceptance of homosexuality amongst North African countries would have meant the possibility of self-expression and fulfilment that he might never have known in his native Scotland. Yet it was not merely the fact that the moral horizons were wider overseas. The social constraints on Hindu India or Muslim Morocco might have been as great (if not greater) as those on Britain. But these applied in each case to the citizen not the visitor. The latter could remain within a community, could experience and enjoy it, but need not ultimately feel bound by its rules.

Moral confinement and sexual escape form a recurrent theme in the lives and literature of travellers, but they are not the exclusive motive. They are merely one facet of a great dialectic between home and abroad, which is at the heart of the travel experience, and which helps explain the personalities of a number of prominent travellers. This process of opposites embraces a multitude of intellectual, social, political, moral and familial issues. In fact, it is a process almost without limits. Some travellers, for instance, have railed, not at British rigidity, but its moral and spiritual laxity. As Jonathan Raban noted in the writings of those Britons who, like T. E. Lawrence, braved the hell of Arabian deserts – they loved its nomadic Bedu 'for his poverty, his spiritual leanness, his ignorance of the "soft" life from which they themselves were on the run'.

> In his desert they found a perfect theatre for the enactment
> of a heroic drama of their own – a drama whose secret
> subject was not really the desert at all but the decadent life
> of the London drawing-room.[25]

Whether Britain actually was soft and enervated, as Lawrence might have thought it to be, or bigoted and repressed, as a man like Burton saw it, is not really important to an understanding of travel and travel literature. The key issue is that, in the interior landscape of the traveller, Britain seemed to represent, and to place on his or her experience, some kind of limitation. This applies equally to their interpretation of foreign places. Whatever it was they claimed to find overseas, whatever it was which seemed more fully expressed in foreign society, is really only the detail. The central, unifying principle in travel books is that abroad is always a metaphysical blank sheet on which the traveller could write and rewrite the story, as he or she would wish it to be.

Chapter II
The Hatter

Although Lieutenant-Colonel Frederick Marshman Bailey is now largely a forgotten figure, there are portions of his legend that might perhaps have been expected to last. One of these was his extraordinary experience in Soviet Central Asia at the close of the First World War. Recalled from Persia in March 1918, Bailey headed a small British delegation across the Pamirs to Tashkent. His object was to try to establish cordial relations with the recently installed communist administration. With an inimitable sense of timing, however, the military authorities had allowed him to reach the city and present himself to a hyper-suspicious Bolshevik government, a week after British forces invaded Russian Transcaspia. As a consequence the Soviets refused to recognise his diplomatic status and accused him of espionage.

Following threats to his life Bailey went into hiding in a series of brilliant disguises, and after twelve months made a dramatic escape across the Transcaspian desert to Persia. An element of this plan had involved his recruitment by the Soviet counter-espionage service under the alias of an Albanian clerk, Joseph Kastamuni. To create the appearance of a Serbian uniform for the purposes of his faked passport photograph, Bailey ripped the shoulder straps off an Austrian tunic, turned his peaked cap the wrong way round and pasted on a simulated badge with apricot conserve.[1] His task, as one of their spies, was to travel to the semi-independent province of Bokhara and communicate all information concerning the elusive English secret agent, Colonel Bailey.[2]

On his eventual return to London in 1920 he was lionised as a hero. King George V received him at Buckingham Palace. His exploits made the front pages of the newspapers. To crown the romance, in the following year he won the hand of Irma Hepburn, the only daughter of the second Lord Cozens-Hardy. With time and repetition his legend metamorphosed. He was the English secret agent the Soviets had asked to capture himself.

What had originally led to this dangerous assignment in Tashkent was Bailey's reputation amongst Indian government circles as a solo explorer of immense courage and resource. Born in February 1882, he had received an education typical of India's military caste. Following the early career pattern of his father, who had later become head of the Forestry Survey Department and then a lecturer at Edinburgh University, Frederick junior went from Wellington to Sandhurst and a commission in the Bengal Lancers. An early interest in India's northern frontier prompted a transfer to the Sikh Pioneers and a place on a military expedition to the Tibetan capital Lhasa in 1903, under the command of Colonel Francis Younghusband. Bailey had a gift for oriental languages and this, coupled with his physical resourcefulness, allowed him to shine at an early stage. Following Younghusband's successful negotiation of a treaty with the Tibetans, the young explorer was given the job of reconnoitring trade routes between India and Tibet. Thus followed a post as trade agent at Gyantse in the south of the country, where he achieved a high degree of fluency in its complex and difficult language.

Bailey's tall lean frame, spare features and fussy Hitler-like moustache gave him a deeply conventional appearance that helped disguise a fascinating streak of eccentricity. His gift for the unpredictable earned him a reputation for madness and his lifelong nickname – the Hatter. An interest in big-game hunting led the teenage subaltern into some early adventures. A typical anecdote concerned the first tiger that he shot with friends in southern India. After bagging the cat from a treetop perch, the group descended to examine their prize. Excited by the achievement, Bailey twisted the creature's tail and made noises like a barrel organ as the others danced round the corpse whooping. All frolics ended abruptly when the animal returned from the dead and stood up growling.[3]

As his career progressed Bailey cast around for larger and more serious projects in which to satisfy his love of adventure. Following long and unbroken service in Tibet between 1904–1909, he found his opportunity in a period of leave that had accumulated to two years. Months before his designated date of return he had secured permission to travel back to India overland. In January 1911 he set off for Moscow and from there continued on the trans-Siberian railway to Beijing. By rail and boat he then made his way south to the Chinese province of Sichuan, which lay almost directly north of India's easternmost province, Assam. Ignoring the more direct route prescribed by the Chinese military authorities, Bailey finally struck out in a south-westerly direction for his principal objective in eastern Tibet.

As a consequence of its dense forests and hostile hill tribes, the northern marches of Assam and beyond had long been *terra incognita* to the British administrators in India. It was also, for reasons not unconnected, a major focus for geographical speculation, which centred on the three large rivers that drained the area – the Lohit, Dibong and Dihang. Converging on the plains of Assam, these eventually formed one of India's great drainage systems, the Brahmaputra. Interlinked with this complex hydrographic situation was the problem concerning the course of yet another river, the Tsangpo. That it flowed eastwards along almost the length of Tibet had been appreciated by Anglo-Indian geographers for many years. However, which one of the three Assamese watercourses the Tibetan river finally joined remained a mystery until the late nineteenth century. When it was eventually established that the Tsangpo and the Dihang were one and the same, there remained one final controversy. During its final 200-kilometre route through the forested valleys of eastern Tibet the Tsangpo achieved a massive drop in altitude of over 2,500 metres. To account for this descent in so short a course, some Anglo-Indian geographers had postulated the existence of falls, possibly rivalling those at Niagara. Bailey's intention on his journey in 1911 was to solve the mystery.

Sadly, on this particular occasion the explorer was to be baulked of his prize. On the verge of the territory he had travelled many thousands of kilometres to see, he was halted by a Tibetan official anxious for the Englishman's safety. Between Bailey and the Tsangpo gorges was a region embroiled in conflict between Chinese troops and a reputedly savage hill tribe, the Po Bas. Refused transport and permission to continue, Bailey could do nothing but retrace his steps and follow the course of the River Lohit home to India.

However, by invoking the support of highly placed contacts in central government, Bailey was able to arrange his return to the region two years later, attached as intelligence officer to a punitive expedition against the Abors, one of the regional hill tribes. Determined to make a break for the Tsangpo again if the opportunity should present itself, he placed the most liberal construction on his written orders and set off for the Tibetan border with only one other officer in May 1913. On this occasion, he and his companion, Captain Henry Morshead, managed to penetrate to the Tsangpo gorges and explored all but a sixteen-kilometre stretch, proving conclusively that the falls were non-existent.

Both physically and intellectually, the particular education and training to which he had been subjected had fully equipped Bailey for this kind of endeavour. The conventional range of nineteenth-century racial and imperial certainties that he had absorbed, had rivetted down the parameters of his moral universe. When travelling in a landscape of such unfamiliarity, it was an immense benefit that his inner world was so entirely known and ordered. It left a decision-making faculty that was swift and unshakeable. His powers of observation were similarly acute. Moreover, the empirical and scientific traditions to which he adhered meant that out of the welter of sense data that confronted him, whatever could not be measured, weighed or collected could simply be ignored.

A more sensitive person may well have had a much deeper and more complex response to the landscapes and inhabitants of eastern Tibet, while any written account of the experiences would have been correspondingly richer. But then a more sensitive person might not have come through. For the journeys were remarkably tough. In the final stages of his trek in 1911, as he neared the Indian frontier, his supplies and finances were seriously depleted. In addition, he was constantly drenched, even at night, by heavy monsoons, which make this region one of the wettest in Asia. These conditions and the severity of the trek at an earlier stage completely rotted his boots, and he walked into India with his feet wrapped in pieces of his canvas bath and the skin of one of his game trophies.[4] Leeches, too, were a problem: in one two-hour period he picked 150 off one leg and his clothes.[5] Some of the people among whom he moved were equally keen to make the most of his presence. The Abor and Mishmi tribes that inhabited the region had had almost no contact with Europeans and had certainly not been weaned either from head-hunting or from the range of poisons with which they tipped their arrows and spears.

The great achievement of Bailey's education was not that it had refined his sensibilities, but that it had blunted them. True, this made him less responsive to his environment, but equally it made him indifferent to discomfort, pain and even danger. By most people's standards he was a deeply courageous and resourceful man. An incident that occurred on the expedition in 1913 is completely typical of the hardships he confronted. Crossing the Pungpung Pass into Tibet, he encountered deep snow on a ridge about 4,300 metres above sea-level. The snow was so soft that they frequently sank up to their waists or set off slides and small avalanches. Negotiating one precipice whose bottom was obscured by dark, billowing snow clouds, he fell and only just saved himself from slipping over the edge with the handle of his butterfly net.[6] Years later, when crossing the Transcaspian desert after his escape from Tashkent in 1920, his party had lost its way and stumbled largely by chance on the well that saved their lives. Even then, it had been entirely fortuitous that they should have found a party of Turkoman pastoralists watering their camels. Without the assistance of these nomads and their animals, Bailey's party would have been unable to haul the water up the 240 metres of the well shaft.[7]

If in his books these incidents were treated in largely the same perfunctory manner as the rest of the narrative, the facts were, at least, fully recorded; he would at minimum attempt to suggest their significance. But the journey to the edge of unknown territory was for him really only an unavoidable prelim, and events that occurred in these parts could be dealt with in a few lines. That pneumonic plague, for example, was raging in Manchuria as he passed through by train in the early months of 1911, was only of token interest.[8] Equally unexceptional was the fact that he had nearly drowned on his passage up the Yangtze.[9] For later travel writers such a train journey through China would have formed the core of their book, a boat accident its climax. Bailey's scale of measurement, however, was that of an explorer. Only lands unknown were of value, only adventures that had stimulated his own unresponsive nervous system could be of interest. His literary agent, aware of the disparity between Bailey's standards and those of his readers, hinted that they would 'not be content to have such interesting material treated so summarily'.[10] But this had little effect.

However, it would be difficult to convict Bailey of failing his readers. He would never have thought it his responsibility to develop his story like the plot of a novel. On the contrary, distortion of the facts for literary effect would have been an abuse of his principal objective, which was to tell the truth. Bailey saw the explorer's role in Promethean terms. He had a duty to carry back to his countrymen, knowledge of a world beyond the confines of their island kingdom. If travel was an excursion into the unknown, travel writing was a means of sharing its discoveries. This strong didactic purpose is almost a common denominator of travel literature and persists in current works. For Bailey, it was paramount, and his wish to communicate his findings was matched by the expectation of the society to which he returned. In 1911–12, for instance, when the story of his first ground-breaking journey filtered back to England, many newspapers printed verbatim chunks from his dispatches. The *Manchester Courier*, for instance, thought it important to relay to the Georgian readers of Didsbury, Trafford Park and Levenshulme that:

> The people [of Drowa Gompa, a sparsely inhabited village on the banks of the Zayul Chu] . . . wear an under jacket of blue cloth edged with red which gives the appearance of a kind of uniform. They carry knives in sheaths of wood, one side being open, and the knife held in leather thongs much as do several of the tribes in the Eastern Himalayas.
>
> The people of South-east Tibet carry primitive chop sticks formed of a single splinter of bamboo bent double and kept in the sheath with the knife.
>
> These people are great snuff-takers. The snuff-box of South-east Tibet is of a peculiar kind: a singular circular wooden box has a piece of cloth stretched tightly across the mouth, on the top of which the lid fits.[11]

This passion for facts licensed a whole array of remarkable details. In western Sichuan he noted bore-holes used to extract salt that were 900 metres deep and which took thirty years to excavate.[12] He went to great pains to work out the loads carried by porters involved in China's tea trade with Tibet, and claimed to have seen one man whose burden was 174 kilos.[13] Bailey was also strong on advice. In *Mission to Tashkent* he thought it important to explain, when holed up in disguise awaiting the opportunity to escape from his Bolshevik enemies, how he had made his pilau rice. Having diced the fat from the tail of a fat-tailed sheep with onions and carrots, and boiled them until all water was evaporated, he would then leave it to stand. 'Then and not till then', he cautioned, 'did we stir it, bringing up all the earlier ingredients to the top and mixing it thoroughly'.[14]

The need for accuracy enjoined him to impart his observations in the narrative at exactly the point he had witnessed them en route. There was no thought of arranging them around a single theme in consecutive, logical order. They were thrown together at random, observation piled on observation, the text only regulated by the dates and localities that punctuated his itinerary. On a single page from *China–Tibet–Assam* he could note and explain the bundles of tea bricks transported to Lhasa; then two methods of fishing, one involving tame cormorants, another a primitive system of bamboo reel. The next paragraph launched onto a highly buoyant type of raft made from bamboo, and the page rounded off with a discussion of an insect, whose boiled body produced a type of wax.[15]

Compounding the random effect of Bailey's narrative style was his apparent failure to apply any hierarchy to the snippets he provided. He could enlarge on the fantastic cruelty of a Chinese official – a man reputed to have nailed the skin of a victim's stomach to his chest and observed the workings of internal organs – and then skip on to the products of a local tannery.[16] The combined impact of his narrative technique was to suggest a man lacking in moral discrimination, for whom the observation of a butterfly or a story of revolting brutality was of equal weight. However, this was far from the case. By the standards of the age, he was in no way an aggressive man. For a Victorian imperialist and soldier of fairly conventional stamp he could show curiously philosophical touches. The Pashto word *Daz* – used to describe the sound of rifle fire – was for Bailey far more expressive than any English word, since it conveyed the sound as it appeared to the target. 'Pop' and 'bang', on the other hand were coined from the point of view of the firer.[17]

The one area where Bailey's information gathering took a more coherent form was his geographical surveying. In areas that had previously never been mapped he would count his footsteps along the route and then calculate the distance between fixed points – a difficult and highly tedious procedure that he would follow sometimes over hundreds of kilometres. Another technique was to time himself and multiply the final figure by the estimated speed of his progress. Careful allowance would always be taken for any kind of delay, even stopping to talk to passers-by. A prismatic compass enabled him to take regular bearings of prominent landmarks, while a favourite activity was reading his hypsometer to establish his height above sea-level. This involved measuring the point at which water boiled: a temperature that varies with atmospheric pressure and altitude. In order to obtain a measurement accurate to within ten feet, the boiling point had to be calculated to one-hundredth of a degree. Bailey's narrative is peppered with variations on: 'We boiled a thermometer at the summit' – a phrase that gives very little indication of the laborious procedure involved in each reading.

On the later expedition to the Tsangpo gorges in 1913 which finally proved the non-existence of the legendary falls, Bailey was fortunate in the choice of his companion, Henry Morshead.[18] For, this man's commitment to the geographer's task was even more remarkable than Bailey's. To work with his theodolite and to complete plane-table surveys of previously unmapped country, he frequently added to the rigours of their itinerary by climbing to the top of important peaks en route. After scaling these, Morshead would then have to ink in each of his resulting sketch maps on his return to camp. As a consequence of this demanding schedule, he and Bailey might only see one another briefly at the end of each evening. One gains some impression of Morshead's dedication to his work from one of Bailey's rare passages about his companion: 'No one can avoid picking up leeches', he wrote. 'Morshead appeared indifferent to them . . . he would stand there covered with leeches and with blood oozing out of his boots as oblivious as a small child whose face is smeared with jam'.[19]

In many ways the product of all this effort – the two-dimensional image of contour lines and trig points – was a version of landscape more important to Bailey than the physical features themselves. In the two books he published on his Tibetan journeys he almost never attempted to convey the power or beauty of the mountain scenery or, indeed, any emotional effect they had upon him.

This restricted response to a foreign land was also carried over into his attitudes towards foreign peoples. In the high, forested valleys of Asia, where the borders of Burma, India, Tibet and China all converge, there is remarkable ethnic diversity. Bailey, active in this region for almost a quarter of a century, encountered many of the remoter hill tribes, as well as the principal nationalities, such as Tibetans and Nepalese. Invariably he judged them in accordance with their usefulness to himself. An important means of assessment was whether they were good or bad porters. He felt, for instance, that the Buddhist Lepchas of Sikkim, were 'a most charming people . . . They make excellent servants, as much at home in the drawing room as in the forest'.[20] Conversely, any suspicions a village might entertain about Bailey's presence in their district ensured that they would be labelled as devious, tricky, greedy.

His independent style of travel made it unwise to apply anything more than diplomatic pressure, and to be fair to him, violent confrontation was out of keeping with the general tenor of his personality. But during his travels he expected, and usually received, courteous treatment. Anything less helpful than passive neutrality could affront his dignity. When a headman from the Mishmi tribe demanded payment for passage through his territory and for the eggs and chickens he had given Bailey, the latter was outraged. This 'truculent savage' then had the audacity to provide him with 'some coolies at the exorbitant rate of one and a half rupees a day'.[21] Similarly, when the inhabitants of a Tibetan village were reluctant to provide him with a free supply of porters and transport he 'waxed furiously eloquent' and threatened them with beatings.[22]

He was evidently unable to see these people as social equals, but in addition, he often failed to recognise them even as individuals. It is perhaps significant that Bailey neither learnt nor used the names of more than a handful of the Asians he met en route (which was in stark contrast to his policy with all other Europeans he encountered, no matter how briefly). He considered them generically – as coolies or porters, or perhaps as representatives of a race, like some natural historical specimen. In keeping with his scientific training he showed deep curiosity about all aspects of their technology, methods of agriculture and even costume. However, elements of their culture which were not immediately accessible, such as their spiritual beliefs, were of no interest to him. A religious ceremony he once witnessed consisted of 'lengthy and monotonous mumblings', and the decapitation of a sacrificial chicken.[23]

A valuable sidelight on Bailey's racial attitudes is provided by his response to the young Tibetan boy who accompanied him for the entire 1911 journey across China, Tibet and Assam. On receipt of a telegram instructing him to meet Bailey in China, the youth, called Putamdu, negotiated on his own the long journey from Calcutta to Beijing, via Shanghai. This voyage alone was no mean feat for a sixteen-year-old. Yet Putamdu then completed the entire trek alongside his employer. Though featuring little in Bailey's subsequent account, there is little doubt that this faithful companion was of valuable practical assistance and an important psychological prop to the white man. Yet in any assessment of Bailey's achievement, either by himself or by his peers, the journey would automatically have been considered a solo mission.

There is little doubt that the explorer expected his readers to understand and share these attitudes to foreign people. To a large extent, of course, they probably would have done. His most likely audience would have been from the officer classes with experience of colonial administration. Bailey seems also to have drawn with great confidence on the assumption that they were fox-hunting, grouse-shooting men, with a background knowledge and interest in wildlife. He himself was a keen amateur naturalist with considerable expertise in butterflies, of which he assembled a large collection. Typical Bailey presumption on this note was his taxing use of scientific nomenclature. Apart from indicating that it

28

referred to a new variety of butterfly, he would often bring into his travel books a name like *Zinaspa todara neglecta*, without any explanation or context.[24] It seems to have been equally unimaginable to him that anyone would not know Asia's various game animals. Names like bharal and serow seemed not to require, and certainly never received, any introduction. Just in case the reader was not sure that the first was a wild sheep of high Himalayan pastures and the second a goat-antelope with a wide Asian distribution, he might include the scientific name.[25]

Bailey was not a systematic naturalist. His observations and collecting were often largely the product of chance encounters along the route. Nonetheless, it would be wrong to underestimate the importance of this work to him. On his 1911 journey he claimed that one of his objectives, in addition to solving the riddle of the Tsangpo falls, was to find a species of pheasant that had previously only been known from a single skin.[26] On his journey in 1913 with Morshead, his colleague's dedication to the geographical surveying left him free to focus almost exclusively on collecting wildlife specimens. He would have seen in this division of labour no imbalance: they were two equal halves of an exploratory whole. The full gamut of the explorer's activities, from counting footsteps to stalking pheasants through the forest, was part of a wider systematic mapping project. The intention in all these things was to pin the universe down and render it intelligible.

It would be unreasonable for a modern audience to expect Bailey to have seen wildlife other than in the most pragmatic terms. The Victorian attitudes he inherited centred around a vision of the earth as an unlimited resource, whose God-given purpose was to satisfy human needs in all their various forms. Any environmental concern for the natural world would have been eccentric. It is even of note that Bailey should have felt that there was any moral question to answer in his shooting, collecting and skinning. Yet, prior to his departure with Morshead in 1913, he had been confined to the shelter of a cave by heavy snowfalls. There, he later wrote:

My friendliest visitor was a shrew, which came on to my table as I was working. I grew fond of it as a companion, and yet the more I looked at it the more I felt that it might be a species which had never been seen or heard of before. As a man I wished it a long and happy life; but as an amateur naturalist I felt that the interests of science came first.[27]

In spite of his momentary doubts, he eventually 'converted [his] friend into a collector's specimen', which 'proved to be a new species and was named *Soriculus baileyi*'.[28]

Of greater interest is the degree to which the natural world was deemed merely an adjunct to Bailey's perceived world – an intellectual stimulus or a physical object to be possessed. Writing of a particular butterfly, for example, he noted that it was 'rare, not because they are few and in danger of extinction, but because the habitat is difficult of access'.[29] Equally, he described an eastern-Himalayan mammal, the takin, as 'Perhaps one of the rarest game animals in the world' because 'it happens that its habitat is almost unapproachable'.[30] In each case when he spoke of rarity he was considering criteria which limited, not the abundance of the living creature, but human access to that population. It was almost as if a wild animal had no independent reality or value: its very existence was predicated upon some human experience of it.

There was no doubt that within the framework he understood, Bailey had a genuine interest in advancing knowledge of the subject. Many of the specimens that he took back with him to India were previously unrecorded, and these discoveries, like those of many other soldier-collectors, were important additions to a valid system of inquiry. However, they also served a more personal end. A species previously unknown to science inevitably required a name, and it was a common practice to call it after the original collector or some person one sought to honour. The shrew that kept Bailey company in the cave was a typical example. Similarly, many of the new butterflies he collected carried his name. One of his more lasting claims on posterity, in fact, was his status as the first European ever to observe a Himalayan blue poppy – a flower which his friend, Frank Kingdon Ward, called *Meconopsis betonicifolia baileyi*.[31] The personal kudos derived from having one's surname enshrined in scientific nomenclature was a powerful motive for many collectors. Similarly it led to frequent rivalry, both amongst individuals and even between nations. The scramble by Europe's scientists to attach their labels and enforce their names on elements of the natural world was at times as hotly contested as the geopolitical scramble for territory.

In many ways it sprang from the same set of chauvinist attitudes. Just as European economic and military supremacy had enabled a handful of nations to reshape the earth according to their own design, so did a European system of knowledge take precedence over other modes of perception and understanding. Giving expression to this intellectual colonialism, Bailey wrote of his second journey that 'Each new place, each new bird or flower or animal, each trigonometrical point or hypsometer reading was an addition to the sum total of human knowledge'.[32] This statement, of course, involved a number of assumptions about what actually constituted human knowledge. It mattered little to Bailey, or indeed to any of the natural scientists who made up the learned societies of Europe, that the white-eared pheasant he had sought, and which had previously only been known to the Western world as a boxful of feathers in the British Museum, had probably been recognised and trapped by local hunters for millennia. Its 'discovery' rested upon Western observers. The very same set of racial assumptions that had previously allowed Bailey and his contemporaries to ignore the presence of the Tibetan boy Putamdu, and think of the 1911 trek as a solo journey, had also made knowledge an exclusively European prerogative.

Ascribing names to birds and flowers could not, of course, directly advance political power, but it was, nonetheless, an important source of national pride. A rough equivalent might be the political purpose which sport has come to serve since the early twentieth century. Just as victory in football can be a measure of national virility, so the pre-eminence of a country's scientific community could be construed as an expression of wider superiority. Moreover, the imposition of nomenclature did carry with it a subtle kind of dominion. This was particularly the case with the renaming of geographical features. Titles like those for a number of African lakes such as Rudolf, Victoria and Albert – that bore no relationship to the physical entities they described and which had no regard for any previous name or historical association – were often simply a means of staking a political claim.

There are perhaps few more telling examples of this symbolic appropriation than the renaming of a mountain, standing at approximately 28°N and 87°E in the eastern Himalaya, and way beyond British jurisdiction. Its three barren ridges converge at the highest point on earth in the upper layers of the planet's atmosphere, where the lack of oxygen, powerful winds and extremities of cold preclude the development of any life form. For centuries this giant had been revered by the peoples of Tibet as *Chomo-Lungma*—Goddess-Mother of the Land. In 1856, however, a change of name and, perhaps more significantly, a change of sex were imposed by the British Government in India. Instead of the bureaucratic Peak XV, which had served as an interim title, it was to be named after a sixty-six-year-old Englishman, who had learned his rugby at Woolwich and ended his days at Hyde Park – Sir George Everest.

In the journeys of a solitary like Eric Bailey there were more obvious political implications for the imperial government he served than those contained in a bag of cured skins and pressed flowers. Although a single Scotsman scrambling through the valleys of eastern Tibet on private means offered no threat by himself to the Chinese or Tibetan authorities, he did so when he returned to India. For his was essentially a reconnaissance mission. The information he took back on roads, routes and topography was a significant contribution to geographical knowledge, but it was also the baseline for military intelligence. Having watched the process of European expansion, independent Asian governments were sensitive to the presence of foreign travellers. It was not just xenophobia that inspired the administration in Nepal, for example, to exclude almost all Europeans, regardless of their claimed scientific purpose, for nearly 200 years. Equally, the rumour that followed Bailey during his passage through China – that a British officer was going to Tibet to report on a road by which the British could invade the country – was not just empty gossip.[33] For, in some sense, this is what Bailey was doing. Although no military operations would be launched on his return, he had still provided the data that might make it possible to do so, should it ever have become necessary.

There is perhaps no more eloquent expression of the close

relationship between the affairs of geographical science and the interests of imperial politics than the roll-call of men who held office in the Royal Geographical Society at the time of Bailey's Tibetan exploration. Three of the six vice-presidents, for example, were variously an admiral, a colonel and a major. The president himself was a field marshal. The honorary secretaries were both middle-ranking army officers. On the council, besides two admirals, four colonels and the renowned explorers Sir Ernest Shackleton and Sir Francis Younghusband (both men wih long careers in the forces), there were Sir Harry Johnston, one of the great colonial administrators in British Africa, and D. G. Hogarth, early mentor to T. E. Lawrence and later head of the Arab Bureau, a Foreign Office think-tank on Middle Eastern policy. The president himself was a future Foreign Secretary, Lord Curzon of Kedleston.

It would be wrong to see the RGS as some covert intelligence agency for colonial government. Its contribution to a scientific understanding of the physical earth has been immense. Yet it also served as a meeting point for men (exclusively men until 1913) steeped in an imperial tradition. For it was precisely these colonial officials and military personnel who were in a position to contribute fresh knowledge about little-known portions of the globe. And their interest in geography naturally overlapped with their concerns as government servants. Testimony to this is the fact that when Lord Curzon praised Bailey's 1911 journey during an RGS meeting, he also speculated on whether the young explorer had opened up the route by which the Indo-Pacific Railway would reach the eastern coast of China.[34] Equally, in the volume of the *Geographical Journal* containing Bailey's account of his Tibetan travels, there was a paper by a British consul in Yunnan which considered geopolitical developments in China and their implications for the Indo-Chinese frontier.[35] Bailey's own piece started with the sentence: 'The following account of a journey through a small unsurveyed portion of south-eastern Tibet and the Mishmi Hills may be of interest in view of the military and political measures recently taken in consequence of the murder of Mr Williamson and Dr Gregorson by the Abors'.[36]

In all of Bailey's varied activities during his periods of exploration, it is possible to detect a concern to 'acquire' personal experiences in a form that had currency once he returned to his place of origin. His note-taking, his measurements of distance or altitude, his skins and pressed botanical specimens were methods of converting intangible experiences into physical commodities. One senses occasionally that the moment of consummation on his remarkable journey was not so much when he crossed the border into Tibetan territory, or when he finally glimpsed the unexplored portions of the Tsangpo, but the day of his return to civilisation. For it was then that he could write up his intelligence report and receive the congratulations of his superiors; or have his skins analysed and his name attached to new species. It was when he returned to London that he could mount the rostrum at the RGS and earn the respect of men he himself respected. Some of the principal reasons behind his journeys to the unknown were rooted in the homecoming. These would probably also have been his ultimate public justification for undertaking them.

Yet, in addition to the social credit derived from travel and his genuine sense of service to his fellow countrymen, it is almost certain that there were other personal, largely undisclosed motives for his journeys. These undoubtedly gave satisfaction to his quest for adventure, and offered him the opportunity to pit himself against trying and dangerous conditions. Even through the thick veil of his prose, it is possible to detect his genius for improvisation and for survival. One senses that in the exercise of these talents Bailey experienced life at its most vital. Moreover, they were talents that would have found little scope for expression in an Indian landscape ordered and unified by roads, railways, telegraph lines and *Pax Britannica*.

Satisfying his love of adventure (outside of sport and hunting) demanded that he move across the border. Occasionally this led him to disregard the very authorities that he felt his exploratory travels would ultimately serve. During his journey through western China in 1911, for example, he was happy to ignore the instructions of the Chinese authorities in order to enter the region of Tibet through which the Tsangpo flowed.[37] Equally, the lengthy detour that this involved delayed his return to India until several weeks after the expiry date of his leave. Both these transgressions got him into trouble. For all the valuable survey work he might have performed, Simla's politicals were at pains to emphasise the extent of viceregal irritation. After praising his efforts, a telegram dated 6 November 1911 continued:

> At the same time your proceedings were in contravention of the instructions given to you by Sir John Jordan and it is impossible that you should have been unaware of the stringent rules about exploration in tribal territory beyond the outer line of the Assam border; moreover it cannot be overlooked that your infringement of the rules referred to might have led to grave consequences. I am accordingly to convey to you an expression of the displeasure of the Governor General in Council at your having contravened these rules.[38]

Disobedience was in evidence prior to his departure for Tibet with Morshead in 1913. As intelligence officer to the punitive expedition against the Abor tribe, Bailey's personal orders ordained his exploration of the region. However, they did not make clear whether this included penetration of foreign territory. Lest any further communication definitely forbade this, Bailey made off for Tibet without waiting for clarification.[39]

Evidently, he was prepared to forego official sanction for his actions and take career risks to gain the immediate and alternative satisfaction derived from travel. Indeed, he himself later believed that he had acquired opponents in the Indian government's foreign office. In later life his streak of rebelliousness was offered by his friends as a reason for his lack of advancement.[40] In spite of a fairly distinguished diplomatic career as resident in Sikkim, Kashmir and Nepal, Bailey was never knighted. His biographer Arthur Swinson also suggested that some had seen in the explorer's long spell in Tashkent in 1919–20 a deliberate attempt to lengthen out the excitement.[41] Bailey himself expressed contempt for more hide-bound officials. 'I have always found', he once wrote, 'that if there is anyone more timorous than a civil servant, it is two civil servants'.[42] Similarly, in the irreverent name – 'mugwumps' – used by Bailey and his wife for the political officers on the Indian plains, one can detect an obvious disdain for their more conventional and ordered diplomatic lifestyle.[43]

Even in a highly sympathetic biography, sanctioned by Bailey's wife, Swinson was prepared to spell out the poor quality of Bailey's relations with higher authority and why this was so.

Whether [his] reports were late, it is difficult to ascertain, but they definitely found little favour. On at least one occasion they were described as 'models of what reports should not be'. The attitude in Simla is not difficult to understand. The vast majority of officials in the Indian Civil Service had an identity of experience; they had spent their years doing mostly routine work, in administering their districts, handling taxation, and presiding as magistrates in court. Bailey had little experience in these fields, and in many matters was quite ready to confess that he was not only ignorant but uninterested. He was a specialist with his own values and his own methods. He despised the little men in their offices, and regarded the vast flow of paperwork as merely a nuisance. The job as he saw it was to get around Sikkim and meet people and deal with problems as they arose. To him problems were more important than reports on problems, an attitude which in Simla appeared highly idiosyncratic.[44]

Except for periods of leave, all of Bailey's thirty-eight years' service was spent overseas; and for the vast majority he served on the mountainous northern borders of British India – in southern Tibet, Assam, North-West Frontier Province, Sikkim, Kashmir and Nepal. In the outline of this career one can perhaps detect a preoccupation with borderlands: a point of contact between the highly organised regime in British India and the relatively un-tamed, often unknown territories beyond. On each side of the dividing line Bailey found an environment that satisfied different, and possibly opposing, elements in his psychological make-up. This might be seen to introduce a paradoxical element into Bailey's forays into Tibet and other outlands. For while his journeys were undertaken out of a desire to strengthen his government's position, had the territory he explored been brought under British control, the very structured nature of this administration would have exorcised the element of the unknown on which his spirit of adventure thrived. Travel and exploration for a figure like Bailey were at once a wish to extend British power, and an escape from its consequences. Despite the very long interval between the period of his adventures and the time that he wrote them up, it was a contradiction that he himself never seemed to consider.

Chapter III
Lords, Arabian Ladies and Members of the Athenaeum

While many travellers and travel writers of the twentieth century have exhibited some element of this inner contradiction, there are few more striking or complex examples than Harry St John Bridger Philby. This gifted and prolific eccentric is among the century's greatest British explorers. As a traveller in the peninsula of Arabia he has few rivals. Of the other great figures of Middle Eastern exploration – Charles Doughty,[1] T. E. Lawrence, Bertram Thomas,[2] Wilfred Thesiger – none can equal his record either in terms of the distances covered or the sheer range of his discoveries and volume of his writings.

In so many of his exploits Philby strove to outshine his rivals and invariably succeeded. In 1917 he became the first European for a hundred years to cross Arabia from the Persian Gulf to the Red Sea. In 1932 he was only the second European ever to explore the vast waterless tract in southern Arabia known as the Rub al Khali – the Empty Quarter. That his own journey had been preceded twelve months earlier by Bertram Thomas's north-south traversal of the region was a source of bitter disappointment to Philby; he sought consolation in a first crossing from east to west and in making his journey longer, more difficult and more fruitful. The full complement of his travels was achieved over a remarkable thirty-five-year period. When represented on a single map, they interlace the peninsula from Baghdad to Damascus in the north, from Hufuf on the Gulf, south to the borders of Yemen and through the Hadramaut onto the shores of the Arabian Sea. Most of his journeys were in areas previously unsurveyed, and by piecing together the vast range of topographic information he acquired, he was able to produce many of the country's first accurate maps, for which he was justly acclaimed.

Covering more than three million square kilometres, this arid region in south-western Asia is almost as large as India, much of it a sun-baked wasteland of stony plateaux and sandy deserts. From the classical period onwards it has exercised a strong fascination for Europeans. For the Greeks and Romans it had been *Arabia Felix*, a fortunate land rich in frankincense and spices. In the Middle Ages it was renowned as the cradle of Islam and the heartland of a Muslim empire that had once stretched from the Pyrenees to the borders of China. By the time of Philby's birth in 1885, however, it remained almost completely unknown. Except for the two poles and portions of the forested interior of South America, it represented one of the two largest blank spaces on the European world map. The religious fanaticism of its people and the deeply hostile reception they gave to most non-Muslims found a natural correlative in the country's barren, often waterless terrain. Together, the landscape and its inhabitants presented a formidable barrier, not only to military and political conquest, but to any kind of foreign penetration. Almost inevitably, the screen of secrecy around Arabia excited European interest and enticed a handful of adventurers to try to slip through. Their journeys necessitated great physical hardship, personal risk and, to escape detection, frequent subterfuge. Almost all the principal Arabian explorers of the nineteenth and twentieth centuries, from Richard Burton and Lady Anne Blunt to Bertram Thomas and Wilfred Thesiger, were at times obliged to adopt disguises. Of these, Philby alone had moved largely unhindered.

The key which had given him unprecedented access to Arabia was his long-standing association with the region's eventual ruler, King Abd' al Aziz ibn Saud. Lasting for thirty-six years until the latter's death in 1953, this friendship had been made possible by Philby's fluency in the Arabic language, his deep knowledge of the country's history, culture and tribal lore, and by an unstinting political support that had, at times, alienated him from fellow countrymen. In 1926 he took up residence in Jedda as a businessman, adopting Arab dress and customs. Photographs of

Philby in middle age, revealing his trim, pointed beard, dark arched brows, deeply-lined cheeks and the faint down-turn in his nose, suggest an almost physical effort to assume Semitic identity. In 1930 he gave notice of a larger, inner transformation by adopting the Islamic faith. A house in Mecca itself in the same year was the first of many presents from ibn Saud and indicated the royal favour that gave Philby almost constant access to the King and his household. Through these developments the explorer had also removed all obstacles to his Arabian travels.

Rather curiously, perhaps, Philby's deep preoccupation with Arabia and Islamic culture, which culminated in the convert's journey to Mecca, had been prefaced by several years in one of the most efficient agencies of white imperial rule – the Indian Civil Service. Similarly, when he had first left for the east in November 1908 he could look back on a school record remarkable for its achievement and its high orthodoxy. He had won a Queen's scholarship to Westminster in 1898 and established himself at the top of his class – a pattern he maintained for the rest of his academic career. At Westminster he was elected school captain, then won, in typical fashion, an exhibition to Trinity College, Cambridge. A first in the modern languages tripos proved the springboard for yet another scholarship and entry into the Indian Civil Service.[3]

In India itself his remarkable capacity for work, spurred on by his family's chronic financial difficulties, earned Philby 10,000 rupees for brilliant results in examinations.[4] He had an omnivorous appetite for languages, devouring six – Arabic, Baluchi, Hindi, Persian, Punjabi and Urdu – in almost as many years. It was this same industry that urged his superiors to overlook a number of youthful misdemeanours (including what was considered an over-hasty marriage to his wife Dora); it would also secure him by 1914 a highly-paid post as head of the language board.

In later life Philby claimed that his conversion from conventional civil servant to rebel had occurred as early as the summer of 1906. After delivering an undergraduate lecture on 'The Convenience of Convention', he apparently recognised the fallacy of almost all that he had said.[5] However, if this moment had been the 'swansong of [his] orthodoxy', then the first real expression of a new faith did not occur until 1917, after his initial encounter with ibn Saud, then the

Sultan of Nejd, a region in central Arabia. In this dashing warrior Philby may have recognised a gift for leadership and the easy exercise of power that he himself had hoped to enjoy. Certainly his adherence to the Saudi cause was an almost instantaneous affair and remained one of the few permanent fixtures in his turbulent career.

In the concluding years of the First World War, Britain's two-pronged assault on the Turks – in Mesopotamia and Palestine – had forced the Ottoman empire into a state of final collapse. In the vacuum that ensued, the largely Arab populations pressed a range of demands upon their liberators, inspired in part by the new ideals of independence and self-determination which had carried across the Atlantic from the United States of America. The political confusion in the Middle East was matched by the rivalry amongst the various British government departments that had a stake in the region. While the India Office, for example, had at times fought a rearguard action for the imperial status quo and outright annexation in the Middle East, the Foreign Office favoured a more liberal approach, with the establishment of quasi-independent nations under European, preferably British, tutelage. Their strongest client was the head of the Hashemite family, Hussein, and his four sons, whose power was centred on the Hijaz, a region in western Arabia. As Sherif of Mecca, Hussein commanded significant tribal support and had organised a revolt against the Turks that had been of strategic and political value to the British campaign in Palestine.

Given Britain's support for policies that would lead to Hashemite pre-eminence in the region, Philby found himself increasingly at odds with the flow of post-war events. For he had come to the conclusion that only the Sultan of Nejd had the necessary qualities to unite and govern an independent Arabia. The political isolation these views almost inevitably entailed – an isolation that may well have been exacerbated by the unrestrained nature of Philby's lobbying – rather than curbing his advocacy of ibn Saud, hardened it almost into a governing principle of policy. He was equally distressed by the settlements that were eventually imposed on the region, which seemed to reflect European imperial interests rather than Arab national aspirations.[6] Nor was he reconciled to British officialdom when his hero's final and resounding triumph over King Hussein in 1924 proved that he had been correct in his analysis of Arabian affairs all along. For Philby saw in Britain's continued support for Hussein's sons, and in France's subsequent military conquest of Syria, a cynical betrayal of post-war promises to the Arabs.

On two occasions during his short political career his unorthodox views led to clashes with the administration he served. The first of these came in 1921. Acting as Minister for the Interior in Mesopotamia, he took issue with the policies pursued by the British High Commissioner, Sir Percy Cox. Reeling from the effects of a widespread and costly rebellion, the British had hoped to stem Iraqi opposition by the appointment of an Arab leader and national administration. Their candidate was the Hashemite prince, Feisal, recently exiled from Syria by the French, and previously an important leader of the Arab revolt. However, Feisal had few links with the Iraqis and small claim on their throne. Philby sensed, in this imposition of an outsider, blatant imperial manipulation – a charge confirmed by the dubious ballot that secured Feisal's nomination and the enforced exile of his only serious rival. Philby's opposition to these measures, known to the British High Commissioner, and also to Feisal himself, demanded that he must go.

Three years later, while serving as Chief British Representative to Abdullah, the second eldest of the Hashemite princes and Britain's appointee as head of the fledgling state of Transjordan, Philby fell out with his superiors over pay and policy. Once again, he gave up the post to salve his pride in a position made untenable partly by his own intransigence. His repeated expressions of support for Arabs, which widened to embrace both Indian and Egyptian calls for independence, eventually evolved into a bold anti-imperial posture, much like the one Wilfrid Blunt[7] had adopted a generation earlier. Completely out of tune with the Indian Civil Service he had served for sixteen years, he brought his chequered career to a final close and resigned in 1925.

His resignation was a logical, if not unavoidable, step and he later claimed that he never hesitated in taking it. However, it left himself, his wife and their four children in a precarious economic position. It also closed the avenue of opportunity for which he had felt himself best equipped, and which he had seen as his optimum route to the top. For the sheer ability and industry on which his brief career had been founded were matched by ambitious designs on political power. Yet given his maverick views and history of intransigence, those ambitions were also a measure of his capacity for self-deception.

The hopes triggered by the election in 1929 of a Labour administration he believed sympathetic to his views, serve as a valuable illustration. To his wife he confided that the protracted and seemingly insoluble Arab-Jewish conflict that arose out of a Zionist policy in Palestine could be laid to rest if only the government would appoint a commission consisting of a Jewish historian and himself. In another he claimed that the breakdown in negotiations for an Anglo-Egyptian treaty could have been saved if only they had called for Philby. No doubt, however, they would appoint him first British minister to Jedda with freedom to act entirely as he saw fit. 'They must surely realise now', he explained, 'that in my judgement of the Arab situation I have never made a mistake'.[8] On two occasions he had sought to intervene in Middle Eastern disputes on an entirely freelance basis – once between ibn Saud and the Hashemite family, and then between the Jews and Arabs in Palestine. On neither occasion did he seem to think that official sanction for his actions was a prerequisite for success; and in both he was sternly rejected.[9]

The towering egotism from which these actions and statements emanated was ultimately the undoing of Philby the politician. For while it gave him supreme confidence in his own undoubted abilities, it also gave the sharp edge to his rancour and his arrogance. Often his favourite means of address was the personal lecture. For all Philby's erudition, charm and abilities as raconteur, where matters close to his heart were concerned, one-to-one conversation could easily become little more than a unilateral declaration of *the truth*. Once, during a heated dispute in Mesopotamia, he is reputed to have said: 'I can't hear what you say, Edmonds, but I join issue with you.'[10] This classic remark was quoted against him for years as evidence of unreasoned contrasuggestibility. Given the particular course of his political career, it is easy to believe that Philby's personal intransigence and love of argument were fuelled in part by frustration at his failure to get on. Equally, one senses that in his frequent attacks upon British foreign policy and in his championship of the underdog, he had perhaps harnessed his own personal disappointment to the larger, more dignified vehicle of political opposition.

Yet, despite all his sympathy and support for his Arab hosts, Philby was not above biting the hand that feeds. Even his life's hero, ibn Saud, was not safe. Once, during an evening's audience, the Arabian King, drawing a parallel between his own autocratic rule and the British system of government, said, 'we discuss everything here in complete democratic freedom and we even have an official opposition. Philby'.[11] This anecdote was no doubt dear to the Englishman's heart, for true to his own perverse form, Philby looked upon his inability to hold his tongue as a badge of merit. He was the man who spoke the truth regardless of time, place or personal circumstances.

Given his constant and privileged access to the Arabian royal court there is little doubt that ibn Saud enjoyed the Englishman's company and his wide-ranging conversation. He must also have valued his forthright advice, possibly as some sort of corrective to the usual court sycophancy. As the reign wore on, however, Philby's strictures intensified to intolerable levels. The Arabic taste for luxury, previously checked by the frugal conditions of the desert, was given licence by the large revenues that accrued from the country's recently discovered reserves of oil. The King's unwillingness to control the excesses of his family and his inability to regulate the nation's economy led to a good deal of extravagance and corruption. Philby, who had himself played a major role in introducing the Arabs to European and American oil companies, and who had also exploited for his own commercial ends an Arab taste for Western goods, was yet unable or unwilling to acknowledge his part in these developments.

With a typical disregard for consistency, he condemned them as symptoms of decadence. Even in a book written to celebrate the fiftieth anniversary of ibn Saud's triumphant return to Riyadh – *Arabian Jubilee* – he could not resist tackling the issue. However, on the King's death in 1953, Philby was deprived of the personal bond which had been at the core of his attachment to Arabia. The loss of his friend also rendered his position at court less secure. And when his accusations were renewed, this time in a series of lectures to

American oilmen and their families, ibn Saud's son and heir, King Saud, decided to expel his noisy critic. Thus, in 1955, the old favourite went into exile, entirely unrepentant.[12]

One of the most commonly repeated patterns in the lives of travellers is some degree of personal transference to the cultural identity of the people whose lands they wandered. This new sense of self could leave them unable or ill-equipped to resume permanent residence in their country of origin. Following their initial encounter with Africa many nineteenth-century explorers like Livingstone, Selous and Stanley returned again and again. It was perhaps more than a simple issue of dangerous circumstances or ill-health that the first two should end their lives there. T. E. Lawrence, although hardly returning to Arabia in the final seventeen years of his life, was unable to shrug off his Arabic legend. Wilfrid Blunt frequently wandered his Sussex estates at Crabbet in Bedu robes. Of all twentieth-century travellers, Harry St John Philby and the pattern of his cultural allegiance present perhaps the most complex picture.

Despite, for example, his obvious political and religious adherence to ibn Saud's Arabia, socially he remained very closely in touch with his own country and the mores of the British middle classes. Even during his desert journeys he would sit, ear jammed up against the wireless, straining to catch the faint commentary on his beloved cricket. Long periods overseas were punctuated by regular visits to Britain. Summers with his wife and four children were spent in a Welsh cottage. In London he divided his time between the learned societies, Lords and the Athenaeum – one of the oldest and most exclusive clubs with a membership reserved for those of high literary or scientific achievement. Moreover, he retained late into life an ambition to enter the House of Commons as an MP.[13] Where his children were concerned he was the model of paternal conventionality, desiring the best of educations and the most suitable matches for his three daughters. For his son Kim it could only be Westminster and then Cambridge, and perhaps a career in the Foreign Office.

In matters of sex, Philby's curious and unstable synthesis of two cultures precipitated out into an almost stark schizophrenia. He had always been a deeply sensual man and had long strayed beyond the boundaries of monogamy. His long-suffering wife Dora, for years the sheet-anchor for her husband's disordered life and with formidable personal qualities that are deserving of a separate biography, had put up with a full catalogue of extra-marital affairs. On his adoption of Islam these liaisons were laid aside, only to be replaced with the greater sexual freedom that male Muslims traditionally enjoyed. In 1931, accompanying ibn Saud's gift of a house in Mecca was a *jariya*, a slave girl – Miriam bint Abdullah al Hasan. She remained in Philby's home for many years and in 1946 was replaced by Rozy al Abdul Aziz. This light-skinned teenager had been selected for Philby by one of the King's wives from the girls in the royal household. A year later, at about seventeen years old, Rozy became the mother of Fahad. The happy father was then sixty-two. At sixty-eight he was dandling on his knees his fourth son by Rozy. Sadly, only two of their children survived. Despite the newly acquired responsibilities of fatherhood, Philby was still leaving Rozy in summer to take holidays in the West. And just as he would change at the border from dish-dasha, aba and head-cloth into western clothes, so he seemed able to exchange the role of Muslim father doting on his baby son for that of ageing patriarch, distinguished amongst his English grandchildren and grown-up offspring.

In Philby's published books on Arabian themes, fifteen in all, one encounters much the same level of inconsistency. He clearly saw himself as an important channel of contact between Europe and the Middle East, and in particular a middle man who could be of service to the Arabs. In a number of works, such as *Arabia of the Wahhabis* and *Saudi Arabia* he evidently sought to educate an English-speaking audience about his adopted country and its culture. Increased British understanding would improve the Arabs' position. The books were, in effect, a form of international advocacy on behalf of his friend King ibn Saud. It is interesting, however, that he never wrote anything that examined English or European culture for the benefit of an Arabic audience. Equally important, only one of his books – *Arabian Jubilee* – was ever translated into Arabic.

In his works of travel adventure the pro-Arab purpose was far less pronounced. One of the distinguishing features of the genre is the assumed identity of outlook of both narrator and audience. Without a range of common cultural and moral assumptions, the observations made by the author during the course of the imaginary journey would resist full understanding. Reader and narrator also share, in effect, a common ignorance. Without some sense of what his audience lacked, Philby would have been unable to select the information necessary to satisfy their curiosity. This narrative focus made Philby appear, like most other travellers, very much as the outsider looking on, and not as one on the inside, as he himself might have hoped. There was also another factor helping to confirm this impression. Philby was a classic example of the Victorian polymath. His curiosity radiated outwards with an almost indiscriminate, centrifugal energy. Geology, geography, cartography, all aspects of natural history, history, philology, literature, ethnology, archaeology – it seems that only music and machines failed to inspire his interest. Yet this deeply Western, empirical approach to life meant that Philby, on the printed page, at least, seemed to have little or no access to the emotional fabric of Arab-Islamic culture. It is also interesting to note that his scientific interests also culminated in a secular version of reality quite outside that prescribed by Islam. This was perhaps an indication of how little his own conversion had transformed the settled pattern of his beliefs.

His written justification of his adoption of Islam perhaps provides a further valuable insight into his true cultural identity. Although he spoke of the 'orgy of intellectual and spiritual self-surrender'[14] experienced in Mecca itself, in explaining the background to the step he used very much the language of a pragmatist rationalising a strategic compromise. He acknowledged, for instance, that as a Christian in a Muslim kingdom, he was prevented from 'any great expansion of [his] sphere of activity'.[15] He also confessed that he had long ceased to have religious feelings or convictions, but was 'prepared to admit that for the vast majority of mankind religion was an inescapable necessity'.[16] In searching for the formula of words that best expressed his reasons for apostasy he alighted on that of the British envoy in Jedda as most accurate: 'Mecca and Islam will give Philby the background which he has needed ever since he quarrelled with the Government'.[17]

This might have served him as a perfectly good explanation, but they were not the words of a man compelled by religious conviction.

Although he received considerable criticism for his change of faith he never sought to disguise that he had become a Muslim. In his travel books he frequently depicted himself stalking the foreground in Arab dress, attentive to the details of Islamic law. Yet in these portraits he often appeared highly self-conscious. In *The Empty Quarter*, his account of his crossing of the Rub al Khali, he was at pains to explain his pious observance of Ramadan, the ninth month of the Muslim year during which a fast is observed for all the daylight hours. No doubt wishing to demonstrate what a good and true Muslim he was, particularly in view of the laxity of many of his Bedu companions, his emphasis on this issue also perhaps served to illustrate that an Englishman fashioned at Westminster and Cambridge was made of as stern a stuff as any desert nomad.[18]

If the attempt to pin down Philby's final national allegiance becomes increasingly confused, in an examination of his preoccupation with travel one perhaps comes closest to the mainsprings of his being. Throughout his career as an explorer he remained entirely true to a single habitat – desert. It was one that best suited his passionate, iconoclastic temperament, and a choice that explains so much about his behaviour. Although the pattern of his life – resignation from government service, removal to Arabia, adoption of Islam, and hero-worship for a foreign ruler – accords with that of a man in rebellion against his own country (like his more notorious son Kim), in the final analysis, Philby senior exceeds such a definition. In his hunger for power and fame, in his persistent need to speak his mind whether to Briton or Arab, in his ultimate lack of allegiance, except to a highly personal version of reality, one senses a figure of almost Faustian proportions. At times it seemed that Philby was in revolt against the limitations of life itself. It was in the desert that he found an opportunity for absolute liberty and absolute command of his destiny. While his conversion to Islam cannot be easily construed as evidence for a strongly spiritual nature, the desert does seem to have been an environment that expressed his innermost nature.

He frequently used religious language and religious images to

describe himself and his relationship with the desert. It is symptomatic of this trait that his final autobiographical work is entitled
Forty Years in the Wilderness. In the book he even suggested parallels
– no less significant, perhaps, for his dismissive tones – between
himself and John the Baptist.[19] In a lecture to the Royal
Geographical Society on his journey across the Empty Quarter he
described his disagreements with his Bedu companions. When
unable to meet their demands, he said: 'I was like Moses in the
wilderness but without his miraculous gifts'.[20] The same image
found its way into his full-length account of the journey, *The Empty
Quarter.*[21] When discussing his support for ibn Saud in the teeth of
opposition from his British contemporaries, he again wrote: 'I was
the voice crying in the wilderness which they laughed to scorn'.[22]
In the preface to the autobiographical *Arabian Days* he wrote of the
consequences of his disagreements with T. E. Lawrence and A. T.
Wilson concerning British policy in Arabian territory: 'I owe a debt
of gratitude to Lawrence and Wilson, who knew not what they
were doing when they drove me into the desert'.[23] Here, grandiose
religious parallels are evident, if not explicit. So often he saw
himself as the prophetic outsider, one whose vision of the truth
exiled him from his own kind, and for whom the desert was the
ultimate sanctuary.

Yet this burning ambition to travel in foreign lands was not
exclusively about a deep spiritual need for wilderness. Two
sentences in the introduction to *The Empty Quarter*, describing his
obsessive concern to cross the Rub al Khali, provide a crucial
insight into another of his principal, underlying motives:

> For fifteen years my life has been dominated by a single
> idea, a single ambition – rather perhaps a single obsession.
> Faithfully, fanatically and relentlessly through all those years
> I have stalked the quarry which now, in these pages, lies
> before the reader – dissected, belabelled and described.[24]

Philby's sweeping image billed him as the great hunter. It also
reduced 650,000 square kilometres of the most forbidding landscape on earth almost to the condition of a showcase filled with
butterfly specimens – 'dissected, belabelled and described'. More-

over, one senses that it was a showcase not so much for his own delectation, but for that of his audience. Like many hunters his pleasure was as much in others' admiration of his trophies, as in the actual stalking of the quarry.

Philby had given more direct expressions of his reasons for exploration in letters to his wife. 'My chief aim', he wrote in 1928, was 'to secure the immortality to be gained by the accomplishment of some great work'.[25] Just prior to his first attempt at the Rub al Khali he explained: 'My ambition is fame, whatever that may mean and for what it is worth'.[26] In an age when human-made rockets have travelled 1.3 billion kilometres into outer space, circled Venus and photographed the mountains and plateaux on its surface, it is perhaps difficult to comprehend the acclaim enjoyed by those who had found some portion of this planet previously untrodden by Europeans. Even a failed journey like Eric Bailey's 1911 attempt on the Tsangpo attracted the attention of over twenty national newspapers. David Livingstone's triumphant return from Africa half a century before developed into an almost royal progress around the country.

If Philby had hoped that his conquest of the Empty Quarter would be his ticket to immortality, then he should have been well satisfied by the immediate results. News of his crossing made him a national and even international celebrity, dined, fêted, requested and honoured wherever he went. It was a reputation that would help secure his personal and financial stability; it would also smooth his access to politicians, publishers and newspaper editors. Indeed, it was probably because of the respect he commanded as an explorer that so many of his countrymen and women overlooked his occasionally treacherous condemnation of Britain abroad. Yet it is interesting to note that the reputation he sought was one that would ensure his story was exchanged, not during the desert night over the campfires of the Bedu, but over brandy and cigars in the clubland of St James.

Finally, it is valuable to compare Philby's response to travel and the purposes it served him with those of Eric Bailey. As characters they initially appear fundamentally different. While one was a brilliant talker and an extrovert, the other man was highly modest and unassuming. Compared with Jack Philby, the Tibetan explorer, for all his rumbling discontent with mugwumps and civil servants, appears an extremely mild version of the explorer as outsider. If Bailey revealed an instinctual preference for border-lands – a region in which he might comfortably attain strikingly different political and physical landscapes – Philby's need was quite literally for the wilderness, for regions way beyond any boundary.

A number of their motives were also radically different. Clearly the Arabist would never have seen himself as performing any service for his king and country. There were no geo-military reports for the general staff, like those Bailey prepared on his return from Tibet. Philby's journeys could hardly have furthered his country's interests at all, except perhaps in the most peripheral manner. His maps were of value to geographers, his discoveries would interest various scientific specialists and perhaps some of the glory that went to Philby as an individual would redound to the country of his birth, but otherwise the value of his travels was personal. Yet in his strong concern to convert his adventures and experiences in Arabia into a currency that had value at home, in their joint preoccupation with the moment of return, and a shared assumption that travel in unknown lands achieved much of its purpose once they had got back, Philby and Bailey come to resemble one another more than one might have expected. However, it is perhaps only when set against the achievement and concerns of a much younger explorer in Arabia that the full nature of Philby's travels can be properly appreciated.

Chapter IV
Old Stone Age

That younger explorer, now in his eighties, is Wilfred Thesiger. He is Philby's natural heir as the great British Arabist and desert traveller; the only man, perhaps, whose travels could be said to rival Philby's.

In any consideration of the two it would be difficult to ignore a number of interesting parallels in their backgrounds and family circumstances. Each, for instance, was one of four boys, each born abroad, just north of the Equator: Philby on a coffee estate in Badulla, Ceylon; Thesiger just outside Addis Ababa in June 1910 – the first British child to be born in Abyssinia. Both came from families with a tradition of distinguished imperial service. Philby's great uncle had been Lieutenant Governor of the Punjab, while his grandfather had helped suppress the Indian uprising of 1857, and been nominated for a VC for his part in the relief of Lucknow.

Thesiger's lineage is even more elevated. His father had been British minister in Addis Ababa; his uncle Frederick, Viscount Chelmsford, had been Governor of Queensland, then New South Wales and then Viceroy of India from 1916–1921. Their father, the second Lord Chelmsford, had also seen military action in the Indian uprising, and in Abyssinia. As Commander-in-Chief of forces in South Africa he had overseen Britain's final triumph over the Zulu nation. Both the young explorers had eventually followed their forebears into colonial service: Philby in India and Thesiger in the Sudan. These careers had been prefaced by a classical British education. Philby, as we have seen, progressed from Westminster School to Trinity College, Cambridge, Thesiger from Eton to Magdalen College at Oxford.

Most striking of all the family parallels, perhaps, is the absence of a father in the Philby and Thesiger households from a very early stage. Philby's mother May, exasperated by her husband's debts and fast living, left their failing plantation in Ceylon after only eight years of marriage, and returned to England. A successful London boarding house provided a degree of financial security for the single-parent family, and from then on the four boys had almost no contact with their father. Jack Philby saw him only once, when he was at Westminster in his early teens, before his father's death in 1913.[1] In 1920, when Thesiger was only nine, his father, also called Wilfred, had had a heart attack while shaving, collapsed into his wife's arms and died at the age of forty-eight. Until her remarriage to a childless widower eleven years later, Thesiger's mother, Kathleen Mary, had brought up her four sons singlehanded at a house in Radnorshire, Wales.

By contrast, both explorers enjoyed long and happy relations with their mothers. Once he had become a bread-winner himself, Jack Philby was an important financial support to the courageous and enterprising May. According to his biographer, Elizabeth Monroe, he was her favourite son, and despite his many unortho-doxies and long periods overseas, they remained close until her death in 1950, only ten years before his own.[2] Thesiger too has acknowledged the importance of his mother in his life. In the introduction to *Arabian Sands* he wrote: 'Only I know what my mother's interest and encouragement have meant to me . . . she has always understood and sympathized with my love of exploration'. His second book, *The Marsh Arabs*, which he dedicated to her, repeats the acknowledgement. In addition to encouraging her son's travels, she herself was imbued with a spirit of adventure, and accompanied him on a number of journeys. Even when she was eighty-eight they travelled together on the fringes of the Sahara Desert in Morocco.[3]

It is tempting to speculate that these common childhood circumstances, particularly the absence of a father, indicate some of the origins of Philby's and Thesiger's thirst for travel and their disregard for a more conventional lifestyle. In Sigmund Freud's traditional tripartite model of the human pysche – id, ego and super ego – the last operates as a mechanism to curb and regulate the urges

of the instinctual id. During the early stages of psychic development, Freud believed that it was 'the authority of the child's parents
– essentially, that of his autocratic father, threatening him with his
power to punish – which called on him [the child] for a renunciation
of instinct and which decides what is to be allowed and what
forbidden'. The super ego was 'the successor and representative of
the individual's parents . . . it carries on their function almost
unchanged'.[4] In the case of the two Arabian explorers the absence of
a father at a very early age may well have inhibited the development
of any internal restraining mechanism. (Is it perhaps symptomatic
of this process that Thesiger's autobiography is entitled *The Life of
My Choice*?) Such an interpretation meshes completely with their
disregard for societal norms, and would help explain Philby's
occasionally ferocious opposition to authority. Equally, one can
perhaps detect in their passion for landscapes of the utmost austerity
a quest for self-identity and an effort to prove and realise their
masculinity – a maleness that they failed to absorb organically
through long-term relations with a father figure.

Thesiger's passion for austere landscapes and his attachment to
'primitive' peoples, when set against the customary lifestyle of
those from his elevated social background, has thrown up some of
the contradictions so evident in Philby's life. In his account of their
journey together in the Iraqi marshes, his friend and travelling
companion, Gavin Maxwell, gave expression to this element in
Thesiger's personality:

> The knowledge of his years of primitive living in the Sudan,
> Ethiopia, and Arabia, of ordeals and hardships past, had led
> me, perhaps, to expect someone . . . with a contempt for
> conformity to the conventions of a European social group.
> The bowler hat, the hard collar and black shoes, the never-
> opened umbrella, all these were a surprise to me.[5]

Maxwell might easily have added the ancient cut of his dark suits,
Thesiger's gold pocket watch and chain, his routine attendance,
during his periods in England, at the Travellers' Club, his well-
appointed flat in the heart of Chelsea and his precise Oxford diction.
However, any attempt to equate these apparent incongruities

with the wild oscillations between East and West performed by Philby would be inappropriate. Nor could one take this conventional side to his nature as evidence that his travels were merely a self-conscious pose – an effort to secure a hero's reputation in the drawing-rooms of London. Wilfred Thesiger has probably pursued his ambition to tread the remote places of this earth more fully than any other British traveller, alive or dead.

Approximately three-quarters of his life has been spent abroad, much of it in inaccessible regions inhabited largely by pastoral communities whose allegiance was initially to the tribe or clan, and then, perhaps, the Islamic faith. Until the age of nine he lived with his parents in Abyssinia. The longest period of continuous residence in England was the thirteen years of his education between 1920 and 1933. Apart from this he has seldom stayed for more than a dozen weeks. For the whole of his brief political and military career – amounting to approximately twelve years – he was home for only nine months. Many periods of leave during foreign service were simply an opportunity for further travel. During his years in Sudan as a political officer, for instance, his furlough was devoted to journeys in Syria, Morocco and the Tibesti mountains in French-controlled Chad.

The vast majority of Thesiger's time overseas has been spent in Africa, particularly since the 1960s, when he made his home in the previously remote northern provinces of Kenya, among the Samburu and Turkana tribes. Yet the legend most frequently attached to him concerns his status as 'the last and certainly one of the greatest of the British travellers among the Arabs'.[6] Philby was invariably generous in his tribute to fellow Arabists; his assessment of his friend's achievements was typical, though perhaps playfully barbed. 'Wilfred Thesiger', he wrote, 'one of the most outstanding desert travellers during the few years he devoted to Arabia, has long since jilted his old love to wander in search of other charms'.[7] Those 'few years' actually amounted to forty-five months of continuous exploration in and around the Rub al Khali, in Oman, the Hadramaut and the Trucial States. This had included not one but two crossings of the Empty Quarter, following routes that neither Thomas nor Philby had used. All of this amounted to an explorer's record in southern Arabia not too far behind the latter's own.

Furthermore, the charge of infidelity suggested by Philby was completely unfounded. It was the political opposition of a number of Arab rulers, notably ibn Saud and the Imam of Oman, that had finally forced Thesiger, unwillingly, to leave the Arabian peninsula.[8]

When he did so, he simply moved further east into Arabic Iraq. There, a fortnight's duck shooting in the marshes at the confluence of the Tigris and Euphrates in 1950 opened up a pattern of life which only came to a close with a republican coup and execution of the Iraqi king in 1958. Seven years with the Marsh Arabs, combined with his five years in Arabia, comprise the period for which he is best known; they are also the principal focus for four of his five books.

It is perhaps ironic that political considerations had eventually debarred him, firstly from the deserts of the peninsula, and then the marsh world north of the Shatt al Arab. For of all the important explorers of the twentieth century, he is one of the least politically concerned or motivated. Although it was his father's and then his own position as a servant of the British empire that had provided him with his first opportunities for foreign travel, Thesiger had little interest in furthering imperial ends. His journeys in Arabia and Iraq were initially undertaken as an employee of a UN-based research programme, and then as a self-financed individual travelling entirely for pleasure. While a deep conservatism would probably determine any political allegiance, his outlook is rooted, not so much in a party creed relevant to conditions in the United Kingdom, but in a desire to engage and also preserve the ancient lifestyles of non-white, non-European communities, such as the Bedu or the Ethiopians. It is a position that Thesiger has termed as traditionalist.[9] Indeed, it is only when seen as a last stand on behalf of such principles that his adherence to the social rituals of an older England, during his periods in this country, appears less at odds with the rest of his lifestyle.[10]

His boyhood years in Abyssinia appear to be central to this abiding preoccupation. The absence of any European society, apart from that provided by the legation staff, and daily contact with Ethiopians seem to have imprinted on him a predilection for the life of black Africa, rather than that of his own biological race. Thesiger himself singled out the importance of experiences in 1917, when he witnessed the triumphant return from battle of the national army after it had successfully defeated the political opponents of their ruler, Ras Tafari. Watching the procession of victorious troops, often armed with the weapons of the Iron Age, implanted in him 'a lifelong craving for barbaric splendour, for savagery and colour and the throb of drums, and . . . a lasting veneration for long-established custom and ritual'.[11] Possibly reinforcing this development was the rejection he suffered at his first preparatory school in England, where his tales of everyday life in Abyssinia and India appeared to the other children as the fantastic romances of a little liar.[12]

His choice of childhood heroes is also a clear measure of early unorthodoxy. They were not the Victorian military figures idolised by his contemporaries, but precisely those African and Asian leaders whose campaigns of resistance had so troubled the empire, and whose final suppression would earn the opposing British commanders their *Boy's Own* immortality. On learning of General Kitchener's sweeping victories at Omdurman, for instance, the young Thesiger could not help but feel the tragedy of the Mahdists' defeat. Even family loyalties did not countermand this pro-African position. When Cetawayo's Zulu impis annihilated a portion of Lord Chelmsford's forces at the battle of Isandhlwanaland, his grandson felt that it was a victory they 'had jolly well deserved'.[13] With role models like the commander of Moroccan guerilla forces, Abd el Krim, and the Druze leader, Sultan Pasha el Atrish, Thesiger was perhaps always destined for an unconventional life.[14]

Running in tandem with his reverence for the pre-industrial communities of central and south-western Asia or Africa have been his rejection of 'Western innovation in other lands and a distaste for the drab uniformity of the modern world'.[15] Even as a youth he claims to have recognised in the motor car and other forms of mechanised transport the agents that would eventually diminish the rich cultural diversity that these undeveloped communities represented. Add to these misgivings an acute sensitivity to loud noise, and it is hardly surprising that airports have come to represent for him 'the ultimate abomination'.[16] An anecdote Thesiger delights to quote against himself concerns an exchange between him and his adopted son, Lawi Laboyare, a member of the Samburu tribe, traditional pastoralists of northern Kenya. Chiding Lawi for his love of cars, transistors and pop music, the explorer was check-mated when his adopted son replied: 'Of course, the truth of the matter is that you are Old Stone Age, and I am modern man.'[17]

It is perhaps Thesiger's deepest personal misfortune to have been born at such a crucial moment in the development of the internal combustion engine. Prior to 1900 the motor car had merely been the eccentric plaything of a wealthy few. Yet by 1909, as his father and mother travelled to the Abyssinian capital by mule, an American called Henry Ford had put the finishing touches to the first mass-produced vehicle and fine-tuned his assembly lines. In the year of the explorer's birth, the Englishman Charles Rolls, one half of a famous engineering partnership, became his country's first martyr to an even newer transport technology, when his prototype plane crashed near Bournemouth. And by the time, as a young man, Thesiger was set to travel up to Oxford, there were already fifteen million Model T Fords on the planet. It is against this background of the motor car's massive proliferation that his career as an explorer has derived much of its significance. The transport revolution that it has effected worldwide has made him, for many people, the last traveller in the tradition of the eighteenth and nineteenth centuries. Equally, it is when set against the profound and universal social changes which have carried in the motor car's wake, that Thesiger's writings on his life amongst pre-industrial societies have derived much of their drama and their pathos.

Despite such heartfelt opposition to the process of modernisa-tion, he has never felt it necessary to disown the society that initiated it, or move further away from his own cultural back-ground, as Philby appeared to do. Thesiger never converted to Islam. He was even highly ambivalent about the adoption of Arab dress, which in some travellers has been little more than a theatrical pose. In Arabia an exchange of costume had been an essential element in his efforts to secure the co-operation and respect of his Bedu companions.[18] In Iraq, however, it was several years before he gave up his customary Western dress – a delay in sharp contrast to Gavin Maxwell's enthusiasm, from the very outset of his two-month visit, for the dish-dasha of the marshmen.[19] Thesiger's unwillingness to adopt Islam or even to pose as a Muslim led him into considerable difficulties in Arabia. On one occasion he was unable to enter a settlement to obtain supplies, for fear of discovery and possible conflict. The alternative was a gruelling seventy-two hour wait without food.[20] On another occasion he was forbidden access to a mountain area he had long hoped to explore, and then forced to leave the region or face armed opposition.[21] By contrast, Philby's royal favour and his wide acceptance by the Arabs as one of their faith freed him entirely from this category of inconvenience.

One might also have expected that Philby's partial assimilation of the Arabic way of life would have enabled him to achieve closer relations and a better understanding of his Bedu travelling companions than other Europeans visiting the region. Yet this was not the case.

It is important to recognise that disagreements are common in the stressful conditions that travel often involves. Amongst the dangers and wearing anxiety of desert travel they are inevitable. To be fair to Philby, for much of the time his relations with his entourage were based on a fairly easy, if coarse, camaraderie. It is equally to his credit that he was unwilling to disguise any difficulties he had with his Bedu entourage. Yet some of their clashes were extraordinarily explosive, and on one occasion his Bedu companions contemplated his murder, despite the severe royal retribution they would certainly have faced on return.[22]

British Arabists have sometimes been accused of bringing home an overly romantic impression of the region's desert inhabitants, recreating them in their travel works as nature's aristocrats, dignified by rigorous codes of conduct, by a fabulous generosity and by their indifference both to physical discomfort and the excessive material concerns that so obsessed and etiolated the West. Of all British writers on Arabia, Philby has perhaps contributed least to this legend. He was often disparaging of their qualities, and spoke of their 'greed of filthy lucre',[23] their 'petty' or even 'evil, envious souls'.[24] When he was forced to retreat from his first attempt on the waterless heartland of the Rub al Khali, he was scathing of what he regarded as their pusillanimity.

In such circumstances the Arab does not show up to
advantage. He clings frantically, desperately, to life,
however miserable, and, when that is at risk, loses heart and
head . . . And now it was waterless desert, the fear of thirst
and death, that made women of these men. . . . A third of
the journey was behind us and a steady effort would carry
us through if only they would play the man.

'Could one be anything but critical', he questioned, of 'companions
who would readily have sacrificed the whole object of our
endeavour to their own miserable comfort'.[25]

Although, as Philby claimed, the 'endeavour' might have been
shared, the 'object' of the journey was exclusively his, and this was
at the heart of the problem. His Arabian travels were one-man
expeditions. Their principal purpose was the accumulation of
scientific data. His remarkable dedication to collecting, note-taking
and investigations involved frequent delays or extensions to their
intended route. Why he should seek precisely those areas that no
one knew much about was often incomprehensible to his companions, whose own thoughts were for water, supplies, pasture for
their camels and, naturally enough, the avoidance of difficulties
greater than they need encounter. At times the gap between their
respective concerns widened into bitter conflict. On their way
southwards through the Empty Quarter, Philby was increasingly
urged by his entourage to abandon their course. However, he was
adamant:

For many days now I had endured the constant and
inevitable friction engendered by the struggle between the
insistent urge of my own fixed and unalterable purpose and
the solid weight of the innate national inertia thrown into
the balance against me by the united body of my
companions . . . Step by step we had progressed ever away
from their home fires, but each step had been achieved . . .
as the momentum of a purposeful mind triumphed . . . over
the inert mass ever ready to recoil from any arduous
objective.[26]

Such passages reveal the demonic energies and self-will that enabled him to achieve his goals, but they also confirm how little identity of purpose there was between the two nationalities. Ironically, the fact that the journey was sponsored by ibn Saud militated against smooth relations. The royal gold that paid his companions' wages made Philby, not just *primus inter pares*, but their temporary master – Sheikh Abdullah, whose private tent and personal servant confirmed the gulf between them. This did not alter the fact that to go anywhere in the desert environment, Philby was totally dependent upon their guiding skills. Yet their indispensability to him was entirely functional, their relationship like that of rubber tyres to a motor car. Had they not been so essential for his purpose there is little doubt that he would have driven on without them. Indeed, his switch, in the thirties, to the use of motorised transport, particularly Fords, in his exploratory journeys, may have been an expression of his unwillingness to be tied to the wants and concerns of others.

During those years and in those portions of Arabia where he was obliged to travel by camel with Arab guides, he would go to almost any lengths to ensure that they did precisely as he wished. Physical coercion was seldom a part of his repertoire, although he once struck a man for a minor misdemeanour,[27] and when damage was done to a hare skin he wanted, Philby allowed his retinue to beat the man responsible.[28] More common tactics involved some kind of financial bribe, or exploitation of the Bedu's deep preoccupation with their self image to shame them into submission. If they refused to march in the fashion he required, Philby would dismount and walk, even in the heart of the Empty Quarter, until they fell in with his plans.[29] On another occasion, his men, disgruntled that Sheikh Abdullah had reserved for himself the lion's share of some camel's milk, placed with elaborate ceremony the two equal bowls of liquid side by side – one for him and one to be divided amongst ten. Philby responded by turning their ruse on its head with a vow not to drink any more milk on the trek until they were safely home. The outcome of the fracas was an unexpected double portion for the saluki bitch that accompanied the party.[30] During a journey to map Arabia's south-western frontiers he used the same stratagem and refused food for days to exact moral retribution.[31]

It is perhaps only when set against these methods and attitudes that one can fully appreciate Wilfred Thesiger's very different response to his Bedu companions. He may not have shared their faith, or achieved Philby's consummate fluency in Arabic, but he was able to establish deep friendships with his companions that have endured for over forty years.[32]

In his assessment of the respective crossings of the Empty Quarter by Philby and Thomas, it is significant that Thesiger, while offering the laurels to the former for his longer and more difficult journey, stressed Thomas's achievement. His capacity to win the confidence of potentially hostile tribespeople, without the backing of official Arab authorities, spoke of Thomas's great personal qualities.[33] Such emphasis typified Thesiger's own egalitarian and co-operative approach to his Arab associates. Immersed in the paraphernalia of collecting and geographical surveying, Philby saw the Bedu as an essential vehicle, or perhaps impediment, to his goal. For Thesiger the relationships established with the members of his party were an end in themselves. Without them, in fact, 'the journey would have been a meaningless penance', as easily accomplished in the inhuman ice world of Antarctica.[34]

It is also of interest at this point to compare Thesiger's attitude to personal names with that of Eric Bailey. While the latter was seldom concerned to give individual status to local people he encountered, and usually described them by tribe or even nationality, Thesiger's books have long and rather complicated lists of *dramatis personae*. *Arabian Sands*, for example, has a main cast of twenty-nine, *The Marsh Arabs*, thirty-five, and both have numerous individually named extras.

Given the depth of his feeling, especially for two young Rashidi, Salim bin Ghabaisha and Salim bin Kabina, it is perhaps inevitable that his generalised statements about the Bedu would differ widely from those of Philby. While the latter often found them faint-hearted, greedy and too concerned with comfort, Thesiger was in awe of their courage, dignity and generosity. Frequently in *Arabian Sands* he noted their remarkable selflessness, even in conditions of considerable hardship; how they often argued at meal times if they felt they had been given more than their share.[35] A moment of humour in his otherwise austere account occurs when they kill and roast a hare after weeks of only bread and dates. At the last minute they are forced to go without by the unexpected appearance of three strangers, and the Bedu custom that they feed their guests before themselves.[36]

In Peter Brent's *Far Arabia: Explorers of the Myth*, the author argues that British travellers by living

> in the manner of the beduin fed western convictions that
> nothing was beyond the European, that no conditions could
> not be mastered, that he could survive in any environment.
> Thus the achievements of the Arabian explorers in
> humbling thirst and desert hardship played their part in
> reinforcing European assumptions of superiority; for if a
> Burton, a Leachman, or a Philby could live like an Arab,
> was it not at least possible that any clerk in Putney or
> Birkenhead might do likewise if he chose?[37]

In Philby's case a sense of superiority is possibly true. When his companions failed to keep the fast of Ramadan or baulked at the idea of travel in particularly dangerous regions, he was not slow to point out their failings. However, Brent's argument can hardly be extended to Thesiger. If anything, his comparisons of respective standards emphasise his own inadequacies. The nephew of India's viceroy, educated at Eton and Oxford, he hoped that his background had fully equipped him for life amongst a people proud of their ancient and noble lineage. 'Yet in their tents', Thesiger confessed, he 'felt like an uncouth, inarticulate barbarian, an intruder from a shoddy and materialistic world'.[38] In his introduction to *Arabian Sands* he acknowledged that he 'owed everything to the Bedu'.[39] Even amongst all the ceremony of the 1948 AGM at the Royal Geographical Society, when Thesiger was awarded the gold medal by Lord Rennell of Rodd, he acknowledged that without an entourage of long-haired, ragged Bedu he 'should not have gone ten miles'.[40]

A tone of deference and polite words of acknowledgement from the honoured individual are perhaps a natural part of such occasions. However, in his book he provides an unequivocal and compelling expression of Arab courage. After a long day's march during the first crossing of the Empty Quarter, Thesiger discussed with his guide, Muhammad al Auf, the latter's journey across the region two years earlier. 'Who was with you?' Thesiger asked:

> and he answered, 'I was alone'. Thinking that I must have misunderstood him, I repeated, 'Who were your companions?' 'God was my companion'. To have ridden alone through this appalling desolation was an incredible achievement. We were travelling through it now, but we carried our own world with us: a small world of five people, which yet provided each of us with companionship, with talk and laughter and the knowledge that others were there to share the hardship and the danger. I knew that if I travelled here alone the weight of this vast solitude would crush me utterly.[41]

It is the author's reputation as a traveller in some of the most remote landscapes on earth that gives this passage its peculiar resonance. If travellers are ever, as Peter Brent suggests, representatives of their race, then it is in this statement, if anywhere, that Thesiger speaks for us all.

It is not just their differing responses to the Bedu that separate Philby's and Thesiger's books on their desert travels. The production of any written account was in itself an issue on which they were fundamentally divided. Philby's *The Empty Quarter* was an inevitable consequence of his journey. It was, after all, his chief aim 'to secure the immortality to be gained by the accomplishment of some great work'. Having completed such a task it was a personal and financial imperative to announce the fact. The disciplined preparation of notes throughout the Rub al Khali had been a portion of this objective, and it allowed him on his way home to write to his wife that he was already 'bursting with [his] epic in embryo'.[42] Equally, Philby's speedy negotiation of a contract with the publishers Constable and then a commission to write articles for *The Times* were the hallmarks of a professional travel writer busily converting his experiences into concrete and saleable assets. It was also perhaps a measure of his remarkably rapid methods that he had produced a

400-page manuscript in the summer after his return from Arabia and had delivered it to Constable for publication in early 1933.[43]

Thesiger, like Philby, saw in the Empty Quarter 'the chance to win distinction as a traveller'[44] – a reputation he has been at some pains to protect. His friend and companion on a number of journeys, Gavin Young, has remarked on his 'tart tongue in private for some well-known British Arabists who based pretentious claims to great courage and adventurousness on relatively easy and riskless journeys'.[45] Between 1945–49, during the intense heat of the Arabian summers, Thesiger returned home to London, where he gave four papers on his journeys at the Royal Geographical Society. However, it is an indication of a larger indifference to the commercial possibilities of travel or to the wider acclaim his adventures could earn him, that for years these papers constituted the extent of his written record. The preparation of a full-length account had never occurred to him, largely because it would have interrupted the periods he had begun to spend in the Iraqi marshes. Even in 1959, Jack Philby could write of his fellow Arabist:

> He has yet to pay his full tribute to the country [Arabia] in a volume which is long overdue, though it is perhaps never likely to materialise. His occasional articles . . . are perhaps all we can expect to have from his pen, less accustomed to moving on paper than his bare feet on the desert sands.[46]

Ironically, by the time Philby's words were in print, *Arabian Sands* was poised to appear. In 1957, Gavin Maxwell, inspired by some of Thesiger's many excellent photographs, had suggested he have them published. However, the Arabist manfully resisted all encouragement to take up the pen until, faced with the combined efforts of Maxwell's agent, Graham Watson, the publisher Mark Longman and his own mother, he finally agreed to attempt a larger work.[47]

Although Philby's suggestion that his friend was no professional writer is essentially accurate, Thesiger had already given notice of some literary ability in his various papers. These were written in a spare, simple and exact prose. In his own book, *A Reed Shaken by the Wind*, Gavin Maxwell had already unearthed an early Thesiger nugget. On the inevitable consequences of modernisation for the marsh Arabs' ancient lifestyle, Thesiger had written: 'I regret the forces which are inexorably suburbanising the untamed places and turning tribesmen into corner boys'.[48] His gift for synecdoche and almost epigrammatic concision are dominant features of his style. Take two other sentences on the disappearance of traditional Bedu culture:

'Salala had been a small Arab village adjoining the Sultan's palace; now it was a town with traffic lights.'[49]

'The values of the desert have vanished: all over Arabia the transistor has replaced the tribal bard.'[50]

It was surely no mere coincidence that one capable of such frugal prose, and whose preferences are for black-and-white over colour photographs, or for line drawings over paintings, should be drawn to a landscape of such powerful simplicity.

Thesiger was disadvantaged in his first literary project by a lack of contemporary travel diaries. The cursory notes he had jotted at the time of his journeys had been to ensure the subsequent accuracy of his RGS lectures, but they were not the basis for a book.[51] A crucial substitute to help recollect the details of journeys undertaken sometimes more than a decade ago was his large series of photographs. The process of remembrance was further assisted when he subjected himself to a winter in Copenhagen and then the deep tranquillity of a relative's country house in County Wicklow. Even then his production was remarkably slow. A practice of writing, rewriting and then rewriting each portion at least five or six times meant that 250 words was an average daily output. During the night a pencil and notebook were always handy to capture the adjective or phrase that had eluded him during the day.[52] This slow and exacting system of composition resulted in a hard-won, word-perfect style, whose economy is well matched to the task of describing desert life. It is also perhaps these unusual background circumstances to the book's preparation that have helped make *Arabian Sands* one of the great books on Arabian travel.

To examine such a claim it is first valuable to consider Philby's

66

methods of composition. His *The Empty Quarter*, while documenting one of the outstanding desert journeys, is a travel work typical of the age. It is essentially a hybrid of science and journalism: a book compiled to capture the maximum contemporary interest, in which its author took considerable pains to ensure its accuracy. Yet it was written at great speed in Philby's competent, though somewhat prolix style. Indeed, this wordiness was suggested by his biographer as one reason why he is so little read today.[53] It is also perhaps worthwhile to reflect that, in addition to his fifteen published works, he produced almost as many that were not. Just one of these, *Out Of Step*, which chronicled the war until 1943, amounted to over a million words.[54]

In his standard works of travel Philby, like Eric Bailey, and in fact most of his Victorian contemporaries, made the physical itinerary the basis of his book's narrative structure. Working with a grid of dates and localities, he inserted descriptions of events or observations exactly as they occurred. Refashioning the journey in any way, to maximise the interest of the book, was something Philby would probably never have considered. For one, it was close to deception; it would also have complicated, and so lengthened, its preparation. It was the drama inherent in the journey itself that would provide, almost incidentally, all the book's narrative tension. When Philby wrote to Dora of his 'epic in embryo' he was probably thinking more of the long and gruelling nature of the trek he would describe, rather than any literary merit he might exhibit in doing so.

From the outset Thesiger identified that a core problem of a work on desert travel was how to convey the vast emptiness of the landscape without inducing a feeling of monotony in his readers.[55] He was also at pains to maintain some sense of uncertainty and drama about a route that had been successfully completed a decade ago. It is typical of his effort that background factual information on the region and its people is carefully integrated with the events of their march. An extended essay on the prehistoric origins, the history and cultural traditions of the Bedu is presented as the thoughts induced by the steady sway of a moving camel.[56] Desert lore about pasturage and grazing is passed off as a brief conversation en route.[57] In this way the education of the reader about unknown parts is not allowed to interrupt the forward momentum of the journey itself.

Another of Thesiger's dramatic techniques is to draw his audience into an elaborate anticlimax. A crucial element of the first crossing of the Empty Quarter was a formidable series of sand mountains called the Uruq al Shaiba. His party's ability to cross these becomes Thesiger's *idée fixe*, and when finally confronted by a solid wall of sand, he speculates aloud:

> What were we going to do if we could not get the camels over it? . . . Our water was already dangerously short and even more urgent than our own needs were those of the camels, which would collapse unless they were watered soon. We *must* get over this monstrous dune . . . But what was on the other side?[58]

Having then brought the reader to a state of great relief by their successful ascent of this sand mountain and the apparent completion of the most dangerous part of the route, Thesiger stages a moment of masterly bathos. While resting, he commented to his guide, al Auf, on their improved situation: 'He looked at me for a moment and then answered, "If we go well tonight we should reach them tomorrow". I said, "Reach what?" and he replied "The Uruq al Shaiba", adding "Did you think what we crossed today was the Uruq al Shaiba? That was only a dune".'[59] The stage is thus set for one of the climactic scenes of the book and their encounter, the following day, with the true mountains. It is this manipulation of the journey's dramatic possibilities that gives *Arabian Sands* a much stronger claim to epic status.

The ten-year interval between Thesiger's journeys and his written account meant that even had he wished to, he could not have employed the blow-by-blow, inch-by-inch reportage of Philby's works. The long gap had effected a natural editorial process, which left only those elements of deepest personal significance. This harder substratum of memory had also been allowed to accumulate additional meaning. By 1957, twelve years after his first journey in Arabia, Thesiger had spent a substantial part of seven years in the Iraqi marshes; he had also made four lengthy expeditions to the Hindu Kush and Karakorams, as well as two three-month treks in Kurdistan and a journey in the High Atlas of Morocco. In spite, or perhaps because of all these experiences, he was able to identify his time in Arabia as his happiest period – an opinion which he has never altered.[60] From the longer and wider perspective of the late 1950s, his desert years seemed the natural climax to a life of travel. 'All my life', he wrote in the opening chapter of *Arabian Sands*, 'had been but a prelude to the five years that lay ahead of me'.[61]

Throughout the book one has a sense of an attempt to give expression to the deeper personal significance of this period in the desert. As a consequence many scenes seem to carry an importance that is greater than their immediate and obvious content. Take, for instance, this passage describing a portion of the return route to Salala on the Arabian Sea:

> Once more we rode across an empty land, but now it was not only empty, it was dead. Shallow depressions in the limestone floor held sloughs of glutinous black mud, crusted with scabs of salt and sand, like putrescent patches on a carcase rotting in the sun. We rode for seven and eight and nine hours a day, without a stop, and it was dreary work. Conversation died with the passing hours and boredom mounted within me like a dull ache of pain . . . I watched the sun's slow progress and longed for evening. As the sun sank into the haze it became an orange disc without heat or brilliance. I looked at it through my field-glasses and saw the sun-spots like black holes in its surface. It disappeared while still a span above the horizon, vanishing in a yellow sky that was without a cloud.[62]

The journey theme, which so readily translates into a metaphor for life itself, in Thesiger's case becomes almost a voyage through purgatory. In particular it examines what remains to humans at such levels of deprivation, and at the limits of endurance. *Arabian Sands* is a quest for and celebration of both the masculine severity and atavistic pleasures of the pagan world: 'the richness of meat; the taste of clean water; the ecstasy of surrender when the craving for sleep becomes a torment; the warmth of a fire in the chill of dawn'.[63] It is passages like the one above which have inspired another traveller in Arabia, Jonathan Raban, to talk of 'the enormous power' of Thesiger's writing.[64]

In its highly visual, at times almost vision-like quality one can possibly detect the author's use of black-and-white photographs as an *aide-mémoire*. It may also provide access to the entire cast of his creative imagination – expressed both in his writing and his photographs. So frequently a landscape or scene or human figure is pared to a minimum of details. By illuminating these apparently random fragments, he manages to convey the whole, undisclosed background. A passage on the migrations of the Bakhtiari tribe from Itan, in a much later book, *Desert, Marsh and Mountain*, is typical:

> I climbed above the wood and sat beside the track, to watch the migration pass. Below me were the lights of many fires, and from the darkness of the valley I heard a rising, falling roar, a flowing river of sound, as the migration moved forward. Flocks of sheep pushed past, their fleeces luminous in the near dark; and separate flocks of black goats, a moving darkness, darker than the hillside. Men and boys passed, pale figures in white coats; and dark, barely discernible women interspersed with scrambling, straining mules and cattle. The light grew stronger. I could distinguish bedding, pots and pans, sacks of grain loaded on mules and cattle, a puppy on a cow's back, babies in cradles or bundles, carried by the women. Then the birds began to sing in the wood, and the sun came over the mountains. I climbed to the pass; ahead, the track was solid for miles with a thread of slowly moving men and animals.[65]

If there could be said to be unifying principles in Thesiger's *oeuvre* then it would be his passionate – some would say romantic – sense of dignity and value in the lives of nomads and 'primitives', and his deep sense of loss as their ancient cultures succumb, one by one, to the impact of a global, technological advance. With the eloquence and perversity almost of a tragic hero he announced in his first book: 'I craved the past, resented the present and dreaded the future'.[66] The central self-drama of his life has been his role as last witness to a vanishing golden age. It is in this wider autobiographical context that his writing on pre-industrial communities has been invested with its crowning emotional charge. Descriptions like the one of the Bakhtiari convey not only the morning passage of a migration, but the ancient past of an entire people, as well as the imminent demise of their pattern of life.

Thesiger has at times suggested that he has lived in the wrong century: his preferred year of birth is apparently 1836.[67] Yet he was also deeply fortunate. Born in 1910, he had just time to find and explore a part of Abyssinia – the Danakil Desert – that had never seen a white person, and then encounter Bedu tribespeople whose only knowledge of the West were personal memories of two men, Philby and Thomas. Even in an age of Soviet space probes, of the Stones and Beatles and teenagers in mini-skirts, Thesiger could still describe a people in *The Marsh Arabs* whose lifestyle had gone unchanged since the empire of the Assyrians. Even well into the sixties, in Kenya, Iran and North Yemen, he could satisfy the purist's concern for travel on foot or with pack animals, amongst communities uncontaminated by the 'drab uniformity of the modern world'.

In many people's eyes, including perhaps his own, these final glimpses have made him the last explorer in the tradition of the past.[68] Yet those individuals that are most frequently numbered in that tradition – men like Speke, Burton, Livingstone, Stanley – were invariably a vanguard for imperialism. Their maps, established routes, and treaties led to subsequent European penetration, colonisation and then finally those very processes that have suburbanised the untamed places. In Thesiger's resentment of this pattern, in his reverence and his sensitivity to the lifestyles of nomads and so-called 'primitives', and also in his adaptation of the travel genre to express their disappearing values, he appears wholly distinct from the explorers of the past. It would perhaps be more accurate (to borrow Alan Moorehead's judgement of Sir Samuel Baker) to describe him as a kind of fulcrum in twentieth-century travel: one of the first in a line of generous, sympathetic travellers who are also writers of great ability –men and women such as Lawrence Durrell, Patrick Leigh Fermor, Norman Lewis, Dervla Murphy, Colin Thubron and Bruce Chatwin – than as a final exponent of the old.[69]

Chapter V
Truth Stranger than Friction

One of the great strengths of travel writing, and one of the reasons why it commands attention in a way that fiction might not, is that it purports to be a record of fact. Moreover, it frequently chronicles real lives at their most extreme – the most daring or dangerous actions and the most extraordinary incidents in a setting of rich unfamiliarity. It is perhaps a hallmark of the successful travel work that it can convey its audience to an environment entirely outside their experience, which is yet authentic and even sometimes extant. In *Arabian Sands* the average European reader encounters a realm almost as remote and mythological as purgatory itself, whose impact is redoubled by the very fact of the Rub al Khali's existence, and the actuality of its hardships. Equally, the heightened sense of drama in Thesiger's account of the crossing of the Uruq al Shaiba partly derives from the notion running at the back of the reader's mind that these events really took place. There are even occasions when the author of travel adventure, almost paradoxically, is unlimited by conditions that might restrain the fictional writer. The guiding principle in the narrative need not be a sense of what the audience will accept as plausible, but a fidelity to what happened, no matter how incredible this might seem.

Frederick Bailey's *Mission to Tashkent* is an excellent example of this. During his period in Soviet Central Asia at the close of the First World War, he was a witness to the extraordinary conditions of early Bolshevik rule. The fears and confusion unleashed by the revolution brought into being a looking-glass world in which Soviet intelligence services unwittingly arrested their own agents;

in which Bailey's dog, Zep, a gift from the Maharaja of Dholpur, was trailed by spies as it sniffed along the streets of Tashkent; in which a man could be arrested and executed for destroying his own piano with an axe. During these years Bailey eluded the secret police in a succession of disguises – at one time as a sausage-maker – sustained fractures in both knees in a falling accident that prevented him from making an early escape, and was eventually recruited, on his recovery, into the Soviet counter-espionage service with a brief to gather information on himself.

Although Bailey was not able to exploit the full possibilities of his remarkable story, the very authenticity of the tale tends to compensate for any literary deficiency. In fact, the events of real life provide the basis for a narrative that is perhaps more extraordinary than one that was entirely a product of the imagination. It was precisely this reversal of an accepted norm that inspired the headline in an issue of *The Englishman* newspaper after his successful escape:

THIRTY-NINE STEPS
TRUTH STRANGER THAN FRICTION [*sic*]
BAILEY ROMANCE
INDIAN SECRET SERVICE[1]

The recurrence of real-life dramas in travel literature is an indication, perhaps, of exactly how dangerous the business of travel can be. Bailey, Philby and Thesiger each encountered circumstances in which they might easily have lost their lives. Bailey revealed, with typical understatement, how in 1913 he saved himself from a potentially fatal fall on a mountain pass, by digging the handle of his butterfly net into the deep snow. During Philby's crossing of the Rub al Khali his entourage, disgruntled at his high-handed leadership, seriously contemplated murdering him. In Thesiger's *Arabian Sands* he described a narrow escape from two hostile parties of Bedu tribesmen. Ironically, his safety had hinged on his inability with a rifle. For had he not failed to shoot an oryx at under 200 metres, his party, unaware of the danger, would almost certainly have stopped to skin and dry the carcase. The delay might then have permitted his assailants to overtake and kill him.[2]

It might be argued that in the journeys of some of the twentieth century's greatest explorers, danger was to be expected. Yet even travels undertaken in a post-exploration age, amongst relatively settled communities, have involved situations in which life was clearly at risk. During Dervla Murphy's wanderings in the Ethiopian highlands she was confronted by a gang of thieves in an isolated locality and relieved of a number of her possessions. It is typical of the traveller's acceptance of these occupational hazards that Murphy deprecated the fuss made by the local police on her behalf, pointing out that Ethiopia was merely the sixth foreign country in which she had met robbers.[3] When Gavin Maxwell visited the Iraqi marshes with Wilfred Thesiger he was spared very serious injury and possibly death, when the charge of an immense wild boar was deflected by a shallow depression in the ground.[4] Marooned in the remote southern Arabian town of Shibam, and stricken first with measles, then dysentery, Freya Stark lived to see her forty-third birthday only because of the prompt action of the Royal Air Force pilot who flew her to a hospital in Aden.[5]

Given the level of threat from both natural and human elements, it is perhaps more remarkable how few of the most daring travellers have lost their lives during the course of their journeys. Two outstanding Arab explorers of this century, Gerald Leachman[6] and William Shakespear,[7] both fell to Arab guns, but their deaths were in conditions of war or rebellion. Yet the death of travel companions is a frequent source of drama in travel works. In those of a violent martinet like Henry Stanley, to whom retainers were little more than disposable assets, loss of life amongst his entourage was almost commonplace. In Thesiger's *Arabian Sands* he describes how a companion during one of his early journeys in the Hadramaut, Bin Duailan, was murdered by opposing Arab tribesmen.[8] The shooting accident that killed Falih bin Majid, Thesiger's friend and frequent host in the Iraqi marshes, forms a central episode in his book, *The Marsh Arabs*, and appears also in Gavin Maxwell's *A Reed Shaken by the Wind*.[9] In Laurens van der Post's *Venture to the Interior* the drowning of a companion is a tragic event at the heart of one of the most elaborately constructed travel books in the post-war period.

Venture to the Interior was also one of the most successful. Van der Post's second book, it earned him immediate recognition, a *Who's*

Who entry and substantial royalties. After the first week of publication the first two printings of 40,000 copies were all but exhausted, and it continued to sell at 1,000 copies a day.[10] Only weeks after its release in January 1952, the *National Review* had already decided it would be 'one of the outstanding books of the year'.[11] According to the *Daily Telegraph* it was 'a masterpiece' on a par with *Seven Pillars of Wisdom*.[12] Of the period's triumvirate of literary taste – Cyril Connolly, Raymond Mortimer and Harold Nicolson – the last two were happy to announce on the same day that 'everybody will enjoy this book',[13] and that its author was 'brave, modest, thoughtful, imaginative and eminently humane'.[14] The novelist Howard Spring went one step further: it was 'one of the noblest books of travel written in our time, and one destined . . . to have a permanent place in English literature'.[15] This praise for a work describing travels in Nyasaland (Malawi) was echoed in van der Post's native southern Africa: 'one of the best books put out in recent years';[16] 'This is one of the most significant books yet written about Africa';[17] 'the most thoughtful and penetrating writing about the real essence of Africa since Conrad's *Heart of Darkness*'.[18]

The journey which the book described was undertaken by van der Post on behalf of the Commonwealth Development Corporation, to examine the agricultural potential of two little-known areas of Nyasaland – a region of forest close to the border with what was then Portuguese East Africa (Mozambique), and the Nyika Plateau, 2,500 square kilometres of high-altitude grassland, a portion of which lay across the border in Northern Rhodesia (Zambia). In a relatively small, densely populated country like Nyasaland neither area was totally unknown, although Nyika was uninhabited and without a road at the time of van der Post's visit.[19] Mount Mlanje, on the other hand, had long been an important source of timber for the country's forestry department. Van der Post's relatively straightforward agricultural reconnaissance, completed in little more than three months and undertaken largely in mechanised transport, had little of the glamour that surrounded the explorations of a solitary like Philby or Thesiger.

Accompanied by the chief district forester and his subordinate, who were given the fictional names of Peter Quillan and Richard Vance respectively, van der Post led a short investigative trek across the forested mountains around Mlanje. Caught on the fifth day by unexpected and violent rainstorms, the party of about thirty-five was forced to spend the night on the mountainside in a disused lumber camp. The following day conditions on the steep slopes had become treacherous and the last portion of the trip was abandoned. During the return hike, in an area known as the Great Ruo gorge, the abnormally swollen waters of a mountain stream halted progress until the young forester, Vance, volunteered to cross it with a rope. Using a large stick to test for footholds, Vance waded out into the stream. After he had gone some distance and with the water up to about his navel, the young man then deviated from the procedure which he and van der Post had agreed he should follow. Releasing his stick he called for the others to let out the rope.

> Before we had even properly grasped his meaning he had thrown himself on the stream and was swimming a breast-stroke. As was inevitable, the stream at once caught him and quickly swept him to where it foamed and bubbled like a waterfall over the edge of the track. The unexpected speed with which all of this happened was the most terrifying thing about it. Even so, Vance had got to within a foot of the far bank, was on the verge of reaching it – when the water swept him over the edge and he disappeared from our view.[20]

The young man was never seen again. The force of the water pressing on him as he was suspended by the rope swept him sideways back towards the bank from which he had set out. In so doing the rope frayed on the sharp-edged stones and eventually snapped before the others could reach him.

Not surprisingly, this tragic misadventure served van der Post as an emotional climax to which the sequence of events naturally builds. Yet the accident has a significance greater than just as a source of dramatic tension, since it lies at the very heart of an elaborate symbolism which underpins the narrative. In order to appreciate fully the way in which the Mlanje incident functions in van der Post's story, it is initially valuable to consider the author's personal background.

Laurens van der Post, born in South Africa in 1906, is a member of a prominent Afrikaner family, whose lands at one time apparently totalled 500,000 acres.[21] By the outbreak of the Boer War his father, Christian Willem Hendrik van der Post, had become chairman of the executive council of the Orange Free State parliament, and was also a highly successful lawyer, maintaining the largest legal practice in the state.[22] Laurens, the youngest of thirteen children, following a period as a journalist with the *Natal Advertiser* and a brief, though influential, visit to Japan, left South Africa in 1927 with a new wife and an ambition to advance his writing career in London. Further years of journalism both in England and South Africa were the prelude to his well-received first novel, *In a Province*. This dealt with a theme that dominated the author's early writing – the relations between black and white in colonial Africa.

Brought up in a liberal and apparently multi-racial farm environment, van der Post has claimed immunity from the poisoned racial attitudes of Afrikanerdom.[23] Opposition to his country's segregationist policies was the background to his early work on a radical literary and political magazine, *Voorslag* (Whiplash), started by two writer friends, Roy Campbell and William Plomer. Despair at national injustice also lay behind much of his effort as a journalist, and was the goad for his frequent periods of exile. For much of the thirties, until the outbreak of the Second World War, he moved back and forth between South Africa and England, and spent much time walking and travelling throughout the African continent.[24] This pattern of life was apparently resumed when hostilities ceased, van der Post alternating 'between Africa and Europe in a state of suspended being like a ghost from some unquiet grave, shocked almost as much by the ruthlessness and brutalities of peace'.[25]

In *Venture to the Interior* he identified his restlessness as the result of a conflict between two opposing elements in his make-up: the 'conscious and unconscious, male and female . . . On one side, under the heading "Africa", I would group unconscious, female, feminine, mother; and under "Europe" on the other: conscious, male, masculine, father'.[26] For van der Post this personal antinomy was an expression of a fundamental dialectic in life, whose impact rippled outwards to encompass almost all human experience. In particular, he offered it as a means of comprehending what was, at the time of the book's publication, a gathering crisis in relations between white colonials of European origin and black Africans.

Europeans, according to van der Post, had been immersed since the Renaissance in cultural traditions that laid overwhelming stress on the masculine, rational, extrovert aspects of human experience. This bias had led to a profound neglect of the dark, preconscious, elemental side of human nature which psychologists like Freud and Jung had 'rediscovered' and identified as the unconscious or the 'shadow'. A refusal to allow this dark half of the self legitimate fulfilment had resulted in a profound schism in the European spirit.[27] Africa, on the other hand, a deeply ancient landscape and the original birthplace of the human race, was an environment where the preconscious and non-rational had had full rein in the lives of its inhabitants. These largely Negroid people were termed 'primitive', which in van der Post's vocabulary carried no pejorative overtones, but was intended to convey 'a condition of life wherein the instinctive, subjective and collective values tend to predominate'.[28] However, having given full expression to one half of themselves, Africans had hitherto failed to develop precisely those rational faculties and values so dominant in European culture. Only through a synthesis of the two patterns of experience could blacks and whites achieve inner and outer harmony. Yet this resolution had not taken place. Confronted by Africa's human and natural landscape, colonial settlers had simply hemmed themselves in behind a palisade of racist attitudes and policies, and projected onto the external world – especially the subject black inhabitants – the fear and hostility felt within for their own dark selves. Racism, in effect, emanated from the whites' self-rejection or, at least, rejection of a portion of themselves.

It is quite clear that in *Venture to the Interior* the young forester Richard Vance is intended to symbolise the European self divided by personal experience and cultural background. Accordingly he is presented as a man with an unhappy childhood, burdened by a deep sense of inferiority, for whom the forested mountains are a refuge from inadequacies within. Living in an isolated log cabin with his young wife and baby daughter, he hopes to find in Mlanje the setting for deep and lasting fulfilment. It is significant that when he and the author first meet in the book, their initial conversation includes the following exchange:

> 'This is very beautiful, well-nigh perfect [says van der Post, pointing to the mountain]. Might be somewhere in Europe,' I said, realizing it was a half-truth but not yet aware of the full one.
> 'Yes,'. . . [Vance] said, with a warm look that took in the whole valley. 'Yes. It is absolutely perfect.'[29]

Even in this apparently innocent small-talk, however, the author marks the trail that leads to Vance's fatal accident, since perfection, in van der Post's parlance, can be deeply negative. 'To love only perfection', he announces towards the end of the book, 'is just another way of hating life, for life is not perfect'.[30]

Vance, cut off from the dark half of his own being, and therefore capable of only a lop-sided understanding of life, is at the mercy of Africa's dark forces, of which Mlanje, ironically, is an archetypal expression. Long before the accident occurs van der Post describes the mountain as:

> a great, grey, compelling Jurassic sort of personality, a character of ill-suppressed rage, a petrified brontosaurus-like grinding and gnashing of teeth, that made everything near it shrink and cower; it presented itself to my senses as a giant striding through time with the plain, like a mongrel, at its heels.[31]

When these hidden 'realities' are unveiled by the author, the reader is made to feel that rather than being a mere product of chance, Vance's death has about it a deep inevitability. 'Accident and disaster without', van der Post informs us, 'feed on accident and disaster within'.[32]

Following a fruitless search for Vance's body, the expedition eventually returned to the forestry headquarters and, after preparing a report on the storm-troubled mountain, van der Post set off for the Nyika Plateau and the second leg of his mission. In *Venture to the Interior* he marries to his account of this survey a further inquiry into the philosophical ideas articulated in the circumstances of Vance's drowning. Several days into the expedition's trek and lying one morning almost rooted to the primal African earth of Nyika – a locale deeply appropriate to the author for introspection – he recalled experiences endured exactly seven years before in a Japanese prisoner-of-war camp on Java. Van der Post and other officers had been forced to stand and observe the brutal execution of two fellow internees, one of whom was decapitated, the other run through by Japanese soldiers with fixed bayonets. At the moment of slaughter, the officer standing next to the author was overcome by the horrific spectacle and on the point of collapse. 'In this moment', van der Post wrote, 'lies the real significance of that afternoon'.

> For as I put my arm round [the officer] Horobin, a stranger,
> in order to support him, I felt to my utter amazement how
> near he was to me. There seemed to be no barrier between
> us; we might have been the same person under the same
> skin; and in spite of the dreadful circumstances of the
> moment, a tremendous warmth and reassurance welled up
> within me, like wine and song. All sense of isolation . . .
> my desperate twentieth-century awareness of isolation and
> doom vanished. I was out of it all in a flash, and far beyond
> in a world of inseparable nearness.[33]

Reconsidering these events from a fresh African perspective and in the light of his recent tragic experiences in Nyasaland, he finally came to an understanding of why the Japanese, for all his own sense of transcendent unity with his fellow prisoners, were yet so distant.

> It seemed so clear to me that morning . . . Those Japanese
> did not know what they were doing . . . They thought they
> were performing their duty nobly, beautifully, and justly.
> Yet they were doing the opposite and doing it because their
> awareness of themselves, and of life, was inadequate. For
> this unreality starts in an incomplete awareness of ourselves;
> it starts in the elevation of a part of ourselves at the expense
> of the whole. Then, out of this dark gorge which we have

allowed to open up between the two halves of ourselves, out
of this division between the Europe and the Africa in us,
unreality rises up to overwhelm us.[34]

The spiritual schism which, according to van der Post, lay at the
heart of problems in colonial Africa, and which he saw at the root of
events on Mount Mlanje, also explained a wider disharmony in
human affairs. White Europeans and black Africans might embody
the two extreme poles of human consciousness, but no single
people had achieved a satisfactory integration of the two modes of
perception. The Second World War, from whose destructive
impact the author felt himself only just emerging, was itself a
profound expression of the same spiritual crisis.

Venture to the Interior, true to the travel genre, is a linear narrative
of journey experience, whose author's preoccupations were largely
appropriate to one particular time and place. Its underlying
message, for instance, must have seemed freshest and most
pertinent to an audience for whom six years of conflict constituted
the very recent past. Equally, it dwelt on a crisis in race relations
which, while of paramount importance then, has now changed out
of all recognition. Of all the African states existing when the book
emerged, only four (Ethiopia, Egypt, Liberia and Libya) enjoyed
independence. Yet within fifteen years only Angola, Mozambique
and South Africa (with Namibia) were still under European
dominion. However, the book would not have remained almost
continually in print for the last forty years if it had merely
contributed to an outworn debate. It has enjoyed a consistent
popularity shared by very few other works of travel (Lawrence
Durrell's *Reflections on a Marine Venus* and T. E. Lawrence's *Seven
Pillars of Wisdom* are two of them). If this longevity rests on
anything then it is perhaps on van der Post's successful fusion of an
individual tale of travel and a spiritual odyssey of much wider
relevance. If, as Howard Spring claimed, the book is destined to
have a permanent place in English literature it is because its vatic call
for self-examination is as appropriate now as it was then.

Despite the huge success of this book both in Europe and
America, the aspect of van der Post's work with which he has
become most closely identified has been that on the San, the so-

called Bushmen (apparently a derogatory term coined by early Boer settlers) of the Kalahari Desert in southern Africa. Tradition-ally considered some of the continent's oldest inhabitants, the relict communities of these small, Mongol-featured nomads, with a technology representative of the Stone Age, have been the focus for three of his non-fictional works, for two of his novels and for a famous series of documentary films. It is interesting to note that, like Thesiger, he has claimed that the origins of his fascination with non-white 'primitives' stemmed from his earliest childhood experiences, especially his contact with his nurse Klara, a woman with a San mother. In the autobiographical *A Walk with a White Bushman* he wrote:

> It started almost before I could speak, from the moment the sunset inflamed the necklace of beads round the throat of Klara and I would see her antique face as she put me to sleep. I was committed from that moment on, to a very special and profound interest in the Bushman and his fate . . . there is almost nothing of importance in my life which does not owe something to this commitment.[35]

However, it was not until after the expedition to Nyasaland in 1949 that van der Post participated in a series of government surveys of the Kalahari Desert, which is shared between Botswana (then the British protectorate of Bechuanaland), Namibia (formerly South-West Africa) and South Africa. These journeys revived his interest in the San and he returned there with an expedition in 1954 to make a film of their rapidly vanishing lifestyle.

Dominating van der Post's written account of his mission, *The Lost World of the Kalahari*, and possibly looming over his entire *oeuvre* is his mythic representation of the San. His outline of their culture and tragic history, which occupies the first quarter of the book, is rendered in a naive, almost Biblical language, and presented as the fragments gleaned during a childhood quest for information; and full, therefore, of a child's mythopoeic sense of wonder. Physically, the San were the stuff of legends. 'His ankles were slim like a race horse, his legs supple, his muscles loose and he ran like the wind fast and long . . . There has never been anyone who could run like him over the veld and boulders'.[36] His skin colour, unaffected by the intense sunlight, was 'a lovely Provençal apricot yellow', while the deep brown colour of his eyes was only to be matched by those of an antelope.[37] His prowess as a hunter followed along much the same idealised lines. He was an unerring shot, a natural botanist, an expert in chemistry and unrivalled tracker, while his powers of vision had 'become part of the heroic legend in Africa'.[38] To cap it all, the last refuge for this dispossessed and fragmented tribe, the Kalahari Desert, was a final Eden:

> its deep fertile sands are covered with grass glistening in the
> wind like fields of gallant corn . . . It is filled too with its
> own varieties of game, buck of all kinds, birds and lion and
> leopard. When the rains come it grows sweet-tasting grasses
> and hangs its bushes with amber berries, glowing raisins
> and sugared plums. Even the spaces between the satin
> grasses are filled with succulent melons and fragrant
> cucumbers and in the earth itself bulbs, tubers, wild carrots,
> potatoes, turnips and sweet potatoes grow great with
> moisture and abundantly multiply.[39]

However, the San were not merely noble savages living in a state of pre-lapsarian innocence. Withdrawing before a succession of stronger invaders, both black and white, they had still put up a fierce and dogged resistance. The Bushman, van der Post proclaimed on the opening page of the book, was 'gay, gallant, mischievous, unpredictable and to the end unrepentant and defiant'.[40] Their inner lives were also highly sophisticated. Rock paintings worked on cliff sides and cave walls were 'the purest form of a truly organic art the continent has yet known'.[41] Their music similarly had no equal in Africa. With an orchestra of drums, rattles and stringed equivalents to the fiddle, harp, bass violin and cello they produced a complex music. This, together with a variety of games were the heart of a pattern of life that put many 'so called "superior" cultures to shame'.[42]

Although perhaps highly coloured, van der Post's description of the San and their culture was rooted in hard fact, and has since been corroborated by the work of numerous anthropologists. When not constrained by the encroachment of Europeans, the San lived in family units of about thirty individuals and wandered across the desert, their worldly possessions amounting to no more than twelve kilograms each. This lack of material wealth had previously provided European colonists with their argument that the San were cultureless savages, little better than apes. Another long-held belief maintained that their life in the desert was one endless, animal battle to fend off starvation. Since then research has proved these ideas to be inaccurate. What the San lacked in technology and material culture, they made up for with a remarkable array of survival skills and unparalleled knowledge of their Kalahari environment. Moreover, the average period per week devoted to work has been estimated at about forty hours (with women doing somewhat more than men) – far less than in modern industrial society. Their considerable leisure time had permitted the development of their abundant songs, stories, dances and games and the richness of their social lives. Egalitarian, free from exploitation, from serious violence or dispute, San society had a great deal to commend it.

During the 1950s, especially in southern Africa, van der Post's more idealised portrait of the San in *The Lost World of the Kalahari* could be justified as an essential corrective to long-held prejudices. The book, along with the expedition's resulting films shown in a BBC series of six to large audiences in 1955, was also a straightforward piece of international advocacy, raising concern for the San and eventually leading to government action on their behalf.[43]

Yet, it is evident that van der Post intended this portrait in the book to go beyond the merely educative. It is striking, for example, that his description of the small, authentic community encountered and filmed occupies a mere forty-eight pages at the very end of the work. The remaining four-fifths of the narrative are absorbed by the sketch of San history and of the genesis of his own preoccupation with their culture, but primarily by a detailed account of the expedition's long and initially fruitless quest for its subject. Much of *The Lost World of the Kalahari* is, in fact, a description of the search for the San, rather than an account of the San themselves. In particular, van der Post seemed preoccupied with the various setbacks that hampered his party, such as the difficulty of his relations with a contracted cameraman, Eugene Spode, and the hectic chase to find a replacement photographer once Spode resigned.

When the book was released, its author received considerable criticism for apparently wandering from his principal theme. 'One has an odd feeling', complained the reviewer in the *Economist*,

> that the book's object was to offer some devious apologia for Colonel van der Post's having failed to make the best of Mr Spode. There are moments – and they are far too many – when the book might better have been called 'the lost film of the Kalahari' . . . All this may be well enough told, but is irrelevant and annoying because it has little or nothing to do with the matter in hand. [44]

The matter in hand for most people, it seemed, was describing the San and illustrating their lives as his films had done several years earlier. In the *Times Literary Supplement* the criticism was even more intense. In a final paragraph, the anonymous critic concluded that 'This is a book like a heavy doughnut. The jam in the middle is excellent, but there is an awful lot of dough. (And in the less eminent literary circles, in the ruder, more shameless, less mystical branches of the writer's trade, they sometimes call it padding)'. [45]

These remarks, however, showed little regard for van der Post's multi-layered treatment of his subject. *The Lost World of the Kalahari* is on one level a straightforward narrative of action, on a par with Bailey's *No Passport to Tibet* or Philby's *The Empty Quarter*. But it is also – like *Venture to the Interior* (whose title implies an alternative stratum of meaning) – at a more fundamental level, a psychological drama. In particular it is a contemporary version of the quest myth. In the context of this classical model, the author's record of the expedition's tribulations all approximate to the trials which confront the quest-myth hero, and which he or she must overcome in order to gain the ultimate goal of the spiritual journey. [46] At the heart of the Kalahari quest are the San themselves, contact with whom provides a route back to 'the First Man in ourselves'. [47] For a number of reasons they are a deeply appropriate element in van der Post's iconography. Their uncontrolled decimation by colonial invaders mirrored exactly the fate of the dark shadow of the human spirit, driven into near extinction by a European obsession with reason. 'They are both an example', van der Post has written,

> of what we should recover in our own spirit. And they are also a warning to us, that if we do not recover this sense nature will turn on us one day, and we will be eliminated as the Bushmen were eliminated – because you cannot eliminate something precious in life without killing something in your soul.[48]

Yet their fate offered a lesson not just to the obsessively rational European colonials. Successive invasions of tribes like the Bantu, Zulus, Hottentots, Karrani, Basuto and Griqua had all taken their toll on their smaller, less aggressive San neighbours. They were, therefore, 'the one historical mirror . . . in Africa wherein both black and white can look and see their fallible human faces'.[49] The story of the 'Bushman' and his lost world of the Kalahari are simultaneously a measure of the deep flaw in the human spirit, and a lodestar for our ultimate redemption.

It is interesting to note that there is a number of striking parallels between *Venture to the Interior* and *The Lost World of the Kalahari*. In both books the expedition initially met serious difficulties, misfortunes that van der Post attributed to a lack of preparedness amongst his party for the African environment. In each the sense of dissonance is largely projected onto one person, an individual who seems also to serve as a foil for van der Post himself. In the case of *Venture to the Interior* the unfortunate was Richard Vance. In *The Lost World of the Kalahari* it was the cameraman, Eugene Spode, the very sound of whose fictional name seems to convey something of the rôle he was intended to play in the narrative. Of undisclosed European nationality, Spode was apparently a painter, musician, scenario writer, composer, producer and cameraman of uncommon talent. Van der Post was also told of the 'intensely heroic rôle he had played in the resistance movement of his country', and that his suffering under the Nazis, Communists and Fascists went some way to explain why he seemed such a 'profoundly unhappy man'.[50] However, swayed by Spode's war record and his avowed love of Africa, the author agreed for him to join the party.

Unfortunately, their collaboration started to founder even before the expedition left Bulawayo in Rhodesia, on the issue of who should control direction of the film. This discord becomes almost a touchstone for the party's wider atmosphere of disintegration. Spode, unwilling to film effectively and apparently unable to face the harsh conditions imposed by African safari life, moons through the narrative, cast in a mood of undisclosed resentment, until the party's fortunes reach their nadir in a chapter entitled 'The Swamp of Despond'. Searching for relict communities of river-dwelling San, the expedition advanced 330 kilometres into the Okovango Swamp, accompanied by a host of native paddlers. When they were left on a small reed island to look for traces of Bushmen, the party of Africans rapidly became dejected, issuing mutinous threats, while one of the expedition was bitten by a poisonous spider. Others, including Spode, fell ill, and at this point the cameraman begged van der Post to release him from his contract: 'You must send me back to Europe. This life is too brutal . . . for me.'[51]

Spode, like Vance in the earlier work, appears to serve the author as a psychological archetype – the super-rational European whose unhappy divisions within are found out and exploited by Africa's formidable energies. And just as Vance's vision of Mount Mlanje as a place of perfection is, in van der Post's parlance, a measure of personal bad faith, so is the cameraman's vaunted love for Africa. For Spode's emotion is merely the 'popular, pink marsh-mallow conception of "love" which considers it a lush force that does for human beings the things they are too lazy or greedy to do for themselves instead of the call to battle that it is'.[52]

Even when Spode left the group the expedition's fortunes hardly flourished. Informed of a Bushman sacred site in a range of hills to the south of the Okovango, the party made its way to the spot. However, when members of the group shot game animals en route they unwittingly flouted conditions imposed by the medicine-man who had agreed to guide them. Despite locating great frescoes painted by early San artists, the living nomads they had hoped to find were absent. Moreover, van der Post was denied an oppor-tunity to film the paintings, the cameras inexplicably breaking down time after time, despite every effort to clean and repair them. Even an attempt to tape the 'strange night sounds that wailed around the hills' failed as the recorder and its microphone went dead and refused to work. And the whole time that the expedition was present at the site, it was assailed and stung by wild bees.[53] It was only when van der Post wrote to the offended spirits of the hills – 'We beg most humbly the pardon of the great spirits of these Slippery Hills for any disrespect we may have shown them'[54] – and had exhorted all his party to sign the document, that they were finally released from the jinx.

In *The Lost World of the Kalahari* the author more than suggests a causal link between the group's unintended impiety towards the site's ancient spirits and their unfortunate setbacks. Earlier in the book, during their temporary confinement in the Okovango Swamp as they awaited the return of a motorised launch, van der Post attributed a capacity to shoot game, despite his colleagues' almost complete failure, to factors that were similarly supernormal.

> . . . to this day the way I shot . . . and the full extent to which it served the imperative mood of that part of the journey, for me holds something supernatural . . . For days it was the only positive force in our midst, and the decisive factor in our fortunes . . . I knew without question that those who hunted with me, particularly Samutchoso . . . when they held the gun their fingers curled reverently about it as if it were a living and magnetic object. And of course I, too, was endowed with something of the gun's 'magic'.[55]

The author's extraordinary powers also extended to prophecy – a gift he shared with his wife Ingaret Giffard. In search of a replacement cameraman following Spode's resignation, van der Post made an unscheduled journey to Johannesburg. There, shortly after entering his customary hotel and having been completely out of touch with everybody for weeks, he received a phone-call from his wife. She had woken up that morning with a hunch he would be there. Earlier in *The Lost World of the Kalahari*, and only two pages after his initial and amicable pact with Spode to make a film about the San, van der Post claimed 'to be vaguely troubled about' him. With uncanny precision, he foresaw the problems the cameraman might present: namely, 'he might not be tough enough for the journey'.[56]

In *Venture to the Interior* he reads the runes with equally suspicious accuracy, picking up a whole trail of clues that point the way to Vance's tragic accident. Within an hour of their initial encounter, for instance, as Vance is given gentle reproof for a small detail of forestry work, van der Post noted how he suddenly looked 'fantastically young and hurt; far too young for the grey, old, pre-human world about' them. The author allegedly felt that this minor and apparently unconnected affair 'might be a kind of warning'.[57] He then confessed to a deeper sense of foreboding, when at the very moment of departure for the fateful trek, Vance and his wife parted with only 'an awkward, brusque, self-conscious gesture quite unrepresentative of their feelings'. Seeing this, van der Post said to himself, 'Dear God, I do hope nothing is going to happen to make those children regret their inadequate goodbye'.[58] Several days later the party reached a native fire-watcher's hut, where Vance mischievously sprang one of the absent watcher's bird-traps as a jest. For the author this incident 'was almost impossible to stomach': not apparently because of any ethical question at stake, but because it seemed a portent that 'we were off the true somewhere if we could behave like that'.[59] As if in confirmation of his vision of disaster, the group then immediately noted a buzzard fighting with an eagle in which the former emerged victorious. Van der Post reflected that had they been ancient Greeks they would have taken a deeper interest in the encounter. He 'could almost hear the Homeric rendering: "Just then Zeus . . . sent a buzzard to defeat the eagle as a warning to the sorely-tried Odysseus that greater perils lay ahead" '.[60]

These unsettling intimations of the future serve on one level to crank up the reader's sense of expectancy and create an atmosphere of suspense. However, for many people they are evidence of the author's all too easy acceptance, even insistence, on the impact of unseen non-rational forces in human affairs. These can only be divined by the most psychically developed, which invariably means van der Post himself. The pervasive supernatural element has led to him being widely regarded as a 'mystic', a label often used by English critics to convey a general ambivalence towards his work. Reviewing *Venture to the Interior* in the *Daily Worker*, Desmond Buckle railed at the book's 'pseudo-philosophy tinged with mysticism'.[61] The *TLS* also called for plain speaking: 'Colonel van der Post is ridden with mystical fancies, with theories of fate and destiny, with high-falutin' analogies, with symbolisms and Meanings and ornate significant metaphors'.[62] Others compared him to the ultimate peddler of obscurity. 'We seem to be edging dangerously near to D. H. Lawrence' was the nervous conclusion in the *Tatler*;[63] while Peter Quennell found van der Post's metaphysic 'As vague as any of the similar prophetic utterances once thrown off by D. H. Lawrence'.[64]

In the other Laurens's work there is undoubtedly a recurring and curiously mathematical or geometric vocabulary of the spirit. When describing the Bushmen, for example, he has written of 'an ancient, centred people',[65] 'contained within the symmetry of the land',[66] their 'own authentic pattern',[67] 'fateful proportions',[68] 'natural sense of discipline and proportion'.[69] Other stock words and phrases – 'wholeness', 'at-one-ness',[70] 'togetherness of things',[71] 'the master pattern within me',[72] 'the master level where all levels are joined',[73] 'instinctive certainty of belonging',[74] 'belonging to the purpose of all around me',[75] belonging to 'the overall purpose of the day'[76] – disclose a constant desire to express unity in nature and between humans and nature.

Indeed, this capacity to articulate an interconnectedness between the seen and unseen leads to a major irony in van der Post's writing. For, in order to show his reader the importance of the unconscious and non-rational in our lives, he must map out its function and mode of operation in the most cogent fashion. In so doing, he tends to make the unknown, known. The travel book, often an inventory of chance encounters and seemingly inconsequential events, in van der Post's hands becomes a tightly woven, ordered, rational fabric. Almost everything that is described – natural phenomena, events, characters, even the random and accidental – is made to cohere in the author's central imaginative scheme. The clarity with which he creates and illuminates a dark penumbra surrounding human experience is one of his major achievements, and it means that the charge of mysticism levelled against him can hardly refer to any deliberate obscurity.

Where criticism may be more valid is the way in which observations and experiences seem to have been manipulated so that they fit the underlying philosophical pattern, a pattern which the plain facts by themselves simply do not support. A classic example occurs in *The Heart of the Hunter*, the sequel to *The Lost World of the Kalahari*. On encountering a carnivorous species of mustellid, the ratel or honey badger, during the journey out of the desert van der Post proceeded to elicit from Dabé, his 'semi-civilised' San interpreter and guide, the folklore surrounding the animal. Dabé tells him of the ratel's symbiotic relationship with a species of bird called the honeyguide. On locating a bees' nest, the bird attracts the attention of the ratel and leads it to the site, joining in the feast of honey once the mammal has broken open the nest. Previously, the bird operated as a similar guide for humans, only to find that they 'more and more took the best and most for themselves and left the least and worst'. Aggrieved by this deception, the honeyguide would later tell the ratel of the offenders' behaviour. This aggressive and powerful animal would then attack the men as they slept, biting off their testicles.

Though much of Dabé's testimony is highly anthropomorphised, the portion concerning the two species' symbiosis is basically correct and well documented. Van der Post, however, reflecting on the story, saw in it evidence of his theory of an all-embracing dialectic of light and dark, rational and non-rational:

No animal is more of the earth than the ratel. It is in a profound sense the earth made flesh. No bird is more of the air than the honey-diviner [the honeyguide]. It is like a sliver of sunlit sky made alive. The two of them represent great opposites of life: one a kind of Caliban, the other a sort of Ariel. For me it was right that in such a reconciliation of opposites, which their partnership created, their reward should be honey; for in the first language of things, honey is the supreme symbol of wisdom, since wisdom is the sweetness of the strength that comes to the spirit dedicated to the union of warring elements of life. Dabé's story held the truth of a parable that has passed the test of time. The account of what happened to the men who deceived the ratel and his friend seemed to me an accurate description of what happens to the human spirit which uses

one opposite to deny the other: like the men tracked down by
the ratel, it is deprived of its power of increase.[77]

In order to prise from these details the hidden precept van der
Post has significantly distorted and misrepresented the facts.
Firstly, the ratel/honeyguide antinomy is unnaturally forced.
Although the ratel regularly digs to locate its prey and sleeps in a
burrow it is hard to see why it 'is more of the earth' than any other
animal. Much of its life is spent above ground and it regularly takes
to trees. Similarly, the honeyguide is more typically described as
drab and inconspicuous rather than a 'sliver of sunlit sky', and is
clearly not the most aerial bird. It has no special adaptations (more
than any other bird) to an aerial life, but inhabits forest or open
woodland, and is at times ground-feeding. The behaviour which
may have led to the verdict that 'no bird is more of the air than the
honey-diviner' is its hovering display, which, together with an
insistent call, is designed to attract the attention of some honey-
eating mammal.

Most misleading of all in this passage is the symbolism surrounding the fruits of the ratel's and the bird's partnership ('For me it was
right that in such a reconciliation of opposites . . . their reward
should be honey; for . . . honey is the supreme symbol of wisdom,
since wisdom . . . comes to the spirit dedicated to the union of
warring elements of life.'). Honeyguides, however, do not take the
honey. Unique amongst birds, they eat and digest the wax comb
itself and also feed on the larvae it contains. Given these facts, it is
possible to argue precisely the reverse of van der Post's claim.
Rather than the bird finding the ideal partnership with the ratel,
symbiosis is most complete with humans, since they seek only the
honeycomb – a food item of no interest to the honeyguide. The
humans also invariably leave some wax comb for the bird as reward
for its guiding efforts. The ratel, on the other hand, will eat not only
the comb containing honey, but also that holding larvae, which is
the bird's principal objective. It is for all of these reasons that the
partner chosen by the honeyguide more frequently than any other is
human.[78]

Although this is only a minor detail in the book, it indicates a
prevalent characteristic in the author's approach to his work. The

underlying philosophical ideas so often have priority and the material evidence is carefully selected to confirm their validity.

Another important contributory factor in the oft-repeated 'mystic' label is the nature of van der Post's prose. This has been widely and consistently praised, and his books are often said to include some of the finest descriptions of the African landscape and its wildlife. However, if this rich, sonorous language is over-burdened with sentiment it can precipitate out in a visceral excess of emotion. Once he had told Valerie Vance, for instance, of her husband's death, he watched as the

> image of Dicky seemed . . . to leave her; it was wrenched
> from her like the topmost leaf torn from a high tree by a
> fierce blast of wind and sent falling down, vainly fluttering
> to retain its height, down below for good; down, down,
> and out of the sunlight of her mind, for ever.[79]

Equally problematic in van der Post's writing is the manner in which he appears able to detect in ordinary experiences and everyday phenomena, profundities that are inaccessible to the ordinary reader. The eyes of African retainers, for instance, become a kind of cosmic looking-glass. In those of his nurse Klara he found 'the first light of some unbelievably antique day'.[80] Those of native labourers on his parents' farm were 'solemn and glowing with the first light of the world's history; warm and content with the secret of man's earliest days'.[81] The eyes of Bushmen were similarly charged with heightened emotion, clear and shining 'like the brown of day on a rare dewy African morning'.[82]

Another characteristic of his prose is the way in which external realities are made to serve as a convenient confirmation of his or the other characters' inner world. Typical of this element are his repeated descriptions of weather patterns both before and after Vance's accident. Prior even to setting foot on Mlanje, he saw a cloud formation over the forested mountain that is a suspiciously graphic representation of the book's central theme:

> as I watched, a whole concentration of cloud rolled down
> on it and . . . had in their possession one half of it,

93

including the highest peak . . . But the eastern half of the
mountain remained astonishingly clear and, as the afternoon
deepened, drew lovely colours and tones into its keeping. It
made the mountain appear divided against itself; one half of it
dark and turbulent; the other bending a shining head over the
evening.[83]

On the day of Richard Vance's death the sunset is once more a
'cosmic schism of light and darkness', in which the clouds appear to
the exhausted author as the 'devils of death . . . charging up and
down those peaks on phantom, skeleton chargers'.[84] Later still it
was 'as if the whole of Mlanje had been dematerialised and
transformed into a kind of Tartar music, riding high, wide and
diabolically handsome across the darkened steppes of heaven'.[85]

If the authenticity of events in travel provides the drama of travel
writing with its primary colours, and even legitimises a truth
stranger than fiction, then that authenticity exacts a price of its own.
In a travel work where the details of a journey seem consistently
over-coloured or completely distorted to satisfy some underlying
philosophy, the reader begins to baulk. The truth, in fact, begins to
sound exactly like fiction. 'One begins to think about the distinction between poetic truth and police court truth', was a concern of
one reviewer of *The Lost World of the Kalahari*;[86] while V. S.
Pritchett, writing of *Venture to the Interior*, felt that 'since this book
is not a novel, but concerns real people, one is a little haunted by the
doubt as to whether [van der Post] has "truthfully" given us the
story'.[87]

When measured against the ground rules of an older form of
travel writing, like those obeyed by the author of *China–Tibet–
Assam*, van der Post's work appears a kind of heresy. For Frederick
Bailey, rigorous exactness and authenticity were his overriding
considerations, even if it produced a jumbled jog-trot of facts and
figures. There was little concern to satisfy any narrative unity or
compel the facts to point an underlying moral. For the explorer in
Tibet, recounting the events precisely as they occurred was the
whole of his ambition. In fact, Bailey was imbued with precisely
that one-sided spirit of reason and empiricism that van der Post had
so lamented in Europeans.

Yet it is important to recognise that even this form of travel writing, no matter how tenaciously its author clings to the facts as he or she sees them, is still an arbitrary and highly specialised version of reality. The whole gamut of Bailey's preoccupations – the detailed empirical observations, the inventory of distances, altitudes, compass co-ordinates, the collection of animal skins and pressed flowers – all redound to European geopolitical concerns and western theories of knowledge. Behind his consistent inability to recognise non-Europeans except perhaps as a faceless, nameless populace best described in terms of race or tribe, lie the central myths of European imperial man and his elevated status vis à vis the rest of humanity. Even something as apparently trivial as his proclaimed discovery of a species of rodent, *Soriculus baileyi*, betrays a whole range of Euro-centric notions about how one confers validity on experience. Even the works of Frederick Bailey, then, are highly selective versions of reality, in fact, a type of fiction. Indeed, it seems a curious confirmation of this fictionalising process that his last book, *No Passport to Tibet*, was not actually written by him but ghosted on his behalf by the novelist Arthur Calder-Marshall.[88]

In Laurens van der Post's travel works the extent to which the raw data have been carefully organised is clearly far greater. One senses at times that he has looked on the experiences during the journey exactly as a fictional writer might consider the plot of a novel. In fact, if one compares van der Post's own novels with his works of travel, there is a remarkable similarity between the two. His African childhood and travels and his real-life experiences of war have been a constant source of idea and symbol for his entire canon of writings. For some, this blend of autobiography and invention represents a new departure. The critic Frederick Carpenter has felt that through all these books van der Post has devised 'a new kind of autobiographical hero, part history and part myth. In the process [he] has rejected the formal patterns of traditional art and criticism in order to create [his] unique literary personality'.[89] Certainly, in the context of the travel genre, the manner in which he has been prepared to shape the narrative and to liberate the work from the confines of absolute verisimilitude, to reveal not merely the circumstances of the voyage itself but also hidden patterns of significance in those experiences, is van der Post's major contribution.

Chapter VI
The Overreacher

At about midday on Thursday, 19 May 1946, off the westernmost tip of the Hebridean island of Skye, a young skipper stood at the tiller of his ten-metre lobster-fishing boat, the *Gannet*. Except perhaps for a distinctive and finely proportioned profile – high forehead, strong aquiline nose, delicate mouth and firm, oval chin – there was very little to indicate this thirty-one-year-old's aristocratic background. Coarse woollen trousers were stuffed into knee-length black military boots. Just below his ribcage a broad leather belt embraced a tatty, thick, chequered polo-neck. His fine hair was unkempt, swept for days by heavily salted Atlantic winds. Superficially he looked for all the world like the rugged, west-coast fishermen who crewed with him.

All week they had pursued their quarry – basking shark, the largest fish in British waters, in fact, one of the largest in the world – without a hint of success. The sharks were all around, breaking the surface at times in great upward surges and, as they fell back beneath the water, the impact of their five-ton bodies produced a heavy crash like the report of a gun. Yet each time the boat had closed on these migrating sharks, the fishermen's equipment had malfunctioned.

The worst offender was a harpoon, which worked on the principle of an ordinary muzzle-loader. Gunpowder was poured down the long barrel, followed by two hard wads of felt pushed down with a ramrod. A heavy metal-tipped stick was then introduced to the barrel, and when one end rested on the powder charge, the other end exposed at the muzzle was fitted with the

96

heavily barbed harpoon head. For some reason, this system had failed them repeatedly in the previous four days.

Yet at Thursday midday, as the skipper eased the *Gannet* towards a large female shark, they were about to try again. At only a metre's distance from her dark back just beneath the water, the harpoon struck home deep into the shark's side. It was the first success of the crew's second season of fishing. For the briefly jubilant skipper, however, this was only the start of a fortnight's problems.

Wary that too much weight on the rope might tear the harpoon from the fish's body, the team took several hours to haul it to the surface. Then a further six hours were spent towing the prize the fifty kilometres back to their factory on the island of Soay. Unfortunately, by the time of their arrival in the early evening the tide was too low for them to reach the factory's slipway. When they started again the next day the intention was to place the carcase on a bogie-cart which ran into the water on rails. Unfortunately they found that these rails did not extend to a sufficient depth for this to be achieved easily. Following several exhausting hours' work, after they had managed to balance the shark precariously on the truck, a winch was hauling the entire load inch by inch up the slipway, when the cart overturned and tipped its contents back into the sea.

Unwilling to wait for a fresh high tide so that they might attempt this whole procedure again, they decided to hack the enormous carcase up where it lay. By the time they had stopped for a break the tide was up to their waists. When the day's labours finally ended, at well after midnight, the young skipper 'had had no food for more than thirty hours, and having struggled all day in that mountain of soft cold flesh and entrails', hoped never to touch it again.[1] The following morning – a Saturday – he started at five-thirty, by which time a second shark had been caught. However the strict observance of the sabbath, so important to the deeply religious communities of north-west Scotland, decreed that all work must cease by midday.

On the following Monday affairs at the shark-processing factory were largely as they had been left two days previously. If anything they were worse. When the skipper returned with the timber and equipment necessary to modify the slipway, he found that efforts to haul the second fish up to the factory had incurred the same problems as the first. An over-burdened cart had derailed, throwing its catch back into the water. And all this time, nobody had bothered to clear away the heaps of carrion left from the first, which had become a battleground for a great flock of hungry gulls.

Taking their cue perhaps from this avian squabble, the factory staff also rebelled. Some of them argued that they had only been employed to cut up the sharks, while a joiner, going to fetch tools from the mainland, failed to return. Another, an engineer's mate, never showed up at all. A recent arrival, an expert, contracted to produce samples of glue from the shark's cartilage, complained that he was there merely to advise, not to skivvy. If the skipper wanted the experiments completed he would have to have the staff currently reconstructing the slipway working for him. He himself would be a labourer for no man; besides he had a bad back.

Exasperated by this final defiance, and barely able to keep himself from hitting the expert, the young skipper 'replied that it wasn't my crew's job to haul wood and build slips, nor mine, but no one made a fuss; all were, on the contrary, anxious to help; that I had synovitis of the right ankle, a duodenal ulcer and an enlarged heart, and that he was likely to survive me'.[2]

These were not the typical physical attributes of the man of action, a man who had chosen as his profession to hunt one of the largest fish in the world. But then Gavin Maxwell, the skipper's name, was not a typical man of action.

Introspective, excitable, subject to rapid changes of mood and deep depressions, he was described by his friend, the writer John Hillaby, who had first met him during his shark-fishing days, as a manic depressive.[3] His business manager, Richard Frere, wrote of him, with careful restraint, that 'the making of new acquaintances was not one of his delights'.[4] Both Frere and another close friend, Kathleen Raine, have described the awkwardness of their first encounters with Maxwell. With the former, his manner had been 'abrupt and uneasy, offhand in a random way, and consequently [had] touched the edge of rudeness'. At the end of their introduction Maxwell had 'stalked away . . . like the offended ghost of Hamlet's father'.[5] Meeting him at her own house, Raine recalled that he had taken very little notice of her, and at the time was 'involved already in one of his periodic crises'.[6]

Yet there was another side to this self-absorbed, neurotic personality. Frere, balancing his character portrait, wrote of a friend 'who was charming, erudite and glittering with sophisticated wit'.[7] Kathleen Raine, whose initial indifference to Maxwell would turn into a deep, consuming and, ultimately, tragic love, also noted his 'vein of genius'.[8] Maxwell was deeply sensitive, not only to his own internal world but to the natural environment around him. As a literary interpreter of British wildlife and landscape he probably has few equals this century. Frere likened him to the nineteenth-century naturalist and writer Richard Jefferies. W. H. Hudson might be another appropriate comparison. He was an enthusiastic, gifted naturalist, while his list of pets was long and varied – dogs of all breeds, cats, wild cats, goats, a ring-tailed lemur, a bush baby, otters, geese, ducks, tropical birds. He seems to have achieved with these creatures levels of intimacy that he perhaps found difficult with others of his own species, and claimed a capacity to think as an animal. Certainly he could make the death of an otter almost a national tragedy, one which left him personally heart-broken and barren for months.

The physical frailty to which Maxwell confessed, almost with a perverse hint of pride, in his altercation with the expert in fish glue, seems highly consistent with an emotional and mental life conducted on a knife's edge. The duodenal ulcer, more regularly found in the upper classes than the lower, and amongst males more than females, is an abrasion or break in the lining membrane of the stomach. Gradually eroded and deepened by acidic gastric fluids, it results in repeated abdominal pain. Like an enlarged heart it is a problem exacerbated by mental strain or excessive physical exertion. It is also adversely affected by tobacco and alcohol. Maxwell, well known for his intake of whisky, was an eighty-a-day chain smoker. Usually the ulcer ensures that its victim remains thin or loses weight. Maxwell was a lean figure all his short life.

The synovitis, like his thromboses in his final years and the purpura that struck him down in his teens, suggest a body whose vessels refused to contain their allotted, vital fluids. Henoch's purpura, manifesting itself in Maxwell in large purple spots on legs and arms, is a condition occurring in children and young adults. The purple blotches are due to extravasations of blood in the skin wherever the smaller blood vessels become unnaturally permeable. In Maxwell's case it was accompanied by great pain and massive loss of blood, which nearly killed him. His convalescence took almost a year and even after this the haemorrhaging recurred whenever he reached a certain level of physical exhaustion.[9]

Despite this history of ill-health and the development of the duodenal ulcer in his early twenties, as a young man Maxwell fashioned an image of himself which took little account of his often poor physical condition. He was intent on, and in some measure succeeded in, leading a life of action and adventure. By the time he had completed his degree in estate management at Oxford, he had made his highly idiosyncratic career choice. 'I wanted, in plain terms', he wrote in the year before his death, 'to be an explorer; not in the grand manner as a leader of mighty expeditions . . . but as a solitary, a lone wolf, using the minimum of my small capital for each journey and then writing about my travels after I had returned.'[10] It was an ambition only partially realised.

Although Maxwell spent a good deal of time overseas, and the majority of his books are partly or wholly set in foreign countries, his travel experience was of a different order to that of Bailey, Philby, Thesiger or van der Post. With the exception of a journey to northernmost Scandinavia and a short trip to Iceland, almost all of Maxwell's travelling was undertaken in the countries bordering the Mediterranean, particularly the Maghreb region of northern Africa. Thirty years ago the emergent states of Morocco and Algeria offered opportunities for authentic adventure. For much of the time, however, Maxwell was seldom far from the conveniences of civilisation and frequently moved around in some comfort, either in his sand-coloured Safari Land-Rover or in some immensely powerful sports car such as his Mercedes Benz 300 S.L. Roadster.

Often it seemed his intended destinations – Assam,[11] India,[12] Sudan, Thailand[13] – exceeded his economic means or failed to suit his wider circumstances, and were never visited. On other occasions it was an apparent inability to organise that seemed to let him down. Following the example of an associate, Maxwell wanted to travel through the High Atlas of Morocco, moving from kasbah to kasbah with pack animals. Only days after setting out, however, he gave up, apparently unable to secure his mule transport.[14] Another trek along the Atlas that was meticulously planned and costed for him by Douglas Botting, his friend and biographer, was similarly never undertaken.[15] The one notable journey of exploration, beautifully rendered in *A Reed Shaken by the Wind*, was to the Iraqi marshes with Thesiger. Yet the most generous assessment of this trip would have to acknowledge that without his companion's assistance, Maxwell would never have been able to undertake it. He spoke almost no Arabic, had little experience of travel amongst such a community and certainly had no entrée to a shy and exclusive people like the Ma'dan.[16]

If one can conclude that Maxwell was not a widely experienced traveller, one must also recognise that this offers little or no grounds for an assessment of Maxwell the travel writer. The challenge and originality of a journey are often key elements in the successful travel book, but they are by no means a guarantee of quality. Frederick Bailey's *China–Tibet–Assam* is classic confirmation of this point. Yet if one examines the nature of Maxwell's writings in some detail, his status as an author of travel books might seem to stand on questionable foundations.

Gavin Maxwell published a total of eleven books. Two of these – *The Otter's Tale*, the children's version of his best-known title, *Ring of Bright Water*, and his least known book, *Seals of the World*, a natural history field guide, a good deal of which was written by someone else – are of very little relevance here. Seven of the other nine have a complete or partial foreign setting. *Ring of Bright Water*, *The Rocks Remain* and *Raven Seek Thy Brother*, Maxwell's trilogy describing his deep involvement with otters, all contain individual chapters on travel abroad. However, these episodes serve largely as a context for, or as relief from, the continued saga of Camusfeàrna, his lighthouse-keeper's cottage in north-west Scotland, where he and a host of friends and animals all lived. There would seem to be very little basis for treating them as conventional travel works. One is left, therefore, with four books that have an entirely foreign setting and which would appear to be the exclusive grounds for considering Maxwell as an author of travel literature.

Yet two of these might with considerable justification be defined as biographies. His second book, *God Protect me from my Friends*, published in 1956, is an account of the career of Salvatore Giuliano, 'a young, savage, violent, idealistic and crudely beautiful' secessionist leader from north-west Sicily.[17] By the time of his death in 1950, at the age of twenty-seven, Giuliano had achieved an international notoriety for the seven-year guerilla campaign he had waged against the island's *carabinieri*. By many of the Sicilian peasantry he had been revered as a latter-day Robin Hood and champion of their cause; to the Forces for the Suppression of Banditry in Sicily he was a ruthless criminal and finally hounded to his death with the connivance of the Mafia. Giuliano's legacy was a confusing tangle of legend, claim, counter claim and deliberate deception. Visiting Sicily over three years Maxwell attempted to pick out the strands of truth, knitting together much of his narrative from the oral testimony of the Sicilian villagers, many of whom had witnessed the events or had been directly involved themselves.

The second of Maxwell's biographical studies, *Lords of the Atlas*, published in 1966, was another product of several years' personal detective work. It chronicled the fortunes of two brothers, Madani and T'hami el Glaoui, members of an obscure noble family from southern Morocco, who during the 1890s and the first half of the twentieth century had manoeuvred themselves into a position of pre-eminence in this French-occupied country. T'hami, the younger of the brothers and the principal protagonist in Maxwell's story, was a personality of immense complexity. Even by the crude standards of his time and nation, the 'Black Panther' and 'Lion of the Atlas' was a cold and ruthless despot, eliminating his rivals or confining them, if politically expedient, to the medieval dungeons beneath his numerous palaces. He was at the same time, a man renowned for his immense wealth, fabulous hospitality and exquisite manners. Courted by European powers, he was a frequent visitor to Paris or the Côte d'Azure, and attended the coronation of Elizabeth II in 1953. The man who could place the heads of his murdered enemies on his gates was also a passionate golfer with his own golf course and a handicap of plus four. From the 1930s onwards – when he befriended and entertained Winston Churchill – he was at the height of his power and the *de facto* ruler of much of occupied Morocco.

With such fantastic material to hand, a gifted narrator like

Maxwell would produce a compelling story and perhaps his finest book, but could it really be described as a work of travel?

The same question must inevitably be asked of his fourth book, *The Ten Pains of Death*. This was almost a natural extension of Maxwell's research for *God Protect me from my Friends* and expressed his deep fascination with the Sicilian people. The author had revisited the Mediterranean island in 1955 and again in 1957, with the intention of writing about the lives of its tuna fishermen. Throughout the spring and early summer, both day and night, teams of Sicilians manned large, static offshore net complexes, spending their time ashore in a communal headquarters, known as a *tonnara*. Maxwell hoped to live and work with the fishermen of the Scopello *tonnara*, next to the coastal town of Castellammare del Golfo on Sicily's north-west coast, and record their shared experiences. In the year of his first visit, however, Scopello suffered 'its worst season in living memory' and Maxwell was forced to alter the character of his projected book, 'in order', as he put it to his publisher Mark Longman, for it 'to survive'.[18]

In June 1955 he planned to write 'more or less a personal journal embracing other subjects, with the *tonnara* of Scopello as the thread to hold everything together'; a work that would have been, in effect, a classic personal travel book.[19] Four years later it was published. However, never one to be bound by his synopsis, even one that had been substantially revised, Maxwell had largely abandoned the idea of a personalised narrative. Instead he transcribed the gritty verbal accounts given to him by a number of consenting Sicilian interviewees. Maxwell served more as compiler, translator and editor of other peoples' words rather than a creator of his own. The end product was, none the less, an extraordinary book and a powerful testament to the poverty, corruption and hardship endemic in Sicilian rural life, but it was a work that had as much in common with a sociological study as a travel book.

The last of Maxwell's foreign quartet, published in 1957, is *A Reed Shaken by the Wind*. He had suggested to Wilfred Thesiger that a book might be written on the marsh-dwelling Arab community that Thesiger had 'discovered' and lived amongst for a large part of the previous four years. The Arabist consented and in January 1956

Maxwell journeyed to Iraq and his friend's 'personal paradise'. His account of the Ma'dan's ancient pattern of life and his two-month spell amongst them was one of Maxwell's most polished works. Certainly, it is one that fully reveals the poetic qualities of its author's writing and earned him the Heinemann Award of the Royal Society of Literature. It is also the one that best conforms to the conventional notion of a travel book – a personal, factual account of the experiences and observations thrown up at the narrator by a journey overseas. Although it is interesting to note that by the stringent standards of his companion in the Iraqi marshes, even his work would have to be disqualified. For in the introduction to *The Marsh Arabs*, his own book focusing on the same region, Thesiger wrote 'this is not properly a travel book, for the area over which I travelled was restricted'.[20]

The heterogeneous nature of Maxwell's four foreign works presents interesting issues for any analysis of the travel genre. It calls into question the means by which this type of book might be identified. That the work should describe a journey, or at least travels of some kind, might perhaps seem the most obvious starting point. Of course, if this were so, then one would immediately have to disqualify three, possibly all four, of Maxwell's foreign books. In fact, as Thesiger did in the case of his own *The Marsh Arabs*, one would have to rule out the large number of travel works where the amount of travelling was negligible. Geoffrey Moorhouse has pointed out that 'travel book' is a designation that has come 'to be attached to any non-fiction with a foreign setting'.[21] While this is true, it would seem far too elastic to operate as a meaningful definition of the genre. Nor would Moorhouse have proposed it as such. Perhaps the most carefully considered examination of what the term might mean is in Paul Fussell's lucid and original study of British literary travelling between the wars, *Abroad*. 'It is when we cannot satisfactorily designate a kind of work with a single word', wrote Fussell,

> but must invoke two (*war memoir, Black autobiography, first novel, picture book, travel book*) that we sense we're entering complicated territory. . . . Criticism has never quite known what to call books like these . . .

Let's call them travel books, and distinguish them initially
from guide books, which are not autobiographical and are not
sustained by a narrative exploiting the devices of fiction. A
guide book is addressed to those who plan to follow the
traveler, doing what he has done, but more selectively. A
travel book, at its purest, is addressed to those who do not plan
to follow the traveler at all, but who require the exotic or
comic anomalies, wonders, and scandals of the literary form
romance which their own place or time cannot entirely supply.
Travel books are a sub-species of memoir in which the
autobiographical narrative arises from the speaker's encounter
with distant or unfamiliar data, and in which the narrative –
unlike that in a novel or a romance – claims literal validity by
constant reference to actuality. [22]

Fussell's evaluation narrows the field of enquiry, but it cannot
solve all travel writing's taxonomic problems. For instance, the
difficulties of separating war memoir from travel book still remain.
A good example is *Seven Pillars of Wisdom*, T. E. Lawrence's
account of his two years in Arabia during the First World War.
Since the book describes both his military exploits and his travels it
is hard to know if it is a representative of the former or the latter.
Similarly, how would one classify *Naples '44*, an account of an
intelligence officer's experiences in Italy during the Second World
War, by Norman Lewis – author of at least four other conventional
travel books? If, in an attempt to lay this problem to rest, one made
a book's wartime setting the basis for its disqualification as a travel
work, then one wallows into a deeper mire when confronted with
something like Henry Morton Stanley's *Through the Dark Continent*. If ever there were an archetypal travel book, then surely this is
it. Yet it contains an account, as Stanley bludgeoned his way down
the Congo, of thirty-two battles between the white explorer's
Zanzibari retainers and the indigenous Africans – thirty-two
episodes in what was, in effect, one long, continuous, private
armed conflict. Could one, therefore, propose the book as a
sub-species of war memoir? Equally problematic is Frederick
Bailey's *Mission to Tashkent*, describing experiences during a period
of political rather than military upheaval.

Professor Fussell's criteria might also run into difficulties with a work like Geoffrey Moorhouse's *Calcutta*. This is a detailed study of India's old capital in West Bengal. At no point in the text is Moorhouse explicitly present as its first person narrator. On this basis it would be difficult to think of it as a memoir; but neither could the book be considered simply as a work of academic geography or sociology. In the bookshop it is almost always to be found in the travel section. It is, in addition, a work of non-fiction, full of distant and unfamiliar data, it exploits some of the devices of fiction, and, amongst other elements, supplies its readers with 'the exotic or comic anomalies, wonders and scandals' which their own time and place might not. Moreover, the traveller's customary first-hand experiences of landscape and people are evident through-out the book. Yet the author describes much of the contemporary city environment as if seen through the eyes of an anonymous visitor. This narrative device achieves an immediate and personal portrait, as in a travel work, yet simultaneously it serves to safeguard the book from the limitations that might attach were it presented as just one man's private view.

If one examines Maxwell's books in the light of Fussell's ideas then only *A Reed Shaken by the Wind* meets the complete definition. In the other three, as in Moorhouse's *Calcutta*, the author was largely the neutral scribe behind the actions and adventures of others. Although they might still contain the exotic anomalies, wonders and scandals of the literary form romance, and could claim literal validity by constant reference to actuality, they could hardly be classified as a 'sub-species of memoir'. What seems even more confusing is that, in the light of Fussell's arguments, it would be easier to make a case for Maxwell's four works about his years of residence in north-west Scotland as travel books, than it would for his four foreign works.

Born and brought up at Elrig, near Wigtown in Galloway, Maxwell had a deep preoccupation with the Scottish Highlands that dated from the Second World War. As a Special Forces officer he was stationed at a training area in the region. Following a visit to the small Inner Hebridean island of Soay off the southern shore of Skye in 1943, he fell in love with the place, decided to buy it and then developed the idea of his shark-fishing business. The original enterprise had been based on the commercial exploitation of the large quantities of oil in the shark's liver. From the average individual he was able to extract eight hundredweights of the liquid, whose value almost tripled to £130 per ton (the equivalent of over £2,000 in 1992), in the course of his four-year operations. Though Maxwell recovered a little from the deeply inauspicious start to his second season described earlier, his income was insufficient to keep the business afloat. Only five months after they had caught that first sizeable female on 19 May 1946, he had been forced to sell the island, boats and gear and become managing director of someone else's company. Within two years he resigned even this post and the business finally wound up after another unsuccessful season.

If Maxwell had not become the lone wolf explorer who wrote up his exotic journeys on his return, as he had initially wished during his days at Oxford, then by hunting one of the largest fish in the world he had at least faced a dangerous challenge of a kind. His home country had provided him with the adventures of a foreign land. It would also provide him with the appropriate environment and the inspiration to write.

Although impoverished after the collapse of the Island of Soay Shark Fisheries, he had retained a foothold on the west coast, when one of his Oxford contemporaries offered him the use of a small cottage overlooking the Sound of Sleat, the narrow channel separating Skye from the Scottish mainland. It was here, several years later, as he combed the beach for a suitable piece of wood from which to make a breadboard, that he came upon

> a small barrel-top, white, smooth, and sea-worn – exactly
> the object I required. I pulled it from the shingle in which it
> was imbedded, and there across the centre of it were the still
> legible letters ISSF – Island of Soay Shark Fisheries. It had
> all the nostalgia of a *carnet de bal* tied with faded ribbon; it
> brought back so many half-forgotten scenes so vividly to
> my mind that I began this book the next day.[23]

The result was *Harpoon at a Venture* – an account of his efforts to make shark-fishing a viable industry. It was also, inevitably, a book about failure. Yet through its portrait of Ulyssean endeavour, its richly poetic prose, and its revelation of error with almost painful honesty, *Harpoon at a Venture* gave this failure a certain dignity. In fact, as a focus for literary enterprise shark-fishing became a considerable success. The book was reviewed and sold well and led Maxwell on to the foreign travels that were the background, in turn, for *God Protect me from my Friends*, *A Reed Shaken by the Wind* and *The Ten Pains of Death*.[24]

Yet it was Maxwell's record of life at his lighthouse-keeper's cottage at Sandaig, given the fictional name of Camusfeàrna in his books, that made him a household name. *Ring of Bright Water* sold in millions worldwide. In Maxwell's *oeuvre* it is, in many ways, odd-one-out: it is a book about happiness and success. *Ring of Bright Water* is a deeply funny and deeply moving celebration of one man's communion with nature, primarily expressed through his joyous relationship with his two otters, Mijbil and Edal. As part of a trilogy, however, it cannot be viewed entirely on its own. If the first book recounts a dream of innocence and strikes an idyllic note of harmony between man and nature, in its sequel, *The Rocks Remain*, it's a note that turns sour. While the last of the trio, *Raven Seek Thy Brother*, is a deeply black book, in which Camusfeàrna and one of the otters are ultimately destroyed. The only thing to stop it achieving truly tragic proportions was the absence of Maxwell's own death. And this followed shortly after, chronicled faithfully by Maxwell's lookalike, Richard Frere, whose prose style, in *Maxwell's Ghost*, curiously resembles his subject's own.

In what ways do these four works resemble travel books? Firstly, Maxwell's personal dramas are set against a rich and, for most of his readers, deeply unfamiliar background. As the crow flew from the author's flat in Chelsea, his cottage at Sandaig (Camusfeàrna) was almost as far away as Copenhagen, Stuttgart, Geneva, or Bordeaux. Culturally it was a good deal further. If any portion of the national landscape could offer Maxwell a sense of adventure and even danger then it was the north-west Highlands of Scotland and their outer isles. Almost severed from the British mainland by a series of deep lochs – Ness, Lochy and Linnhe – it is virtually a separate country. It is certainly the best place to achieve a sense of solitude. Only a narrow coastal fringe was at all populated. The vast majority of the region, the higher moorland interior, had under one person per square kilometre. Its total community in 1951 numbered 178,917, and this declined significantly in the ensuing decade. Even today the telephone directory, for an area equal to one-fifth of all England, is only 268 pages – less than the portion of the London directory for surnames beginning with A and B.

Electricity only arrived in the area during Maxwell's tenancy of Camusfeàrna. Prior to that homes had been lit by paraffin lamps.[25] When he had written *Ring of Bright Water* Maxwell's place was still not on the national grid. For years he had obtained water by bucket from a nearby stream. His house had no lavatory or bath. It could be reached neither by telephone nor even road. To get there initially involved a good deal of walking. His nearest sizeable towns, Inverness and Fort William, were both 160 kilometres away. To obtain even the most basic supplies was a considerable labour. When he first moved there the nearest port from which he could have furniture shipped in to Camusfeàrna was 25 kilometres away. By road the same village was 200 kilometres away.[26]

The region's indigenous community which provided a social backcloth and many of the minor parts in Maxwell's Scottish self-drama is portrayed as enjoying a deeply intimate relationship with the landscape. The Highlanders are ancient, Celtic and Norse stock whose element-bound, tradition-dominated lives are simple and spartan. In *Ring of Bright Water* Maxwell describes human types long extinct elsewhere in the British Isles, like the itinerant peddlers who lived in a cave close to Camusfeàrna.[27] In *Harpoon at a Venture* he wrote of the island inhabitants of Scalpay as a:

> small pastoral community, every visible phase of whose life had a minute and individual beauty, whose every activity enhanced rather than detracted from the wider beauty of their surroundings. Much that the cynical might dismiss as having primarily the shallow appeal of the 'picturesque' is recognisable as something deeper by an eye already long accustomed to these archaic forms of architecture, dress, and speech.[28]

Maxwell's choice of imagery reinforced a sense of organic unity between the Scalpay people and their island. They were 'human herds';[29] twin fourteen-year-old boys have 'fair hair curling like fronds of a fern';[30] a young bare-foot girl dances and gambols with a frisky calf 'as though her own ebullience of spirit must find a common expression';[31] while two old men, Gaelic-speakers, more nature spirits than humans, are described as 'gnomes'.[32]

This paean to a community whose life derived a natural vigour from its intimacy with the physical environment is highly reminiscent of the approach of Thesiger and van der Post to the Bedu and San respectively. And in the same way that isolated communities of Bedu in the former's *Arabian Sands* were often deeply suspicious of outsiders and wary of change, so was the Highlander's outlook deeply restricted by the twin blinkers of superstition and time-honoured habit. Just as the Bedu would eat the desert fox but not the steppe fox, and the Iraqi Ma'dan obey taboos on eating pelicans or plovers while readily taking cormorants or godwits, so would Maxwell's neighbours refuse to work from Saturday midday, or sail with a woman aboard, or use the words 'salmon', 'pig' or 'rabbit' while out at sea. Even more bizarre was a refusal to have eggs on board, or anyone who had eaten them and not cleared them from their system.[33]

For an intellectually gifted and emotionally complex individual like Maxwell there would be, almost inevitably, aspects of this parochial society that he found less attractive. According to Richard Frere, they smirked and gossiped about the constant presence of young male companions, and found a perverse satisfaction in the collapse of his fishery. In *Harpoon at a Venture* the author himself spoke with some resentment of the Soay people, whom he had employed in his shark-processing factory, almost as if their unregenerate insularity had been at the heart of his commercial failure. In the opening pages he wrote of the island's 'troubles, internecine feuds, frustrations, and problems',[34] and – on the final page of the saga – the 'civil wars and demands . . . of its tiny population'.[35]

None the less, it was the rugged wholeness of north-west Scotland and its rural population which served Maxwell as a standard to which he himself could aspire. And it was that coarse, unpopulated, rock-bound environment that operated as a material correlative for his rejection of the modern world. In the opening pages of *Harpoon at a Venture* he suggested that his purchase of Soay and the whole shark-fishing adventure were born out of the squalor and brutality of modern warfare. 'If I'm alive when the war's over', he claimed to have said in 1940, 'I'm going to buy an island in the Hebrides and retire there for life, no aeroplanes, no bombs, no Commanding Officers, no rusty dannert wire'.[36]

In *Ring of Bright Water*, in the opening chapter, he wrote:

Even at a distance Camusfeàrna house wore that strange look that comes to dwellings after long disuse. It is indefinable, and it is not produced by obvious signs of neglect; Camusfeàrna had few slates missing from the roof and the windows were all intact, but the house wore that secretive expression that is in some way akin to a young girl's face during her first pregnancy.[37]

In both books north-west Scotland was a final sanctuary, or as Maxwell himself wrote, 'to me it was Xanadu',[38] 'my Island Valley of Avalon'[39] and 'remote Elysium':[40] an Eden-like locality that permitted a rebirth of innocence. In the recurrent images in Maxwell's Scottish memoirs of a world before the fall, a world free 'from the prison of over-dense communities' and the 'incarceration of office walls and hours', and in his desire to return to the simple and even primitive, one can detect a close relationship between his books and those of travellers like Thesiger and van der Post.[41]

There is another element in the Scottish memoirs, in fact in all of the Maxwell books previously discussed, which is characteristic of many travel books – the theme of a quest. Whether it is a search for understanding about the interior life of Mediterranean peasants, or of a bandit-prince from the Moroccan High Atlas and Sicily's north-west littoral, or whether it is a quest for a chimerical happiness in a passionate affair with nature, the theme is dominant. In two of the books – *The Rocks Remain* and *Raven Seek Thy Brother* – it might be more correct to see their central animus deriving not from a search, but almost its obverse: a swelling sense of disillusionment as the gap between initial aspiration and final discovery is brought fully into focus. Nevertheless, they explore facets of the same theme.

One can detect some confirmation of this questing element in Maxwell in the sheer range of activities and rôles to which this Renaissance figure gave himself. Soldier, poet, journalist, portrait painter, conservationist, fisherman, writer, here was a man who had trained in estate management and in his final months worked to establish a farm for the production of eider-down in conjunction with a British wildlife park.[42] This remarkable rôle-call seems to suggest an urge to satisfy a wider intellectual and spiritual restlessness. In the same way that the traveller finds in each change of locality a sense of inner renewal, so each fresh subject and activity provided Maxwell with the grounds of a new internal landscape.

It is in this sense that one can perhaps view all of his foreign quartet as travel books. While only *A Reed Shaken by the Wind* might be a description of a journey, in the other three some of the physical travelling is replaced by an intellectual voyage. Though to suggest his experience was only *intellectual* is to give it too narrow a definition. In a book like *Lords of the Atlas* Maxwell's complete absorption in the story is obvious. During numerous visits to Morocco in the early 1960s he interviewed many witnesses to the affairs of the house of Gloua and gathered a 'great bulk of verbal communication'.[43]

In the preparation of *God Protect me from my Friends* there was a similar determination to pursue the subject on its home ground. It was not enough to piece together the evidence of Giuliano's extraordinary life from literary sources alone, sat in a study or some well-stocked library. In order to discover, Maxwell must go there, if necessary again and again, and hear the facts from people who had watched the drama or had had a part in it themselves. And ultimately the physical adventures of the traveller and the mental pursuits of the literary detective begin to merge, even to the point where Maxwell himself becomes a player, if only marginally, in the story he unfolds. In the final fifth of *God Protect me from my Friends* it ceases to be a third-person narration and becomes a personal journal – Maxwell's diary account of his 1954 visit to Sicily. This recalls his efforts to interview Giuliano's jailed partner in crime, Gaspare Pisciotta, in the hope of discovering the true identity of Giuliano's assassin. His attempt, however, is initially foiled by official refusal and then finally scotched by Pisciotta's own murder. In his description of this ultimate quest for the truth – from the lips of one living man who would know – the tale of the Sicilian bandit becomes a facet of Maxwell's own.

If the quest theme is a persistent and unifying element in Maxwell's writing, and if one acknowledges that theme as a key characteristic of the travel genre, could one legitimately conclude on that basis that all his works were variations of the travel book?

In a way, it is unnecessary, perhaps even a mistake, to seek to describe them as such. Instead of attempting to fit Maxwell's works into the travel genre, it might be more meaningful to turn the issue upside-down and view travel books as belonging to a broader range of non-fictional writing, of which Maxwell's books are representative. This wider category can include autobiography, biography, history, journalism, sociological or anthropological study and war memoir; or a blend of these different elements. The specific label – travel, war memoir, etc. – is often only a consequence of the production and administration of books: a classification arising out of the librarian's demand for order, or from the publisher's and bookseller's simple economic needs to ensure an author's work reaches its customary audience. It is perhaps this ad hoc arrangement which explains why Gavin Maxwell's *Lords of the Atlas*, Norman Lewis's *The Missionaries* and his *Naples '44*, why Freya Stark's *Perseus in the Wind* and Patrick Leigh Fermor's *A Time To Keep Silence* – books so dissimilar in content and structure – can all be found in the same square metre of shelving.

More important than attempting to define the writing as belonging to one or other category is to give due recognition to a type of creative literature which has tended to reside in an intellectual no-man's land. Travel books, for the want of a better description, seldom obey the elaborate conventions of written expression that might enable them to pass as works of science. No anthropologist, for example, would ever consider van der Post's *The Lost World of the Kalahari* as a significant source for the study of the San people. Nor would an academic specialising in recent Greek history and culture cite Leigh Fermor's *Mani* or *Roumeli* as an essential textbook on the country. As a sub-species of memoir they are placed beyond the scientific pale. The anthropological or historical information they convey is too contaminated with the emotions and personality of the author for it to be truly accurate.

On the other hand, the fact that these books appear to describe a world of actual events and real historical experience has often entailed their dismissal from the realms of 'serious' literature. The inferior status of non-fictional writing, which is enshrined in the very way we define it – i.e. by reference to something it is meant not to be – seems to hinge on the issue of invention. Art, it would seem, equals imagination. Although novelists, like travel writers, might draw extensively on their own personal experiences, the final product is not thought to describe in any literal sense their individual real lives. The work is a product of fancy: internally coherent, self-contained, freed from the limitations of the actual. No critic could condemn a fiction by reference to the material from which it was constructed. At best travel books are a sort of adjunct to this real literature. One might read Lawrence Durrell's *Prospero's Cell* as a means of gaining further insight into his poetry or his novels, but by itself it might not be considered an object worthy of serious attention. To read into it a significance greater than the true events it recounts might face the charge of attempting to trump the book up as something it is not.

However, any rigid and over-simplified division of factual and fictional writing is deeply inadequate when applied to an author like Durrell or Gavin Maxwell. While it might be true that the latter needed the intrinsic organisation of real events as a prop for his creative imagination, as both a poet and a portrait painter he was accustomed to transfiguring life through imagination, and to applying different layers of meaning to a single surface. *Harpoon at a Venture* perhaps most fully expresses Maxwell's instinct for the deeper resonances latent in his own personal story. Within a simple tale of economic gamble and failure on the west coast of Scotland he developed an array of richly suggestive images: the courageous, even dignified fisherman, the subtle unseen powers of his quarry and the unfathomable depths upon which their struggle was enacted. It is interesting that in the same year that *Harpoon at a Venture* was published, another adventurer-writer, Ernest Hemingway, also produced a tale of conflict between a man and an immense fish. Need one assume that only one of these writers was alive to the much more enduring human drama inherent in the fabric of his narrative?

Maxwell was surely conscious of the way in which the actual events of life could metamorphose, once refracted through the poetry of his writing, into something of much wider significance. In the Foreword to *Ring of Bright Water* he acknowledged precisely this process at work in his own story:

> In writing this book about my home I have not given to the house its true name. This is from no desire to create mystery . . . but because identification in print would seem in some sense a sacrifice, a betrayal of its remoteness and isolation . . . Camusfeàrna, I have called it . . . but the name is of little consequence, for such bays and houses, empty and long disused, are scattered throughout the wild sea lochs of the Western Highlands and the Hebrides, and in the description of one the reader may perhaps find the likeness of others of which he has himself been fond, for these places are symbols. Symbols, for me and for many, of freedom.[44]

Yet even he could not have foreseen the manner in which *Ring of Bright Water* 'appeared to touch upon some unacknowledged need in those who read it'.[45] The book's immense popularity must surely be explained, in part, by the fact that it tapped into a powerful urge latent in the soul of urban, industrial society. The fact that Maxwell had given expression to this dream of paradise made him, albeit briefly, a kind of hero figure for the age – one who had successfully reimmersed himself in a world of natural innocence.

However, there are major differences between playing the invented hero in a work of fiction and being the main protagonist in a book that 'claims literal validity by constant reference to actuality'. One of the most striking facets of Maxwell's work is how it reveals, not just the wider possibilities and the deeper value of non-fictional writing, but also the major limitations it imposes on the author. These restrictions, in combination with Maxwell's own extraordinary personality, would eventually have deeply destructive consequences for him.

Somewhat ironically, one of the most valuable places to begin an examination of the personality of Gavin Maxwell, perhaps the most fascinating and complex of recent British author-travellers, is in his least autobiographical works, *God Protect me from my Friends* and *Lords of the Atlas*. Here, one can detect striking parallels between the principal characters in the two books, Salvatore Giuliano and T'hami el Glaoui, and then also between their lives and that of the author himself.

Maxwell's two subjects, although from relatively unexceptional backgrounds, are seen to rise above their peers because of outstanding personal qualities. They are men of courage and daring, with an instinctive gift for leadership. Even Giuliano, the son of an impoverished peasant family, is dramatised as an individual of natural dignity and charisma. Allied to this magnetism is a capacity for action, and even ruthlessness. In a world beyond law and order and settled governance, where physical force was an accepted condition of life, both men used violence to secure their ends. Yet neither is presented as a crude and unsympathetic gangster. Although Maxwell seldom excuses their behaviour, they seem to enjoy, at worst, an ambiguous moral status, and at best the deep admiration accorded to heroes. It seemed that, no matter what other shortcomings an individual might display, primitive manliness and a life of risky adventure earned Maxwell's instinctive sympathy. Giuliano, for example, is repeatedly likened to Robin Hood, a criminal more noble and just than the legal forces arrayed against him.

Through a combination of their native charisma and a dynamic capacity for action, Giuliano and el Glaoui enjoyed a period of pre-eminence. However, central to their respective stories is an irrevocable fall from power. Each saw his position steadily undermined by the inexorable flow of contemporary events, each fell victim to some form of betrayal. Giuliano is finally abandoned by his political allies and assassinated with their connivance; the Lion of the Atlas is sold out by the colonial powers, his fate giving rise to a new adjective amongst metropolitan French, *glaouisé* – betrayed. Through Maxwell's mediation, Giuliano and el Glaoui both assume some of the dignity of the tragic hero: colourful, vigorous, compelling personalities unable to bend or adapt to the inevitable. At root they are also deeply anachronistic, almost medieval figures – a bandit and a prince – crushed by the steady grey tide of modernity.

This same pattern and combination of ingredients – the engaging, if anachronistic or, at least, anti-modern central character, a spell of temporary success, even happiness, betrayal and fall – are fundamental elements in almost all Maxwell's *oeuvre*, whose principal subject, of course, is the life and times of Maxwell himself.

All these themes are fully developed in his first book *Harpoon at a Venture*. In particular the work suggests a deep preoccupation with the life of adventure. There is little question that the shark-fishing business did involve a high degree of physical risk. John Hillaby, accompanying Maxwell as a journalist with the *Picture Post*, described what he saw aboard the *Sea Leopard* as 'almost undiluted derring-do'.[46] This certainly fits the self-image impressed on the reader throughout Maxwell's own account: that of an intrepid frontiersman engaging the unknown. When providing the emotional and geographical setting for his fishing business he describes his home on the west coast as a place 'of a different sort of romance: of herring scales and a million gulls, of energy and squalor and opportunity, of feud and fortune, the "end of steel" – the railhead – beyond which all is gamble'.[47]

By only the tenth page one finds Maxwell stood at his Breda light machine-gun, raking the flanks of the first basking shark he had ever seen with automatic fire. In his description of this incident one has in full a confession of his heroic aspirations. His possession on a private pleasure boat of a weapon, somewhat unlikely even in the final year of the Second World War, is explained as part of 'the rather ridiculous hope of engaging a U-boat' singlehanded.[48] The whole shark-fishing enterprise as presented in *Harpoon at a Venture*, down to its very title, is permeated with the language of conflict and aggression. It is almost as if, thwarted by illness from taking part in his country's wider struggles, Maxwell needed a war of his own to make up. 'Catching', 'killing', 'shooting' and 'attacking' are the dominant actions in the story. Even some of the boats – the *Gannet* and the *Sea Leopard* – have names that carry predatory connotations. And it seems a part of the underlying militaristic theme that when the second of these vessels was found to be unseaworthy, Maxwell offered it a warrior's burial: 'The eye of association lent her dignity as she lay at that squalid wharf, the long scars left by struggling sharks reaching almost to her gunwale.'[49]

Similarly important to Maxwell's self-portrait as fearless man of action is his characterisation of his principal adversary in the story – the basking shark. One of the most striking elements of this presentation is that the fish is always a 'he'; although, as Maxwell himself explained, seven out of every eight fish they caught were females.[50] He even persists in referring to sharks as 'he' or 'him' after he has specifically noted that the individual was of the opposite gender.[51] Perhaps subconsciously Maxwell wished to see his opponent as male, since this suited his adversarial approach to the shark-fishing business. Killing 'women', by contrast, might in some way have diminished his achievement.[52]

Equally significant are things that he failed to say about the species. Although he explains that *Cetorhinus maximus*, far from being the flesh-eating inhabitant of nightmares normally invoked by the word 'shark', is, in fact, a plankton-feeder, Maxwell did little to suggest the essentially bovine character of his victim. No single human fatality has been attributed to the species. And if it has ever caused loss of life, this was certainly inadvertent. It was, of course, large and difficult to catch and, had he ever fallen overboard just as a harpooned individual was struggling desperately to escape, Maxwell may have been at risk from the huge tail. However, the creature would never have turned, *Jaws*-like, to revenge itself on its tormentor. What teeth it had were only the size of a kitten's.[53]

The range of images Maxwell did employ to characterise the creature and his duel with it are of a quite different nature. When confronted with the choice of extracting only the shark's valuable oil and wasting the rest or trying to market the full range of products represented by each captured fish, he wrote:

> I see it now as I saw it at first: an ivory-hunter in the deep
> Congo jungle, standing by the mountainous carcase from
> which he has cut out the tusks and pondering how he may
> capitalise the tons of flesh, the hide, the bones – all the
> apparent and gigantic waste . . . I know now that the
> shark's liver is the elephant's ivory.[54]

Elsewhere he describes the shark as 'gigantic', 'ponderous', a 'creature from a prehistoric world', a 'dinosaur', an 'iguanodon',[55] a giant with gaping jaws and a body covered 'with irregular python markings',[56] 'dark viscous slime'[57] and 'studded with . . . spines'.[58] Most interesting of all are the associations that spring to his mind when he is confronted with a factory pickle-tank of shark flesh that had been improperly preserved and become infested with fly larvae. Looking at the rotted heap of carrion and maggots, he imagined that 'beneath that surface layer of putrescence were the struggling bodies of all the wounded, but resurrected dragons that we had attacked and that had escaped us'.[59] The final chapter of the book is also entitled 'Here Be Dragons'.

The dramatisation of the shark as a mythological monster and himself, by implication, as a dragon-slayer is part of a revealing series of images in the book that hold associations with medieval conflict and the age of chivalry. As we have already seen, Maxwell had called his west-coast home 'my Island Valley of Avalon'. Later, when describing the poor quality of the employees brought in to his Soay factory from Skye, he wrote that this labour merely 'swelled the numbers as dummy figures upon castle battlements did in the Middle Ages'.[60] Expressing his feelings for Harry, the 'strange, contradictory, unclassifiable' captain who sank the company's boat, the *Nancy Clen*, Maxwell thought of him, 'as Prince Hal of Falstaff, "I could well have spared a better man" '.[61]

There were, of course, elements in the author's background which made these historical allusions appropriate. For, although Maxwell was not exactly a prince, he was indeed nobly born and had been, on occasions, escort for a princess. Moreover, on both the paternal and maternal sides of his family, he could gaze back, as far as the age of chivalry, on lines of distinguished military ancestors. In fact, Maxwell was a distant descendant of Prince Hal's arch rival – Harry Hotspur. However, these self-images also indicate the romantic world Maxwell's imagination inhabited. It was almost as if, debarred by his own time and place from pursuing in any literal sense the career of a knight in shining armour, he wished, none the less, to view his life as enjoying some of the glamour of that heroic model. It is surely indicative of the author's urge to be seen in a noble guise, that he could later write of the shark-fishing gamble:

I tried to found a new industry for the tiny and discontented population of the island [of Soay], by catching and processing for oil the great basking sharks that appear in Hebridean waters during the summer months. I built a factory, bought boats and equipped them with harpoon guns, and become a harpoon gunner myself. For five years I worked in that landscape.[62]

Here we have the valiant and socially minded aristocrat braving the deep and tilting with dragons, not for the £130 per ton of liver-oil, but in the service of his vassal tenants and the common good.

It seems inevitable that when devising the moral equation in *Harpoon at a Venture*, the author would place himself, if only subconsciously, on the side of virtue. The slime-bodied, net-rending sharks, on the other hand, seem the obvious candidates as the bad guys, and that idea was fairly well developed. (This, incidentally, would have been much less straightforward had the book been written in the environmentally sensitive nineties, especially in view of the basking shark's decline.[63]) The beast is portrayed as huge, ugly and stupid; while Maxwell exploits the small size of the shark's brain, in a somewhat baffling passage about the nature of pain, to minimise the suggestion of cruelty in his trade.[64]

However, when Maxwell put his shoulder to the wheel of post-war industrial revival and failed, it was not the fish that ultimately defeated him. The shark-fishing enterprise also had other opponents. 'He had to combine in one exhausting act', wrote a reviewer in *The Times*, 'the roles of hunter, killer, industrial organizer and business man'.[65] In the dramatic parts as hunter and killer Maxwell was a considerable success. Towards the close of his time as a fisherman he could catch fifty sharks in eighteen days, and believed he might easily have tripled that tally had he had the facilities.[66] It was when he tried to combine these rôles with the latter two – as a captain of industry, a man of board meetings, of research and development – that Maxwell came up against the chief obstacle to success: simple practical reality. When his noble hopes of revival for Soay and its inhabitants were finally dashed, the real villains in the piece were the small, trivial inconveniences of life: the opposing rhythms of the tide, the malfunction of an engine part, the poor construction of a slipway, the cold, grey and pin-striped rules of commerce, the petty red-tape of an expert in fish glue.

To put it another way he had simply overreached himself. The initial ideal of jobs for his islanders exceeded the flesh-and-blood facts on the ground. As one business corporation had explained to him, Maxwell was attempting to achieve in twelve months with £12,000, what they would undertake in five years with £50,000. In *Harpoon at a Venture* Maxwell's subconscious projection of responsibility for failure onto external forces helped disguise a fundamental aspect of his personality: his aristocratic disregard for practical considerations. Financially, his career passed through a series of high peaks and deep troughs. At a single throw the Soay episode exhausted a substantial inheritance. Subsequently, as an author dependent on his pen, he was frequently living well in advance of his output. Longmans, who published all but the first of Maxwell's books, had the measure of their largest talent very shortly after paying an advance on *God Protect me from my Friends*: 'the author is a likeable person and brilliant writer, but very bad at managing his own affairs, especially money'.[67]

Richard Frere, who acted as Maxwell's business manager in the final years of his life, gave a detailed account in *Maxwell's Ghost* of his rearguard action to stave off creditors and stabilise the financial position of Gavin Maxwell Enterprises Ltd. Behind this somewhat grandiose title was a 'quasi-legal' device to deflect some of the tax burden arising from the huge royalties for *Ring of Bright Water*. When these were fairly rapidly exhausted the title became an ironic commentary on the MD's improvidence. According to Frere, no one took it seriously except Maxwell himself, who found in it an additional benefit. 'If Maxwell had a hangover after a spending spree, or was warned that there was insufficient money for something he particularly wanted to do, he would speak darkly of "mismanagement of company affairs" which relieved him of complicity without actually indicting anyone else'.[68] That Maxwell, an author, should have had a business manager at all was unusual; that there was a board of directors meeting and minuting on the affairs of the one man seems bizarre. On occasions this august body could mull over such urgent issues as whether the Sandaig cottage should be equipped with a dish-washer.[69]

Maxwell's very choice of an isolated lighthouse-keeper's cottage as a place of residence was perhaps an indication of a concern to escape the modern technological age. As he explained in the preface to *Ring of Bright Water*, he felt that industry and urban life were the enemies of Camusfeàrna. They were, by implication, also enemies of its owner. In Sandaig's remoteness and its freedom from association with modern existence, Maxwell found many of the simple experiences and the unhurried quality of life which travellers seek in journeys overseas. However, like most travellers, Maxwell did not find himself entirely satisfied by the rural idyll. Simple economic necessity and, no doubt, his complex social needs demanded that he return to a London residence on a regular basis.

Classic expression of Maxwell's love-hate relationship with the mundane and practical aspects of life was his deeply ambivalent attitude towards mechanical objects. In the biographical blurb on his dustjackets the final paragraph read: 'Gavin Maxwell is an F.R.S.L., F.I.A.L., F.Z.S. (Sc.), F.R.G.S. and F.A.G.S. He is intensely interested in all forms of life, and correspondingly uninterested in machinery.' There was a good deal of evidence to substantiate this light-hearted confession. Richard Frere, for example, could convince Maxwell of his magical powers when, looking at the engine of a vehicle that had just failed, he quickly diagnosed the problem as one caused by an unattached lead, reconnected it without Maxwell seeing, waved his hands and uttered a spell over the closed bonnet, then revived the engine with a turn of the ignition.[70]

By contrast, Maxwell's own unwitting purchase of dud machinery is a recurrent theme in his life. In *Harpoon at a Venture* he described how he put the whole fishing project under a handicap from the outset when he bought 'a worthless and entirely unsuit-able boat' without even looking it over himself.[71] This was a mistake he repeated a number of years later when he purchased the costly and ill-fated *Polar Star*. This vessel required two new engines and a replacement for its highly unreliable transmission before it eventually sank off Camusfeàrna.[72] His bad luck with mechanical objects also ran to cars. When he bought a second-hand vehicle in

Palermo, during his visit to work on *God Protect me from my Friends*, he paid '130 thousand lire for it, then 20 thousand lire in formalities, and finally (to date) 58,000 in repairs. I doubt', Maxwell confessed to Mark Longman, 'whether I shall get more than 80,000 or so when I sell it'.[73]

For all his cavalier ignorance of what lay beneath the bonnet, he was a man keen on the products of the internal combustion engine, especially the sensation of speed. He had a passion for exotic, racy cars such as his Maserati. Frere described how Maxwell, reduced by cancer to a frail invalid, found some of his last moments of pleasure when he took over at the wheel of his Mercedes and drove at top speed down Glenshiel.[74] His boat *Polar Star*, when refitted with a fresh engine and other components, was an expensive luxury Gavin Maxwell Enterprises could ill afford. However, it was retained because of its owner's desire for style on the water.

Another facet of Maxwell that sits oddly with the image of him as mechanical incompetent is a preoccupation in his writing with precise technical details. Over matters of time, distance and dimension he was usually meticulous. In the Camusfeàrna trilogy he could dwell with an almost sensuous relish on the construction of a water tank or the erection of a fence. Another penchant was to insert into the text 'official' reports on an incident. Following the sinking of the *Polar Star*, for instance, described in *The Rocks Remain*, he completed his account of the affair with the reports submitted to the authorities by himself and the coxswain of the local lifeboat.[75] In *Raven Seek Thy Brother* he included the entire text of a highly detailed report he had circulated, which was intended to raise funds for 'a possible new industry for the crofting population of the West Highlands and Islands' – an eider-down farm.[76] *Harpoon at a Venture*, of course, was a golden opportunity to include frequent, detailed descriptions of the equipment used in the fishing business. Take, for instance, this piece on harpoons:

> They were the old type of whaling harpoon, intended to be
> fired from the muzzle-loading guns of the type we later
> employed . . . as our standard equipment . . . The tips were
> spear-shaped, much like a flat stone arrow-head. There were
> no barbs, no holding surface to give the least resistance to

the harpoon's being withdrawn exactly as it had entered; in fact, the rear edges of the arrow-blades were sharpened, as if to cut their way out more easily. Each harpoon was about a yard long; the whole of the shaft was intended to fit inside the barrel of the gun, with only the arrow-head protruding. The length of the shaft was slotted, so that a metal ring for the playing rope could slide to the arrow-head when the harpoon was in the gun, and to the back end of the shaft after it had been fired.[77]

These passages seemed to serve Maxwell as five-finger exercises in clarity, at which he excelled. In addition, however, they suggest an almost child-like fascination with the mechanical and practical. Perhaps for one who was completely immersed from infancy in the life of birds and animals and the Scottish landscape, simple, everyday technology never lost some of its initial mystery. It is equally striking that such a minutely observant and emotional writer on nature had an almost metaphysical feel for the mechanical image: 'she rang a push-button bell and passed me on to another nun who was as human and welcoming as a well-greased cog wheel';[78] 'I had screwed myself up to the point of parting with Edal after years of mutual esteem and now I had to unwind on the instant like a broken watch spring'.[79]

This conflict in Maxwell – his determined eschewal of the modern world and then his need for and apparent fascination with it – is a key source of drama in his Camusfeàrna trilogy. Over the three books the house was gradually converted from a simple two-up two-down, amenity-free and pre-modern cottage to a permanent residence with all mod cons: an establishment Frere later described as 'a modernised holiday camp'.[80] The owner came to view this impact on the house with deep misgivings. What had originally been described as an open, romantic, essential and virginal locality became disfigured with 'straggling prefabricated wings built with the ugliness born of what had seemed necessity and a strict regard for time'.

On the seaward side of the house stood two broken-down jeeps, whose stamina had not proved equal to the boulders and potholes that composed the two-mile track bulldozed four years before. Between these pieces of defeated machinery and the sea the motor launch *Polar Star* lay high and dry on her massive wheeled cradle . . . Telegraph posts and wires descended the hill from one direction, electric conveyances from another. They converged upon Camusfeàrna, and around the house itself were high wooden palings confining two otters that had once been house-living pets.[81]

This transformation of his Scottish home from a paradise almost into a sort of prison was in many ways firmly linked to his celebration of the place in print. *Ring of Bright Water* had been immensely successful, selling in millions around the world. In effect Maxwell's private life, especially his experiences at Camusfeàrna with his otters, became his most valuable literary asset, and possession of the house developed its own incontestable logic. To have sold it or to have disposed of the otters would have been a betrayal of the myth of happiness created in the book. However, ownership of both house and animals involved a major commitment. The otters had to be cared for, especially after they turned savage and inflicted severe wounds on a number of Maxwell's friends. Since he wished to continue his travels and researches overseas, he was obliged to employ otter-keepers and provision a remote cottage on a permanent basis. This eventually set in train the introduction of electricity, water and telephone, the construction of a driveable track and the possession of various sea craft and four-wheel-drive vehicles.

These changes in his material lifestyle could be traced in part to the nature of Maxwell's literary achievement. Most assessments of his writing converge on the issue of its elegant, almost classical, lucidity. It was a style that made for easy reading and instant popularity, which, in some ways, concealed his wider merit. Another dominant characteristic of the autobiographical works was a capacity to reveal his private affairs with remarkable openness. Quite literally anything that happened to him was fair game for his books. A period of intense, neurotic confusion that he experienced in North Africa in the first three months of 1960 was to be the subject of a work entitled *The Haywire Winter*.[82] When he had been prosecuted for libel after the publication of *God Protect me from my Friends* he initially intended 'to publish a complete transcript of his . . . case interspersed with comments by himself on how it felt to be hauled into Court'.[83] His crises, various illnesses, the intense agony of an injection in the groin, even the fading experiences of a man sentenced to death by inoperable cancer – to be called *The Tunnel*[84] – everything could be subjected to the same dispassionate scrutiny and converted into his art.

The supreme confidences that Maxwell entrusted to his audience, the manner in which he quite literally invited them into his home and heart, seemed to establish a deeply personal bond between author and reader. Many people clearly felt they knew him personally, often fashioning an image of him that suited themselves. Indicative of the wide spectrum of interpretations are the existing published accounts. To Richard Frere, for example, in *Maxwell's Ghost*, he was the nobly born near-genius stoically confronting triumph and disaster alike with Kipling's *If* on his lips. To Richard Adams in *The Adventures of Gavin Maxwell* he was the heroic adventurer with the common touch, treating and valuing people as he found them, rather than for what they represented. To many of his readers he simply appeared as a rather vulnerable friend. His cares and joys seemed theirs, his private world became, in effect, their public property.

This affected Maxwell in a number of ways. After the publication of *Ring of Bright Water* he received an avalanche of letters from those he called 'fans'; and when a considerable number had penetrated his half-hearted attempt to disguise the true whereabouts of Camusfeàrna they also took to visiting him in person. Those he managed to hold at bay with a succession of strongly worded notices, the last announcing in foot-high red letters the single word PRIVATE, often resorted to the surrounding hillsides to watch life at Camusfeàrna through binoculars, telescopes and long telephoto lenses.[85] Those whose discourtesy extended to baiting the otters and banging on the door demanding entertainment and a guided tour were often subjected to a severe tongue-lashing. Maxwell claimed in *The Rocks Remain* that his 'days became almost wholly absorbed with warding off unwanted visitors',[86] which put 'the very life of the place . . . at stake'.[87]

However, for all his deep frustration at this behaviour he also felt some sense of guilt when confronted with the need to close Camusfeàrna down. Maxwell apparently received letters in which his fans argued:

> 'Whatever you are going to do, please never say that the Camusfeàrna of *Ring of Bright Water* never was. Say that it's gone, if you like, but not that you lied. I couldn't take that, because it was the only evidence I had that Paradise existed somewhere' . . . 'Whatever you say, Camusfeàrna will always be for me the Camusfeàrna you described. I want to keep that image, even though I will never see it – take it away from me and I don't think I have anything left' . . . 'Your book *The Rocks Remain* shook me . . . it destroyed my great illusion, that somewhere there was happiness, contentment – a world I have never entered in sixty-four years of life'.[88]

The price he had paid for selling his story was a kind of public responsibility for maintaining the fiction. 'If I broke the pattern of my life', Maxwell wrote, 'as they imagined it to be I would be betraying them'.[89] Unfortunately, that pattern of life had become a serious financial burden. He estimated that to support the entire edifice – house, otters, otter-keepers, boats, Land-Rovers, supplies and all – was costing him £7,000 a year – a figure equivalent to the salary of a cabinet minister.[90] This translated into an average of a book a year.[91]

To meet this deadline Maxwell was obliged to work at high speed. The sequel to *Ring of Bright Water*, for instance, *The Rocks Remain*, was written in a matter of only a few weeks, and the haste showed.[92] John Guest, Longman's general list editor, wrote in an internal memorandum that the book was 'a bit of a hotch potch'.

> One feels that the author has pushed himself at it, at various times and in various moods; that he is lacking in self-discipline, and that the success of Ring of Bright Water has gone to his head a bit so that he is less self-critical. He is relying on readers taking anything from his pen, just

because he *is* Gavin Maxwell. There is a lot of unrelated material in the book, and little or no effort is made to pull it into a coherent whole; it is only held together by the fact that it is all autobiographical writing by the same (now famous) character, and that it all appears between the same covers.[93]

To pin the blame for a decline in standards solely on the author was, in many ways, to misrepresent the situation. Maxwell had simply run up against the fundamental limitations of the literary form in which he worked. Non-fictional writing, if it is to be of high quality, requires considerable amounts of research, as in *God Protect me from my Friends* or *Lords of the Atlas*. This detective work, however, is both costly and time-consuming, and Maxwell had precious little of either commodity. Otherwise the author needs to have personal adventures or, at least, noteworthy experiences to provide any book with its content.

Had Maxwell been a novelist then things might have been different. Had he been, for example, like Hermann Hesse, another cult writer whom Maxwell resembled in a number of ways, especially in his Franciscan quest for harmony with nature, he could simply have translated the material and experiences of his own life into his novels. He would have been in no way bound by personal realities: the plot and characters could have been manipulated to serve whatever end or pursue whatever ideas he wished. Nor would his readers, as Maxwell's did, have urged him to steer a course in real life that suited their hopes for the story in the book.

Although Maxwell had attempted to produce a fictional work in the late 1950s – one based, significantly, on true experiences – he felt himself unable to structure it adequately.[94] His imagination seemed to require the pattern of actual events as a framework on which to elaborate. When pressed to deliver the annual manuscripts to Longmans, he simply fell back on the real life story he could most readily exploit – his own. Celebrating the romance of Gavin Maxwell, Richard Adams called him 'a writer-adventurer, a man who – as far as it was possible – lived what he wrote and wrote what he lived'.[95] There was, however, a severe price to pay for that interrelationship. True, his life at Camusfeàrna provided the stuff of his books, but it was the demands of that Scottish home that kept him hard at it, trying to summon up out of his own depths the written material to pay for it all. And the strain could be intense. In the last part of his otter trilogy, *Raven Seek Thy Brother*, Maxwell wrote:

> I felt myself to be a cypher in my own household, and by degrees that is what I became . . . I could take no part in the activity of the others; I wrote for increasingly long hours every day, working simultaneously on *The House of Elrig* and *Lords of the Atlas*, but with an ever growing sense of frustration – and, I believe a growing petulance and ill temper . . . I felt like an aphis, immobile but solicitously kept alive in a cell by ants who tended me assiduously for my daily excretion of written words.[96]

The way in which he ransacked his own experience for literary material, coupled with the financial imperatives imposed by Camusfeàrna, not to mention his practical and financial short-comings, all operated to lock Maxwell into a synergistic downward cycle. At times in his last book it almost seemed as if the very act of writing his story was somehow implicated in his tragically premature death.

In the period covered by *Raven Seek Thy Brother* he had become aware of the fact that Kathleen Raine had cursed him on a rowan tree outside Camusfeàrna, after her passionate love for him had finally been spurned. According to Maxwell she 'had always believed that she possessed great and terrible occult powers'.[97] Though it seems likely that he attached to this no more significance than his natural healthy scepticism would allow, Maxwell built the story of the curse into the book. And without question the catalogue of disasters that beset him during that period lent some credence to the possibility of a malign influence at work in his affairs. His favourite Pyrenean mountain dog, Gus, for example, hanged itself one night on its own choke chain, while another pet, a Great Dane, was shot by a local farmer for worrying sheep. His financial position continued to deteriorate, his long-standing otter-keeper and protégé decided to quit, and before Maxwell was able to close the house and deliver the otters to a zoo, Camusfeàrna and Edal were destroyed in a mysterious fire. The author's health also declined: a car crash left him seriously disabled, adding to the chronic problems generated by his ulcers. Then came the final malignant tumour.

A good storyteller like Maxwell clearly knew how best to exploit the idea of the curse. It suggested a pattern in the otherwise disparate events of real life and provided an element of drama and some of the coherence which all books require. However, *Raven Seek Thy Brother* is more than just a good tale involving the supernatural.

Maxwell was genuinely distrustful of his own success or happiness. Richard Frere recalled him to say 'quite seriously: "Richard, things are going *too* well for us. I don't trust this situation. Someone up there is getting more and more angry, and will strike" '.[98] Kathleen Raine also felt that a sense of crisis was almost an essential condition in his life:

> truth to say, he was ever at his best when, having got
> himself into some desperate situation, he set to work not
> only to extricate himself from it, but to turn it to account
> . . . This was his temperament: for Gavin the very idea of
> security and peace and quiet was unimaginable. That was
> after all why I – and why through his books so many others
> – loved him.[99]

It must surely be a magnificent coincidence or a compelling insight into the character of this man that on the wall of his last home at Kyleakin, Maxwell should have gazed daily on a painting by his friend Michael Ayrton, depicting the climactic moment in the career of Icarus – the archetypal overreacher.[100]

It is undoubted that Maxwell was powerfully predisposed towards a tragic theme. We have already seen it at work in his earlier books, particularly *God Protect me from my Friends* and *Lords of the Atlas*. It was, to a lesser degree, re-worked in *Harpoon at a Venture*, and even in *The Ten Pains of Death* one finds, if not a tragedy, then a catalogue of chronic unhappiness and frustration borne with peasant stoicism. Confronted by the litany of misfortune in his own life and forced by circumstances to shape these events into yet one more literary work, it seems that Maxwell was almost congenitally bound to rewrite the one simple and paradigmatic drama that had always compelled him. In it he would play the central rôle: the noble and heroic individual striving towards his vision, until felled finally by vaulting ambition and a tide of adverse circumstances.

Maxwell's story expresses in the most powerful fashion an issue confronted by many authors of non-fictional books. The dramatic incidents of real life, unlike those of fiction, are easily exhausted. Though few are ever faced by the kind of impasse that frustrated the creator of *Raven Seek Thy Brother*, there is sometimes a decline in quality in the work of the non-fictional writer. Often the most compelling stories of adventure and travel are those in which the experiences described are chance products of circumstance, or which involve journeys and incidents that the author had never initially planned to document. The programmatic completion of a voyage or similar arduous experience so that a book may be manufactured does not diminish the value of the product. The professional travel writer often produces a professional job. Maxwell's *A Reed Shaken by the Wind* proves that. But the element of self-consciousness can compromise the non-fictional book. The interdependence of life and work in the art of the non-fictional author can compel her or him to virtual paradoxes – the chore of escape, premeditated adventure. The travel writer is forced to undertake yet one more journey as a job, with little more sense of spontaneity than a jaded overseas rep. Then the 'exotic or comic anomalies, wonders and scandals' of foreign parts and people can become the stuff of a weary and predictable formula. It is for this reason that John Hatt, author of *The Tropical Traveller* and owner of Eland Books, who has 'done as much as anyone to inspire the current revival of interest in travel writing',[101] believes in the general rule of one consummate travel book per author.[102]

Chapter VII

The Purpose of the Traveller

In any examination of the social value of British travel and the motives that have lain behind it for travellers themselves this century, one obvious line of enquiry is to make comparison between travel as a modern activity and the function it has traditionally assumed in other historical and cultural contexts. Amongst foreign societies and even in portions of continental Europe, one encounters, in addition to the dominant geopolitical, military and economic motives for travel, a recurrent phenomenon – the journey as a mode of religious expression. Very few other activities can serve as a richer metaphor to articulate the essential pattern of an entire human life than the pilgrimage. With its intrinsic sense of linear progress from a known past to an indefinite future, of a complete physical and emotional challenge, and then of a final resolution at the journey's end, travel appears uniquely equipped to communicate what it means to orient oneself towards an ultimate spiritual goal.

It is for these reasons perhaps that pilgrimage has been and remains a fundamental component in all the major world religions. To prepare for and complete the Hadj, for instance, the journey to the Kaaba in Mecca, is an ambition central to the lives of all devout Muslims throughout the Islamic world. Likewise, in Hindu India, religious shrines are ubiquitous, and visiting them confers great merit on the pilgrim. Itinerant holy men, known as saddhus, having abandoned home, possessions and sometimes even clothing, can spend much of their lives walking to these holy sites, some of which can be more than 1,000 kilometres away. Up until the

1950s there existed in Buddhist Tibet a type of pilgrimage which probably exceeded in austerity any other form of religious voyage.[1] The entire return journey was measured out in complete prostrations of the body and could take several years to complete.

In Protestant Britain, however, one encounters a society in which, for several centuries, religious pilgrimage has been of marginal significance. Not only that, British society has witnessed almost the complete extinction of all lifestyles in which the principal motivation is some form of spiritual development. The itinerant holy men and organised monastic communities that were once integral to the structure of medieval society, and are still such a commonplace of contemporary Asiatic life, particularly in the Indian subcontinent, vanished from Britain with the Reformation.

It is tempting to speculate whether the very social processes which extinguished pilgrimage in Britain are perhaps implicated in the growth of later forms of travel and the development of its associated literature. Is it possible that the twentieth-century traveller is an avatar of a much older psychological type? In former times these individuals would have gravitated towards the non-productive, non-domestic patterns of life enjoyed by the wandering ascetic, or the monk, the nun and the hermit. Marooned, however, in a godless society whose national genius is most fully expressed in practical, political and scientific endeavour, this would-be religious community has felt redundant and has eventually been displaced, seeking spiritual fulfilment through journeys overseas.

It is interesting to note that many of the circumstances imposed on travellers are strikingly similar to the principal conditions of a religious career. Both the ascetic and the journeying individual, for example, forego the domestic environment. Emotional and psychological ties with family and friends are temporarily or permanently severed. Both then enter into relationships with communities whose values and objectives can be fundamentally different. Both must abandon excessive material possessions. Travellers are invariably financially independent of the society through which they move. Like the ascetic they are emotionally and intellectually liberated from the demands of economic self-maintenance. These circumstances are an essential prerequisite of the contemplative life, leaving the initiate free to divest earlier values, even an older sense of self, and permitting the development of alternative beliefs and identities. Exactly this same process can impact upon the lone adventurer adrift in the culture of an alien community. Moreover, travellers, in giving themselves to the vagaries of the journey and the unpredictability of its encounters and events, may also come close to the mental attitude of religious devotees, who have made submission to the divine.

There is a scattering of evidence to support the idea that the twentieth-century traveller has a forgotten kinship with the medieval pilgrim. Two prominent interpreters of the travel experience, Patrick Leigh Fermor and Geoffrey Moorhouse, have both exhibited a deep fascination with monasticism, and have written on the subject in their respective books, *A Time to Keep Silence* and *Against All Reason*. Fermor actually spent several months in French and German monasteries. It seems also significant that the work describing this retreat was itself classified as a work of travel.

Moorhouse touched again on spiritual themes in his classic travel book, *The Fearful Void*, an account of his 3,300 kilometre west-to-east trek through the Sahara Desert. Through his study of the navigational techniques essential for this extraordinary journey, he had learnt of the existence of an element in the universe called the Point of Aries. This is the spot at which the path of the sun intersects the celestial equator on 21 March each year. In a passage which gave the book its title he examined the deeper relationship that he sensed might exist between the act of travel and the spiritual quest. He noted that although all the heavenly bodies in the zodiac were related to this point, there is, however, no actual entity called Aries. 'It is, in a way', Moorhouse wrote, 'the invention of astronomers and navigators'. Yet

It is because Aries exists that the navigator is able to make his calculations, and so fix his position on earth. This is the focal point of activity for all those millions of light specks which we call stars. It regulates their relationships. It also gives man, trying to find his way across the wilderness of the earth, a security that he can find it, if only he learns the secret of using Aries correctly.

Perhaps . . . God should be thought of as a spiritual Point of
Aries . . . Without awareness of this God, without a sense of
common relationship with God and with each other through
God, without being able to refer to God, we are quite lost;
people spinning helplessly and hopelessly through a fearful
void of the spirit.[2]

What is so striking about this particular passage in relation to the
theory that travel is a route to spiritual development, and that
contemporary British travellers are a reincarnation of yesterday's
ascetics, is not that it fits so perfectly, but its sheer isolation as a
piece of supportive evidence. It is remarkable how very very few
travellers have ever considered their wanderings a veiled quest for
God. Certainly, for four of the five travellers considered in this
book, religion was a theme that hardly ever surfaced. Neither Eric
Bailey nor Gavin Maxwell showed anything but a characteristic
British scepticism about such matters, while Wilfred Thesiger is an
avowed atheist and denied any spiritual dimension to his journeys,
even in the purgatorial wastes of the Rub al Khali.[3] Philby
converted to Islam, but it was a decision taken largely on pragmatic
grounds. Apostasy liberated him from the restrictions and inconvenience that otherwise hampered Europeans in Arabia, but it was
not an event on which his inner life dramatically turned. Other
travellers – Robert Byron, Norman Douglas, T. E. Lawrence,
Dervla Murphy – have at most professed themselves agnostic.[4]
Richard Burton positively scorned the Christian religion.

One of the very few figures who has made the spiritual
dimension to travel a major theme in his writing is Laurens van der
Post. Yet it is a preoccupation that has elicited a strongly mixed
reaction from the British travel community. A classic expression of
this ambivalence was the response of reviewers to his *Venture to the
Interior*. Although the work enjoyed instant popularity, what
negative criticism there was clustered around a number of key
themes in the book which might legitimately be defined as spiritual.

Van der Post had been deliberately elliptical about the exact
practical objectives set out for his expedition to Nyasaland. Other
than saying that it had been commissioned on agricultural grounds
by a government department he had explained very little. Certainly

he had given away almost nothing about his own conclusions after the surveys. One senses that such an omission was fitting in a work so deeply concerned with subconscious, non-rational aspects of human experience. It shifted the reader's focus away from the obvious, day-to-day material circumstances of the journey, to its underlying psychological significance.

However, for some this left major questions unanswered. One reviewer, baffled by the omission, simply invented an undisclosed geological reason for the survey.[5] Raymond Mortimer was also not completely happy with van der Post's silence on the trip's practical purpose: 'I like to learn about the methods of experts . . . but there is no word here about anything so prosaic'.[6] The mild note of dissatisfaction was much clearer in Peter Fleming's review for *The Spectator*. Fleming was himself an author of several best-selling travel books in the thirties, but these were of a quite different nature. There were no difficult mystical or philosophical ideas in his works. Fleming was a much more familiar British stereotype: 'the cheerful . . . amateur confronting the anomalies of abroad with unfailing pluck, intelligence, good-humor, and modesty'.[7] In Laurens van der Post's book Fleming was clearly irritated by what seemed deliberate obscurity. He 'hardly mentions the main purpose of his journey', Fleming complained, 'and in prosaic minds like mine . . . this omission must generate a feeling of disorientation'.

> To these sublunary readers there is something inherently interesting in the idea of a man being flown into the heart of Africa to examine the possibilities of food production on plateaux 8,000 feet high. We are curious to know what (if any) the possibilities were, how they were assessed and what, as he discharged it, Colonel van der Post thought about his mission. Because our curiosity is not satisfied, we cannot but be mildly irked by a sense of deprivation.[8]

Two other sublunaries, V. S. Pritchett and Peter Quennell, also concurred that the South African's metaphysics were not a habitat in which they felt at home. The former, particularly, thought his treatment of the physical journey fine, but the spiritual voyage was a 'baffling mixture of the naïve, the earnest and the obscure'.[9]

Quennell called these spiritual considerations patches of fog. In all these comments there seems to be an underlying feeling that van der Post had offended against the canons prevailing in English travel writing.

Lesser critics, unable to navigate the text, simply imagined that in those darker regions of prose they failed to penetrate lay their worst fears or their fondest dreams. The reviewer for the *Daily Worker*, somewhat predictably, sensed in *Venture to the Interior* the outlines of a colonial conspiracy. Its author was 'well in the tradition of the liberal intellectual types who so often happen to be on hand when some down-to-earth, materialistic task has to be undertaken to further the aims of British imperialism'.[10] In the *Daily Herald*, on the other hand, the reviewer felt that the book described part 'of the greatest adventure in the world today', which was 'the opening up of the undeveloped lands, growing food in the vast, empty veldt, exploring as cattle country, the lonely lands where no men dwell'.[11] One senses that this is an eminently prosaic and peculiarly British version of the world's 'greatest adventure'.

One of the striking elements of all the reviews, both good and bad, is the frequent note of confusion. Harold Nicolson, immensely cultured and exceptionally well-read in the literatures of the major European nations, displayed not only a characteristic tolerance, but an almost blank incomprehension.

> His [van der Post's] philosophy of life is simple and still
> tentative. 'It is not difficult,' he writes, 'to like people,
> provided they have something in their lives that they
> themselves like . . . The difficult people are the great critics,
> the ones who cannot find anything in life to like.' 'I am sure,'
> he writes again, 'one cannot love life enough; but I believe,
> too, one mustn't confuse love of life with the love of certain
> things in it'. The colonel's *élan vital* is terrific; but it is
> tempered by mysticism and a profound belief in human
> affections. 'How can there,' he writes, 'ever be any real
> beginning without forgiveness?' The only thing that Colonel
> van der Post is capable of hating is *der Geist der stets verneint*. His
> hatred, if one deserved it, would be terrible and fierce; his
> gentleness, a solace to all shattered or unexpressed souls.[12]

It is obviously easier to interpret van der Post's work when the major portion of the *oeuvre* is to hand, and when the Jungian ideas it explores are common currency, rather than when one is confronted by a single, early work. However, what seems most significant about this paragraph, the only portion of the review in which Nicolson offered a key rather than a précis of the narrative, is that none of it really addresses the book's principal themes. Others, unwilling to venture any analysis, and taking their cue from the blurb on the dustjacket – 'Like T. E. Lawrence, Colonel van der Post is . . . a man with a strong personal mystique' – spoke repeatedly of the author's mystique almost as if it were a physical object one possessed, or a quality one cultivated like a literary style or personal charm, which was somehow beyond rational analysis.

Even in the 1990s one finds continuing expression of a British unease for a figure so avowedly spiritual and prophetic as van der Post. The satirical magazine *Private Eye* has lampooned him in the past on an almost weekly basis. Possibly there is something deeply anomalous about the foreign 'mystic' who has yet burrowed his way to the very heart of British society, dining at No. 10 or discoursing on the cosmos with the nation's heir apparent. Perhaps he also provides a stalking horse for the future king himself, who is somehow compromised, as the principal representative of the British people, by his communion with the vegetable world or his interest in what are seen as pseudo-spiritual alternatives. He has abandoned that quintessentially British quality, most appropriately described as being *down-to-earth*.

It is hardly surprising that the British temperament, so archly sceptical of metaphysics, so deeply rooted in the here and now, has been content with the most practical, rationally accessible justifications for travel. Journeys had a logical purpose: they produced a map, yielded scientific data, planted the national flag, opened the region up for trade, relieved a beleaguered mission or found a lost missionary. If practicalities hardly seemed to enter into the enterprise at all (climbing dangerously high mountains, for example), the pat retort about it simply being there has usually served as an effective dampener on any further enquiry. The most elevated purpose and value to travel which the British have traditionally allowed, especially in the ninteenth century, were on a moral character-building note. Wandering overseas tested the individual's mettle. Otherwise, like the grand tour, it had an educational purpose, widening intellectual horizons.

Travel has also provided the enterprising individual with opportunities to attain the status of national symbol, akin to that of the war hero. The resulting love affair between traveller and adoring public brought benefits to both parties. The former enjoyed the heterogeneous advantages of fame. The nation could then wear her or his reputation for courage, resourcefulness and tenacity as if it were their own. The contractual relationship that Peter Brent noted between British Arabists and their audience could easily be extended to all travellers.

> He suffered the difficulties of his journeys not, as he
> thought, for himself and in pursuit of his own aims, but as a
> representative of all those who, reading of his exploits at
> home, passed through sandstorm and foray with him. His
> being there made it, as it were, unnecessary for them to go;
> his achievements proved a general case, and in the light of
> its logic they could all accept something of the aura of
> heroes.[13]

In the ambassadorial rôle overseas travellers were also expected to be paragons of Christian virtue, maintaining civilised standards even in the wilderness. It was his heightened sense of these responsibilities that prevented Henry Stanley, on meeting Livingstone on the shores of Lake Tanganyika, from giving even a cheery wave or a gasp of relief. 'I must not let my face betray my emotions', he wrote, 'lest it should detract from the dignity of a white man appearing under such extraordinary circumstances'.[14] This was despite the fact that in order to make the rendezvous his entourage had completed an exhausting eight-month trek over 1,000 kilometres, through some of the most treacherous East African conditions; a journey that had involved them in a war between the Arab slave-traders and the Nyamwezi tribe, and cost the lives of both of his white companions.

The traveller's status as national hero demanded not only symbolic but also practical functions. Eric Bailey's explorations in

Tibet demonstrated the point fully. By braving 'some of the most mountainous, difficult and inhospitable country on earth' he was a model of British heroism.[15] In counting his footsteps, or repeatedly taking bearings and measuring altitudes – by literally reifying the journeys and bringing them home in a form that made the regions he traversed safe and accessible to his fellow countrymen – he was serving his country's most practical interests. By converting experience into knowledge, both in an intellectual sphere and on a geopolitical level, he permitted an extension of national dominion.

This elevated status of the British and European traveller was, of course, predicated on certain social, political and geographical conditions. There had to be areas of the globe which were unknown, and visiting these regions had to be potentially hazardous, involving risks to health or life. As the number of dangerous unexplored places declined over the course of this century, while the number of people venturing overseas expanded, the myth of the fearless, intrepid traveller became increasingly difficult to sustain. Ironically, however, the legend became itself a motive for the journey, and then a factor in the traveller's subsequent relationship with the public. For a later generation one means of establishing the originality of a venture was to expose the fallacy of the dangerous unknown and to poke fun at the traveller's supposed heroic status. Few authors have better demonstrated this urge than Eric Newby in *A Short Walk in the Hindu Kush*. Nor have they more successfully exploited two cherished strands of the national character overseas – the gifted, if eccentric amateur willing to try anything, and the bewildered Briton amused by the strangeness of foreign parts and people.

The book recounts the author's bid for escape from his family's costumier business and his experiences as one half of a 'two-man' expedition to the Nuristan region of Afghanistan. The intention was to climb a 6,000-metre peak, Mir Samir, then write a book on their adventures. Ill-prepared, except for a few days mountaineering practice in Caernarvonshire, he and his diplomat friend, Hugh Carless, intended to travel overland to Afghanistan from Istanbul. Accident and almost farcical misadventure characterise the journey from start to finish. The car was crashed even before leaving London, and by Tehran the party mistakenly faced charges for seriously injuring an elderly Iranian nomad. Following further trials, including vehicular breakdown and illness, the two men almost achieve their objectives, gaining all but the last few hundred metres of Mir Samir's summit.

The tone of the book is laconic, modest, self-deprecatory. Its author though tough and capable is never quite the achiever he might wish to be. His efforts at heroism are usually flawed, raising laughter rather than the white man's prestige. Diving into an Iranian cloaca, for instance, to rescue a tiny child from drowning, Newby emerges drenched in oriental sewage to find the victim watching him from amongst the gathered crowd of spectators.[16] He is seldom the full master of his circumstances, wandering from one potential hazard to another without apparently grasping the full seriousness of his position. Yet, equally, the reader is never made to feel the true gravity of any predicament, the dangers are always held at arm's length by an omnipresent and deflationary sense of humour. Newby's triumph is not to have visited and returned from a perilous unknown like a Bailey or a Thesiger, but to have emerged from it all with a smile on his face. The heroic endeavours of the nineteenth and early twentieth centuries have metamorphosed into modern picaresque comedy.

Towards the close of his Nuristan trek Eric Newby was vouchsafed an unscheduled encounter with a fellow British traveller; in fact, with 'one of the very few people who in our time could be put on the pedestal of the great explorers of the eighteenth and nineteenth centuries'.[17] In the summer of 1956 Wilfred Thesiger had left the enveloping heat of the Iraqi marshes to travel in Afghanistan. In Newby's humorous sketch made from their meeting this 'great, long-striding crag of a man, with an outcrop for a nose and bushy eyebrows, forty-five years old and as hard as nails' plays the archetypal old-style travel hero and foil to Newby's new man – the traveller as comic anti-hero.[18]

The Arab explorer, after expanding on his great journeys, the continuing decline in Eden's England and the poor workmanship of British goods exhibited in his shirt, trousers and shotguns, invites his compatriots to dinner. While Thesiger appears laconic in speech and commanding in presence, Newby portrays himself and Hugh Carless as footsore and disorganised after their exhausting attempt on Mir Samir. Reversing the standard rituals of colonialism, the white men cadge cigarettes off Thesiger's Afghani interpreter. The explorer, meanwhile, is described moving amongst his locked trunkloads of possessions 'like a housekeeper in some stately home'. In contrast with the latter's neatly arranged luggage – 'dissected, mounted between marbled boards' – Newby's possessions are a 'sodden pulp'. As the evening and the book itself draw to a close the two weary amateurs are shown preparing for sleep, blowing up their airbeds to cushion themselves against the sharp rocks sticking out of the iron-hard ground. Observing these 'effete' modern luxuries Thesiger exclaims: 'God, you must be a couple of pansies'.[19]

This meeting on the banks of the Upper Panjshir serves almost as a symbolic moment of contact between the waning golden age of exploration and the silver age of travel. It did not really matter that Newby's and Thesiger's journeys were equally difficult; the real gap between them was not the nature of the trek itself but one of self-representation. Newby's ironic, self-mockery in the book's final words, which Geoffrey Moorhouse has called 'one of the most hilarious endings in modern English literature',[20] is a measure of their differences. Not for Newby to be placed on a pedestal with the great explorers of the past. Yet he is, in a sense, a type as deeply representative of his race, a national hero of a kind – the common man, the amateur, the escapee from ordinary existence willing to try his hand at anything.

Geoffrey Moorhouse himself has written a book that has many of the qualities found in *A Short Walk in the Hindu Kush*. Like the author of the latter Moorhouse is a traveller in a post-exploration age. Although 'post-exploration age' needs some explanation. For just like Newby's expedition in Afghanistan, Moorhouse's 'solo' camel-trek west-to-east across the Sahara Desert lacked none of the austerity, danger or novelty associated with exploration. He followed a route that had never been attempted before and traversed regions that were almost entirely unknown to European geography. Had he completed the whole intended itinerary it would have been one of the oustanding desert journeys by any Briton. As it was, Moorhouse, running out of time and reserves of energy, was forced to abandon the route in the Algerian town of

Tamanrasset. Even so, from Chinguetti in west-central Mauritania he had traversed almost 3,300 kilometres. This alone constituted a remarkable achievement.

Moorhouse, however, was also at pains to emphasise that his was the travail of an ordinary man.[21] Like Newby in his attempt on Mir Samir, he was an 'amateur' explorer, who had had no previous experience of his chosen form of desert travel, and even a highly limited acquaintance with desert as an environment. *The Fearful Void* is a book that keeps close to the plain, gritty facts. The author reveals his hardships and perceived shortcomings with complete candour. There are no faked heroics, no theatrical postures to uphold the white man's dignity; Moorhouse portrays himself as weary and strained, then finally exhausted by the journey. Nor, on the other hand, are there any of nature's aristocrats in the hard, clean sands of the Sahara. The author depicts some of his Mauritanian companions exactly as they seem to a modern, liberal ex-*Guardian* journalist: unsympathetic, vulgar, and crudely sexist. Worn down by their sullen resistance to his wishes and by the subtle victimisation that flowed naturally from numerical superiority and from their greater familiarity with the terrain, the author struck back in ways of which he was not especially proud. Two of the principal offenders were taught to say, should they ever come across other English-speaking foreigners, 'I am a lanky streak of piss' or 'I am a cunning little shit'.[22]

As in *A Short Walk*, so in *The Fearful Void*, the fact that neither individual completely fulfilled his original objectives is almost an essential condition of their departure from the heroic model. Yet this failure and their own ironic detachment from the intrepid legend of their forebears does not diminish their representative status, it enhances it. Endowed with a more than average sense of adventure and an obvious physical courage, the authors negotiate abroad on behalf of everyone. The successes and the failures are no more, nor less, than we ourselves might experience in that situation. The traveller is no longer an exotic outsider, remote in foreign costume, expert in the mountaineer's technique or the handling of camels, and transformed by fluency in difficult, non-European languages. While Thesiger might recite whole passages of the Koran from memory, or discuss Ethelred the Unready with a

Ma'dan sheikh,[23] Geoffrey Moorhouse attends night classes and struggles, as we might, to pronounce sentences of schoolboy simplicity.

In addition to the ambassadorial purpose of the traveller and its implied relationship between individual and wider society, there can be a function behind the journey of which neither party need be aware. In fact these unacknowledged motives can provide it with greater content and meaning than its more immediate and obvious rationale. Perhaps the most compelling illustration of the point is provided by the sequence of expeditions mounted to locate the sources of the Nile.

The rush to find the origins of this river was a drama that galvanised the Victorian imagination like no other event in exploration. An African traveller from a later generation called it 'the greatest geographical secret after the discovery of America'.[24] Its principal *dramatis personae* – Samuel and Florence Baker, Richard Burton, David Livingstone, John Hanning Speke and Henry Stanley – were given immediate entry to the national pantheon. One was eventually laid to rest in Westminster Abbey, three others were knighted, and all of them – their motives, actions and characters – were subjected to intense scrutiny and endless debate. What is most striking about the entire Nile saga is firstly, the extraordinary privations that all these figures were prepared to endure, and secondly, the acrimony that their actions generated amongst the wider community.

Perhaps its most famous consequence was the mysterious death of John Speke in 1864. Speke participated in the original Nile expedition of 1857–8, under the nominal leadership of Richard Burton. While the two men set out as old companions, their twelve-month journey to the African interior was to transform friendship into implacable enmity. Dogged by persistent ill–health, and divided on methods and interests, Burton and Speke had one major quality in common – an unyielding egotism. As the relationship deteriorated during the return leg of the journey, the younger man left his recuperating companion and made a rapid dash northwards in an effort to locate a vast inland sea known as Ukerewe, of which Arab slave-traders had informed him. What he discovered was Africa's largest body of water. Speke called it Lake

Victoria after his monarch, and was convinced, on no stronger grounds than inspired guesswork, that he had found the source of the Nile. This was indeed the case, but since the claim was unsupported by hard evidence, and since Speke's discovery threatened to eclipse his own achievements, Burton scorned the idea. Thus began a dispute that polarised almost the entire British geographical community.

Its denouement occurred six years later after Speke had made a second visit to the region, with James Grant, a quiet, biddable Scot, who played the rôle of loyal lieutenant to his master. Armed with further evidence to support his original theory, Speke returned to England and a hero's welcome. However, along with the laurels and national acclaim that went to the Nile's discoverer came a great deal of criticism and envious scorn. Armchair geographers, roused by the ruthless self-interest that seemed to mark the thirty-seven-year-old's behaviour on both expeditions, they vigorously disputed his claims. Apparent inaccuracies in Speke's survey work led many to rally to the ideas of his old rival Burton, who suggested his own major African 'discovery', Lake Tanganyika, as the real source of the Nile. Both explorers were invited to do intellectual battle on the subject at a meeting of the British Association for the Advancement of Science, in Bath in September 1864. It was billed by their contemporaries as the 'Nile Duel',[25] while one commentator spoke of the two protagonists as 'blind with rage and bitterness'.[26] However, before a single word could be exchanged, Speke was dead, shot through the chest by his own gun. Two of Burton's later and most important biographers have suggested that his former friend and subsequent enemy might have taken his own life.[27]

This was not the only tragic consequence of the search for the Nile. All of the key explorers suffered in health because of their obsession. By the end of his second trek to the interior Speke had lost the use of one ear, while his sight was severely impaired. On the 1858 expedition Burton had been repeatedly stricken with malaria, and lost the use of his legs for eleven months. Temporarily blinded, racked with fever and often delirious, he was at times very close to death. Samuel and Florence Baker had fared little better. As they travelled southwards through modern-day Sudan to locate Lake

Albert, the White Nile's second major source, they too faced severe danger from several quarters. Both were debilitated by recurrent attacks of malaria and had to be carried on litters. On one occasion their canoe was upturned by a bull hippopotamus, at another Florence Baker suffered a near-fatal sunstroke. By the time they reached Cairo, exhaustion and disease had killed all but one of their servants. As Alan Moorhead noted in *The White Nile*, it had taken the Bakers two years to travel a distance that today might easily be covered in forty-eight hours.[28]

David Livingstone paid the ultimate price for the Nile. After the young Henry Stanley had slogged across East Africa to meet him on the shores of Lake Tanganyika and reprovision him, the fifty-nine-year-old missionary trekked south hoping he could prove beyond question his own theory about the great river. He was, however, on a false trail, and on 1 May 1873 he was found dead in his hut, apparently kneeling in prayer at his bedside.

Why did these men and women push themselves to the limits of physical and mental endurance to solve this particular geographical problem? And why should an entire nation urge them on to such lengths, and then, on their return, bathe them in adulation or crucify them with scorn?

The Nile was undoubtedly the blue ribbon of African geography. It is the longest river in the world, and mystery had surrounded its source since the time of the Pharaohs. Herodotus the Greek historian had set out to locate it in the fifth century BC. Alexander, Caesar and the Roman emperor Nero had all dispatched missions with the same objective. When men like Richard Burton set off almost 2,000 years later they took their place within an immense historical tradition that went back to the very origins of human science.

But where were those practical considerations through which these journeys might be rationalised? The White Nile might be the longer of the two Nile branches, but it was its eastern counterpart, the Blue Nile, that supplied six-sevenths of the river's flow. It was, therefore, the more critical for the fertility of the lower portions of the Nile valley. On any economic or geopolitical grounds it was the Blue Nile that should have received the greater attention from European geographers. This branch, however, had been followed to its Ethiopian source almost a century before, and by the Victorian age it had clearly lost its initial appeal. Moreover, it might be argued that the Ethiopians were a tough, ancient, Christian and, by the standards of nineteenth-century Africa, highly organised martial race – the poorest soil on which to build a new empire. The quest for the White Nile, on the other hand, would lead British explorers through exactly those regions – Egypt, Kenya, Sudan, Tanzania, Uganda – that would eventually form part of the British African colonies. Yet, had such territorial acquisition been at the heart of the explorers' objectives, then to have made a systematic assessment of the original occupants' military capabilities, and then of the land's geographical, minerological and agricultural potential would have been a far more appropriate line to have taken. As the primary component in a British bid for political and economic expansion, looking for the source of the Nile comes to seem increasingly irrational. Even if one discounts these pragmatic considerations in favour of the idea that all these explorers had really sought were the multiple benefits of international celebrity, one is still confronted with the question: why should such an enterprise have brought so firm a guarantee of fame?

The answer surely lies in the immense symbolic valency of the Nile itself. Rivers are, in a sense, a physical analogue of a pilgrimage. Like a journey, the full course of a river embodies the idea of linear progress. Rivers have, in addition, their inevitable beginning, and their inevitable end. Yet as an imaginative symbol they also carry a resonance that no human journey can. Because of their constant physical movement, their persistence through immense periods of time, and their participation in a cycle on which all the planet's life forms are dependent, rivers offer themselves as one of the most appropriate metaphors through which humans can understand and express many deeply abstract ideas about life, the relationship between the individual and the totality of life and even the eternity of life. It is for these reasons that rivers have been deified, worshipped and enshrined in religious cosmology since the advent of consciousness. It is for these reasons that rivers are a powerful motif in all forms of artistic expression. And it is why river journeys have supplied some of the most enduring legends in all European travel: Mungo Park on the Niger; Stanley on the

147

Congo; Lewis and Clark on the Missouri; Francisco de Orellana or Charles-Marie de la Condamine on the Amazon. But to search for the origins of a river, the longest river on earth, one that had exercised geographical curiosity over three millennia, was to tap into a story that touched the deepest layers of human imagination. It was almost a search for the secret meaning of life itself – an idea perfectly conveyed by Samuel White Baker's words, when he came upon the Albert N'Yanza:

> For years I had striven to reach the 'sources of the Nile'. In my nightly dreams during that arduous voyage I had always failed, but after so much hard work and perseverance the cup was at my very lips, and I was to *drink* at the mysterious fountain before another sun should set – at that great reservoir of Nature that ever since creation had baffled all discovery.
>
> I had hoped, and prayed, and striven through all kinds of difficulties, in sickness, starvation, and fatigue, to reach that hidden source; and when it had appeared impossible, we had both determined to die upon the road rather than return defeated . . .
>
> It is impossible to describe the triumph of that moment; – here was the reward for all our labour – for the years of tenacity with which we had toiled through Africa . . . I looked down from the steep granite cliff upon those welcome waters – upon that vast reservoir which nourished Egypt and brought fertility where all was wilderness – upon that great source so long hidden from mankind; that source of bounty and of blessings to millions of human beings; as one of the greatest objects in nature.[29]

Perhaps one indication of the extent to which this peroration has reference to an interior vision is that the physical content of the landscape lying before Baker would not exceed the view one might obtain today from a Chicago skyscraper on the banks of Lake Michigan.

It was the Nile's great numinous power, its almost prismatic symbolic content, radiating outwards in different ways for each separate individual, that induced figures like Baker or Speke to risk their all in Africa. The grail-like importance the explorers attached to the Nile source also helps explain the urgency with which they then fought for their particular theory on their return. And it is interesting to reflect that at the meetings where this took place, with their frock-coated and top-hatted formality and their politely acrimonious debate over water flows, altitudes and geographical co-ordinates, the Victorians were actually giving expression, not only to the advancement of science, but to some of the most ancient human impulses. It might not be going too far to suggest that some of those subconscious drives which impelled early Christians to the banks of the Jordan, or Hindus to the shores of the Ganges, are also implicated in the geographical furore of the 1860s. If this is not to propose the idea of a spiritual motive for British travel, then it is at least to assert that behind the more obvious rational explanations given by travellers for their actions, there are often other pyscho-logical factors of great importance, of which they themselves need not be aware.

One factor, touched upon earlier in Chapter 4, that offers insight into the purpose of travel for a number of individuals concerns the male traveller's contact with his father. The frequency with which one encounters the absence or failure of this relationship is particularly striking. Four of the five figures discussed in this book – Philby, Thesiger, van der Post and Maxwell – had little or no contact with a male parent. Maxwell's father died only three months after he was born, van der Post's when he was just seven, and Wilfred Thesiger senior when his son was only nine.

Although it is not so straightforward to identify instances of failed father/son relationships, there are a number of cases where there is an abundance of evidence. As we have already seen, Henry Montague Philby played a negligible part in the upbringing of his four boys. When the strong-minded mother, May, tired of her husband's financial and amorous adventures on their Ceylon plantation, she returned with her young family to England and brought the children up almost singlehandedly. By the time of his father's death, when the famous Arabist was only twenty-eight, they had had contact only twice, once by letter. Monty's efforts at reconciliation were apparently rebuffed.

Richard Burton's father, Joseph, did not die while his son was an infant, nor did he, as was customary amongst his social class in the nineteenth century, pack his children off to boarding school at an early age. Living with his parents abroad and educated largely by private tutor, Richard saw a good deal of his father until he reached early manhood. However, their relationship was not happy. According to biographer Fawn Brodie, Joseph Burton, 'a weak and lazy man who dissipated his life in boar-hunting and hypochondria, provided no admirable image, and [Richard] had no motivation whatever for imitation or identification with him'.[30] In an unpublished memoir of his childhood, the explorer 'gave no hint of mutual affection, instead complained . . . of the perpetual "scolding and threatening" and "the usual parental brutality" ':[31]

> whatever his father most liked to do [Richard] would first
> try and then come to detest . . . Where the father was
> superstitious, hypochondriacal, and prey to the exponents
> of every medical nostrum, Richard became a serious student
> of medicine . . . with a blistering contempt for the quackery
> inside and outside the profession. Where his father frittered
> away both time and money, giving himself up wholly to
> sloth in the end, the son worked as if pursued by a demon,
> for long periods incapable of even momentary idleness.
> Significantly, when Burton chose a pseudonym under
> which he published some of his poetry, he settled on Baker,
> the maiden name of his mother.[32]

There are a number of other British explorers and travellers whose family relations followed a similar pattern. Henry Stanley, born John Rowlands in mid Wales in 1841, was the illegitimate son of a domestic servant and an unknown father. At six the young Rowlands was abandoned in a workhouse and saw almost nothing of his mother until early manhood.

Although it has been suggested that 'Of all the great explorers, none was more enigmatic and less given to self revelation' than John Hanning Speke, there is evidence to support his inclusion in this category.[33] Speke apparently experienced a childhood 'in which his father was a distant, unauthoritarian and non-interventionist

1 'Mrs Bailey [far left] and the Hatter [second right]',
photographed by life-long friend Richard Meinertzhagen in March 1937,
Kathmandu, Nepal, where Bailey was serving as British Resident.

2 *left*
Harry St John Philby
in 1946.

3 *below* Wilfred Thesiger
photographed in Bedu costume
during his second crossing
of the Empty Quarter,
1947–48.

4 *opposite* Thesiger's party
makes its way to the top
of a high pass in Ladakh.
This area, which is
politically part of
India, is geographically
part of the Tibetan plateau
– a desolate, windsculpted
moonscape, one of the
most barren regions on earth.

5 Laurens van der Post filming in Natal, 1982.

6 *opposite* Gavin Maxwell at Camusfeàrna with his wolfhound Dirk.

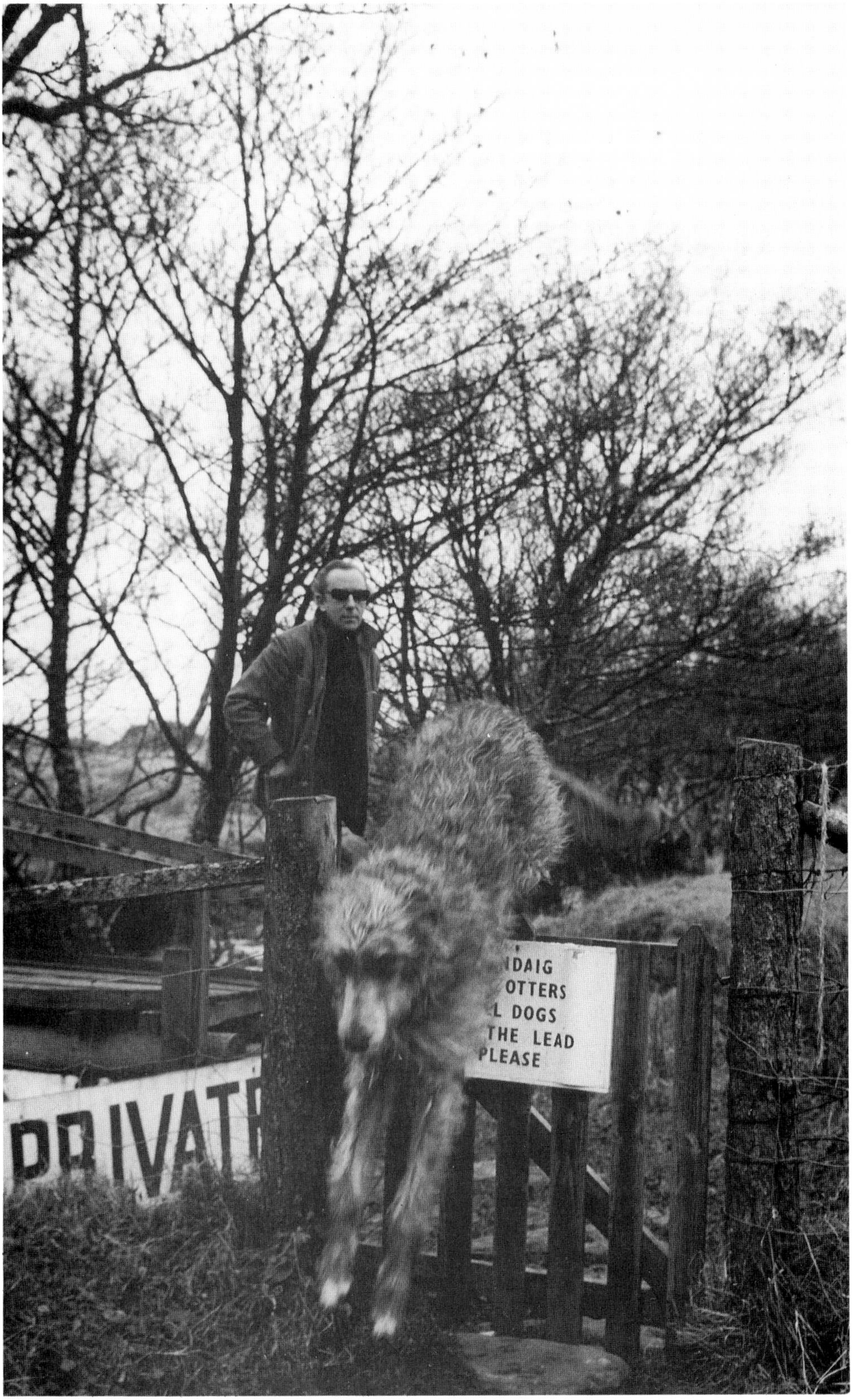

IDAIG
OTTERS
L DOGS
THE LEAD
PLEASE
PRIVATE

8 Patrick Leigh Fermor awaking on a rooftop
in the Maniot village of Phlomochori.

7 *opposite* The final stages of one of Maxwell's shark-fishing expeditions.

9 Henry Miller and Lawrence Durrell
enjoy the warm, comforting, amniotic embrace
of the Mediterranean – Corfu, 1939.

figure, and his mother encouraged an excessively emotional reaction to the world'.[34] Fawn Brodie also spoke of his 'slavish devotion to his mother'.[35] Two other famous twentieth-century travellers, who, if not unable to relate to their father, certainly had a much stronger (sometimes fraught) emotional involvement with their mother, were T. E. Lawrence and Robert Byron. To Charlotte Shaw, the woman who would eventually play a strongly maternal role in his life and whose name he would eventually adopt, Lawrence confessed that: 'Knowledge of her [his mother] will prevent my ever making any woman a mother, and the cause of children'.[36] In Byron's collection of letters to his family there is abundant evidence of his passionate attachment to his 'Darling Mibble'.[37]

From this list of personalities – Burton, Byron, Lawrence, Maxwell, Philby, Speke, Stanley, Thesiger, van der Post – there emerges a number of overlapping characteristics and tendencies. The most obvious was a resistance to authority, which at minimum expressed itself in the unconventional nature of all their lifestyles. In the careers of three – a point to be dealt with later – there seems to have been a highly developed urge to rebellion.

Failure or dislike of school and university is a common expression of the traveller's nonconformism. Speke, for example, 'hated academic learning and had been a rebellious and refractory school-boy'.[38] Both Burton and Byron left Oxford with inglorious results. The former was rusticated, the latter achieved only a third and neglected to collect it.[39] It is significant that Stanley, while above average at his Welsh workhouse school, invented a story of his breakout and escape, which he dramatised in his autobiography as a triumphant revolt against a schoolmaster's tyranny. All these men, with the exception of Speke, made up for any lack of formal academic learning by becoming voracious autodidacts, which in Burton's case blossomed into a quest for almost universal knowledge.

Another characteristic, particularly evident in the lives of three of these figures, was an uncertain or unfixed identity. In Burton's case this manifested itself in a passion for rôle-play and disguise, culminating most notably in his celebrated journey to Mecca under the assumed identity of an Afghan doctor. Frank McLynn has also suggested that his unparalleled talent as a linguist, and his penchant, revealed in his translations, for immersing himself totally in a foreign idiom, were both expressions of his lack of clear identity.[40] The same psychological element was evident in the life of Stanley, when, as the young John Rowlands, he took ship to New Orleans and quickly adopted the name of an English-born benefactor, Henry Hope Stanley, and the nationality of an American. Another illegitimate traveller, T. E. Lawrence, was the son of Thomas Robert Tighe Chapman and Sarah Lawrence. To avoid scandal the already married Chapman adopted the surname of his common-law wife and gave it to each of their five sons. T. E. Lawrence, however, subsequently dropped his name, firstly in favour of John Hume Ross, then later for T. E. Shaw.

Accompanying this early instability was an urge by the last two men to find father substitutes. A prominent figure in Lawrence's early adult life was D. G. Hogarth, keeper of the Ashmolean Museum in Oxford. Hogarth had been instrumental in shaping Lawrence's career as an archaeologist, and during the First World War had been his superior in Cairo, as head of an intelligence unit, the Arab Bureau. On Hogarth's death Lawrence wrote: 'A great loss: the greatest, perhaps, or probably, that I'll ever have to suffer';[41] 'He was really to me the parent I could trust, without qualification'.[42] Other dominant elder males who played the dual rôle of professional boss and father figure in Lawrence's life were General Allenby, Winston Churchill and Hugh Trenchard.

For Stanley there had initially been the New Orleans business-man whose name he had taken, then, most important of all, David Livingstone. The story of their encounter in the heart of Africa is one of the most famous in all exploration history. Not surprisingly it taps into a larger, archetypal myth: that of the young questing hero's encounter with a wise old sage. Stanley's dramatisation of their meeting and subsequent friendship, which he suggested had been preordained by 'kindly Providence', is the complete antithesis of Conrad's *Heart of Darkness*.[43] Plunging into the dark night of the soul – a land of ferocious beasts, fetid, disease-exhaling swamps and barbarous, malevolent savages – Stanley emerged at Ujiji to find an ideal of human civilisation. The Stanley version of Livingstone was a sort of Celtic saint. 'I grant he is not an angel', wrote the admiring disciple, 'but he approaches to that being as near as the nature of a living man will allow'.[44] As an explorer he was acutely observant, 'painstaking and industrious', and showed 'perseverance, doggedness, and tenacity' and 'a wonderfully retentive memory'. Notwithstanding an 'endless fund of high spirits and inexhaustible humor', his faith had 'tamed him, and made him a Christian gentleman; the crude and wilful have been refined and subdued; religion has made him the most companionable of men and indulgent of masters'.[45] 'Livingstone's was a character', acknowledged Stanley, 'that I venerated, that called forth all my enthusiasm, that evoked nothing but sincerest admiration'.[46]

His encounter with the 'lost' missionary was clearly a moment of profound importance to him. In the words of one commentator it was the 'supreme experience of his life. He had come close to moral greatness, and he was startled, captivated, subjected by it'.[47] In the opinion of Stanley's most recent and exhaustive biographer 'the overwhelming element predisposing the two men to forge close bonds was psychological. For Stanley, Livingstone represented the wise and benevolent father he had never known. For Livingstone, Stanley in an eerie way represented the return of the prodigal son'.[48]

The Stanley/Livingstone encounter possibly offers some insight into the travels of all the 'fatherless' figures listed above. Like Stanley, they were in part motivated by a subconscious urge for the parent they never had. In the case of John Speke one finds fascinating support for this idea. Given the Nile's capacity to serve as a symbol for all that was most precious in life, there seems to be a particular resonance in his repeated reference to the river as 'father Nile'.[49] As Fawn Brodie noted, such a conflation was out of line with what she deemed the decidedly feminine character of the river's symbolism and also with the maternal imagery employed by the other Nile explorers.[50] If the idea that all their journeys were a quest for a father is too specific, then at least one could conclude that they were, in part, a response to deep feelings of restlessness, dissatisfaction and of insecurity derived from their failed or incomplete familial relations. Foreign travel was the most dramatic manifestation of this inner experience.

The father/son issue offers insight not only into some of the motives for travel, but also the traveller's wider relationship with a home country. There is a deep psychological association between the place of one's birth and the father. This is expressed in the etymology of many European languages. Both in French and English, the word 'patriot' – defined in the *Oxford English Dictionary* as 'One who disinterestedly or self sacrificingly exerts himself to promote the wellbeing of his country' – derives from the Greek for 'father' – *patēr*. In the writings of a number of travellers there is confirmation of this process of identification.

In the preface to *Venture to the Interior*, for example, van der Post, articulating his sense of perpetual conflict in modern human affairs, cited 'Africa' and 'Europe' as appropriate titles for the two opposites. Under the second of these headings, he grouped 'conscious, male, masculine, father'. Expressing this psychic scheme in terms of his own personal experience, he then wrote 'Africa is my mother's country', while 'My father . . . was of Europe as even my mother could never be of Africa'.[51] Europe (and, by association, the father) was the source of the Dutch Afrikaner apartheid state, which had enforced his own spiritual and physical exile. Equally, European civilisation had given rise to the excessively rational consciousness, which has been the repeated object of van der Post's literary challenge.

In another travel book, Jonathan Raban's *Coasting*, one finds an equally explicit identification of his father with the home country. The author narrates, in an account of a journey around the English coastline, the development of his formerly ambivalent relationship both with his parents and the land of his birth. 'What I saw across the breakfast table', Raban writes in the opening chapter:

> and saw with the pitiless egotism of the thwarted child –
> was not my father, it was England. Towering over the
> stoved-in shells of the pullets' eggs in their floral ceramic
> cups, there sat the Conservative Party in person, the Army
> in person, the Church in person, the Public School system
> in person, the Dunkirk spirit in person, Manliness,
> Discipline, Duty, Self Sacrifice and all the rest.[52]

The fundamental psychic link between male parent and home country perhaps offers some explanation for the traveller's repeated opposition not just to paternal control, but also to institutional authority. This could be expressed as simply the delinquent's ranting at the powers that be – such as Philby's occasional outbursts. Otherwise it could be a mischievous pleasure in shocking, like Burton's delight in his reputation as 'the wickedest man alive'.[53] Yet travellers could also see it as a central mission of their lives to restore to the nation of their birth those aspects of human experience which they found so much more fully expressed in foreign societies. Burton is a classic example. Contemptuous of the stifling moral atmosphere in Victorian England, he was one of the first to unbolt the doors of sexual taboo. According to Fawn Brodie,

> he took it upon himself to bring to the West the sexual wisdom of the East, where acceptance of the naturalness of the art of love came close to religious exaltation. Precursor of Havelock Ellis and Sigmund Freud, he anticipated many of their insights. He translated his sixteen-volume edition of the unexpurgated *Arabian Nights* . . . then risked prosecution and imprisonment to print, secretly, several translations of Oriental erotica, one of which, *The Perfumed Garden of Cheikh Nefzaoui* . . . he was working on when he died.[54]

Two other travellers, both Arabists, who risked imprisonment as one of the natural hazards of their own rebellion – in each case taking the form of anti-imperialist proclamations – were Wilfrid Blunt and Jack Philby. Drumming in the cause of Irish nationalism, Blunt was jailed for two months in 1888. Following his denunciation of the war and further pronouncements that were deemed anti-British, Philby was detained in October 1940 for five months. It was only after the intervention of a number of influential friends, including E. M. Forster, Maynard Keynes and Lord Lloyd, that he was finally released.

One of the most striking facets of Philby's rebelliousness was its importance to him as a means of self-definition. Vehement anti-imperialist he might have been, yet it was exactly those things he kicked against most that, in some perverse fashion, were also necessary to him. For he found in conventional British political life that warped mirror which reflected and confirmed his own highly distinctive self-image as radical outsider. A measure of how seriously Philby took himself and his savage pilgrimage is his frequent use of biblical images to express his critic's rôle. 'I have lived in a setting', he wrote in *Forty Years in the Wilderness*, 'which until quite recently was the very stage on which the greats of the past, like Abraham and Moses, played their part, as I have played mine'.[55] Such historical compression suggested a vision of himself as direct spiritual heir to these Old Testament figures. Describing his journey to the Lebanon after his banishment from Arabia, in a chapter typically entitled 'The Road to Damascus', Philby wrote:

> My guard of honour departed leaving us to our fate; I
> looked my last on the wilderness in which I had wandered
> for forty years and turned away from it without a tear to see
> then the hospitality of other lands, which I had known well
> enough in distant days.[56]

'Fate', 'wilderness', 'wandered', 'forty years', 'other lands', 'distant days' – in this language of the scriptures and in the sweeping, almost cinematic gesture of defiance one senses an author striving to give his story a mythical gravitas.

Another traveller who has shown that same deep seriousness of purpose has been Laurens van der Post. And like Philby he has suggested that his alternative vision, the vital corrective for the fatherland's errors, provoked a deeply hostile reaction in his compatriots. Compare Philby's words on his unheeded advocacy of the Arab cause – 'I was the voice crying in the wilderness which they laughed to scorn'[57] – with van der Post's insistence on the vital importance of dreams and the workings of the unconscious:

> I knew that I was doing the little I did on account of a kind
> of dreaming that clothed the memory of my beginnings, as
> with a Joseph's coat of many colours, and went on
> providing the flicker of such little light as I walked by
> tentatively in the dark hour around me. I knew that
> somehow the world had to be set dreaming again, but what

a laugh that raised for being the whimsy and Barryesque sentimentality it was generally taken to be.[58]

In this particular passage one sees also van der Post's association of his own role with that of biblical figures. Elsewhere he has explained that his deep preoccupation with dreams and their meaning earned him the family nickname of 'Joseph the Dreamer'.[59]

That same moral earnestness is evident in a number of his other books. Towards the close of *Venture to the Interior* his companion on the Nyika Plateau asked the author what he would do once the expedition ended. 'For me', he replied, 'the greatest journey of all was on the move in Europe, and I wanted . . . to add what I had of singleness to it in order to help it on its difficult way'.[60] In *The Heart of the Hunter*, which concludes the story of van der Post's film-making Kalahari expedition, he described his concern to translate the many San stories into a contemporary idiom.

> I had a feeling that I was possibly the only person who
> could start this kind of interpretation; who could be this
> kind of improvised little rope-bridge over the deep abyss
> between the modern man and the first person in Africa until
> the real engineers with proper suspension bridges should
> come along.[61]

One has a fascinating echo of precisely this sentiment in the book of another contemporary traveller who has taken up the cause of the primitive. Benedict Allen, 'who has trudged the remotest forests of the world pursued by a dilemma: how to be an explorer without planting flags, discovering new species and mapping the land', is the author of a travel quartet, intended to document the wisdom of Stone Age people.[62] In the last of these, *The Proving Grounds*, he wrote of his special commitment to a forest tribe of Papua New Guinea: 'damn it, I couldn't walk out now. These people were worth listening to and I was the only person available here to do it'.[63]

In each of these passages, most explicitly in those of Philby and van der Post, it is possible to detect a self-conscious urge to be seen as a prophet-like figure: one who was profoundly concerned for his community, but who was ultimately isolated from it; someone with a deeply unpopular message to communicate, which was yet of vital importance to society. Here one has in its most extreme, not to mention egocentric, form one of the principal functions of the traveller: that of the subversive outsider. This need not take the pattern of foretelling some kind of political, spiritual or environmental Armageddon. Nor need travellers themselves be aware of or seek this particular role. All travellers, even those who have expressed no significant disagreement with the home country, are subtly subversive. By their very actions, their temporary abandonment of ordered society, they ask discomfiting questions about what is important in life. The reader of *A Short Walk in the Hindu Kush* or *Full Tilt* enters into a relationship with one who has cast aside the prudence of a steady career and fixed relations to one physical and human environment. In Eric Newby or Dervla Murphy the reader finds a rôle model for their own escape from society's norms. Peter Brent might correctly assert that in a travel book the audience enjoys a vicarious experience of foreign adventure, and that the author's 'being there made it, as it were, unnecessary for' readers to go themselves. Yet, in travel books there are also whispering siren voices beckoning us to prove that we have the courage to do as they have.

Travellers challenge not only the manner of home life but also the tempo at which it is lived. Their repeated expressions of the luxurious sense of leisure that fills their travel time are surely not merely coincidental, but a gentle if subconscious turning of the knife. Thesiger, for instance, challenges European standards not only in his ability to cross the Rub al Khali but, on completing the journey, then to wait, with little to occupy him, for twenty days in Abu Dhabi and then a month in Buraima on Arabia's south-east coast. For a society where five minutes at the traffic lights is an unbearable delay, to do nothing for fifty days could be literally terrifying. His account of his time amongst the Ma'dan at the Tigris-Euphrates confluence reverses the ideals expressed in Defoe's *Robinson Crusoe*. Instead of blanking out the void with an unceasing activity, Thesiger (justifying his presence with a well-stocked medicine chest) simply wandered the reed-lined waterways and observed for seven years.

During the twentieth century one issue that travellers and travel books have consistently challenged us to consider is the plight of 'shy primitive peoples, daunted and overshadowed by the juggernaut advance of our ruthless age': the conversion of the Bedu or Ma'dan from ancient tribespeople to corner boys in oil-stained rags; the gentle Moï of Indochina absorbed as indentured labour on the plantations of French colonists; the shrinking world of the Kalahari San; the alcoholic disintegration of Australia's aborigines; the quietly efficient annihilation of Brazilian Indians by the Indian Protection Service.[64] It was not always essential to travel to the heart of South America's rainforest or the Arabian desert to find a primitive people besieged by modernity. Norman Lewis, probing the upper strata of European civilisation, found his pagan tribe barely a thousand kilometres from the beaches of Dover. In *Voices of the Old Sea*, his portrait of Tossa de Mar's slide into tourist development, he found a Spanish fishing community which came as close to an acknowledgement of the divine in its deep reverence for the sea.[65] Searching the mountain villages and rugged islands of pre-war Greece, Lawrence Durrell and Patrick Leigh Fermor caught tantalising glimpses of Europe's rich pre-Christian past.

Documenting their time amongst such communities, travellers have found a number of common themes: a cultural sophistication invariably unacknowledged by others, a primal correspondence between the people and their environment, a rich, elemental closeness to one another and, as a consequence of all these, a deep psychological wholeness. In their accounts, the authors have often implied, occasionally made explicit, the belief that they had encountered a community whose traditions, stretching back unbroken sometimes for millennia, expressed layers of humanity that had been covered up and lost in their own modern age; and that the steady disappearance of these primitives was a tragedy that referred not just to a single small insignificant tribe, but one that involved and diminished us all.

The elegiac and sometimes minatory note in travel books like *Arabian Sands*, *A Dragon Apparent* or *The Lost World of the Kalahari* has invariably been met with an equally firm counter-argument. Travellers were coming to sometimes grandiose cultural theories but these were based on occasionally brief and always temporary experiences. When 'one says Mexico', wrote D. H. Lawrence on the limitations in travel writing, 'all it amounts to is one little individual looking at a bit of sky and trees, then looking down at the page of his exercise book'.[66] Another charge was that the travel writer perhaps deliberately neglected to notice the less attractive sides of primitive life – the hardship, disease, the Stone Age life-expectancy that went with a Stone Age medical knowledge, and the crushing uniformity inflicted by cultural traditions that demanded total obedience and predetermined all aspects of tribal life. Inherent in the traveller's overly positive conclusions was a kind of bad faith; it was simply a nostalgic longing for a simpler age, a manufacturing of poetry out of someone else's poverty. 'British Arabism', wrote Jonathan Raban, 'is an old romantic love affair in which a faint glimmer of the perverse is never far from the surface . . .'

> As a historical movement, it coincides exactly with that period when England was a rich country in the first flush of its dependence on industrial technology. For Lawrence and Thesiger, Arabia was an alternative kingdom; a tough utopia without either money or machines. In the bedu tribesman they professed to find all the simplicity, the powers of personal endurance, the stoic independence, which they feared the Englishman was losing.[67]

Raban concluded that the Englishman in Arabia had found in the desert 'a perfect theatre for the enactment of a heroic drama of their own'. That there was a fallacy at the heart of the traveller's experience was an idea in which Peter Brent concurred.

> There was . . . a fundamental difficulty facing those who sought even a temporary identification with the beduin who accompanied them on their journeys. The desert nomad does what he does not by choice, but because of the coercion of circumstance . . . But the man from the west who decides to test himself against the forces of nature, or against the demanding conditions of the world's most intractable regions, finds himself to some extent caught in a paradox. For the more profoundly he plunges back into a

'natural' life, the more artificial becomes his decision to do so
. . . To choose to brave its most demanding wildernesses is, in
these circumstances, to opt for the ultimate luxury.[68]

While there is an element of conflict in the traveller's experience,
it would be inappropriate to insist on only a simple binary system of
either/or – Bedu or playing the part of a Bedu, natural or artificial,
authentic state or self-conscious pose. Such an interpretation would
place unnecessarily severe restrictions on the interior lives of non-
industrial communities. They would be merely noble savages,
contained in an authentic natural state by obedience to unconscious
instinct, without any capacity for reflection or choice in their own
condition. On the other hand, it demands that the only 'natural'
environments for travellers are domestic, urban and modern. To
enter the desert or the forest is to falsify their position automatically. Equally to see their time in the wilderness as only a self-drama
is to insist that they have awareness of all the variables in their
motives.

It is perhaps more accurate to see in the traveller's contact with
non-western cultures, not an attempt to *be* a Bedu or a Moï or an
aborigine, but an effort to satisfy authentic, sometimes unconscious
urges that have no place in the suburbs of Bournemouth, nor even
on the kagool-pocked hillsides of Lakeland. Yet they do find fuller
expression in the lives of these alternative communities. In his
foreword to Victor White's *God and the Unconscious*, Jung wrote:

> There are people [in contemporary society] who,
> psychologically, might be living in the year 5000 B.C., i.e.,
> who can still successfully solve their conflicts as people did
> seven thousand years ago. There are countless troglodytes
> and barbarians living in Europe and in all civilized
> countries, as well as a large number of medieval Christians
> . . . So it is psychologically quite 'legitimate' when a
> medieval man solves his conflict today on a thirteenth
> century level.[69]

What some travellers are perhaps attempting is to fulfil the
troglodyte and barbarian in themselves – an idea that finds its echo

in Thesiger's self-proclaimed 'life-long craving for barbaric splendour, for savagery and colour and the throb of drums'. Equally, in giving us in their travel books an account of those experiences, they provide opportunity for a wider audience to participate in that same process.

For all their celebration of the pagan and the primitive, travellers cannot be discounted simply as latterday savages addicted to exciting action. One of the striking facets of many figures is the multiple direction of their intellectual interests. Once again, Richard Burton serves as an archetypal example. His scholarship was on an Olympian scale, producing forty-three volumes of travel, two volumes of poetry, over a hundred articles and twenty-eight volumes of translation including his celebrated sixteen-volume *Arabian Nights*. Frank McLynn has suggested that 'One would have to conflate the careers of Stanley, Vámbéry, Frederick Burnaby, Mark Twain, Edward Fitzgerald and John Paine to distil the essence of Burton. Even then, many pessimists have concluded, one could not do justice to his career'.[70] Similarly, in this century, T. E. Lawrence stands at the meeting point of several cultural vectors. His two volumes of letters, themselves considered some of the finest in the language, provide a veritable *Who's Who* of literary, military and political figures in the first third of this century. In the diaries and letters of Freya Stark a similar inventory continues into the second third.

Laurens van der Post has counted amongst his friends an equally wide spectrum: men and women as diverse as Lord Mountbatten, Virginia Woolf, T. S. Eliot and C. G. Jung. Philby's curiosity, even towards the close of his life, was constantly opening new doors. It was not until he was in the final decade of his life that he embarked fully on his study of pre-Islamic culture in Arabia. Wilfred Thesiger is also a man of developed sensitivity. His photographs of nomadic and pastoral peoples must constitute one of the finest and most important collections of its kind in the world. Peeping into his luggage on the Upper Panjshir, Eric Newby noted that as Thesiger trekked through part of the greatest mountain chain on the planet, he had been dipping into *La Chartreuse de Parme* and *Du côté de chez Swann*.[71] Amongst current travellers this tradition of intellectual vitality continues. Author of six books of travel or place, Geoffrey

Moorhouse, with his other works on rugby, nineteenth-century missionaries, cricket, contemporary monasticism and the British raj, strongly resists the simple travel-writer tag.[72]

Possibly it is out of a desire to communicate these all-round abilities, or perhaps a concern that their physical exploits will be noticed at the expense of their mental attainment, that travellers have developed the habit of revealing in travel books their own reading lists. Dervla Murphy, for example, itemising her Himalayan equipment in an appendix to *Where the Indus is Young*, slipped in that she had taken with her *War and Peace*, *Anna Karenina*, *Literature and Western Man*, Simone de Beauvoir's *The Mandarins* and an anthology of Shakespeare.[73] It seems of a piece with the epic nature of the journey that Thesiger's camel should have carried volumes of Gibbon and Tolstoy across the Empty Quarter.[74]

With a whole cabin to fill rather than just a saddlebag Gavin Maxwell gave a fuller picture of his diverse mental furniture. Describing the contents of his boat, the *Sea Leopard*, in *Harpoon at a Venture*, he wrote:

> I find an inventory . . . of the contents of the bookshelf – as ill-assorted a list as one could well imagine. Eliot's *East Coker* was, I remember, stained by the damp kiss of its green-covered neighbour, *Le Tannage des Peaux des Animaux Marins*; *Adamastor* rubbed shoulders with its avowed enemies *The Condemned Playground* and *Enemies of Promise*, and next to them came Hogben's *Principles of Animal Biology*, Empson's *Seven Types of Ambiguity*, Huxley's *Evolution*, and *A History of the Whale Fisheries*.[75]

Expressing exactly the same breadth of focus was the 'explorer's library' taken aboard Jonathan Raban's *Gosfield Maid* in his book *Coasting*: Saul Bellow, R. T. McCullen, MacNeice, Ian McEwan, Evelyn Waugh, Machiavelli, Sterne ('in the ten-volume calfbound 1780 edition'), Trollope, Thackeray, Dickens, Cobbett, Defoe, G. M. Trevelyan, Nikolaus Pevsner, Arthur Mee, as well as books on British history, geology, birds and flora.[76] What seems at times a type of intellectual name-dropping has reached its climax, however, in Patrick Leigh Fermor's *A Time of Gifts*, where the author provides a three-page list of those works in English, French, Latin and Greek that he could recite from memory alone.[77]

Wide-ranging and cultivated it might be, the travel sensibility is not a flower that opens in the small, dry air of Bloomsbury. In the lives of many travellers a recurrent pattern is the restless and centrifugal dynamism of their intellectual pursuits. Knowledge, so often acquired as a by-product of experience, becomes almost a facet of their physical activities, part of a wider life adventure. Writing of Peter Beckford, a Jamaican landowner, friend of Voltaire, Rousseau and Sterne, one who ' "would bag a fox in Greek . . . find a hare in Latin, inspect his kennels in Italian and direct the economy of his stables in exquisite French" ', Patrick Leigh Fermor suggested that such a man was 'a stinging rebuke . . . to the present irreconcilable antagonism that severs the active from the intellectual way of life'.[78] This could almost serve as a manifesto for the traveller: one who refuses to fall neatly into one camp or the other, or even to adhere to the conventional hierarchies that govern so many cultural spheres. T. E. Lawrence's *curriculum vitae* provides classic illustration. As aircraftman Shaw, Lawrence was involved simultaneously in preparing an English version of Homer's *Odyssey* and improvements in the design of the RAF's high-speed rescue boats; each activity equally valued, each absorbing his entire attention. Burton spanned similar divides: the consummate swordsman who translated Catullus's love poetry; the organiser of irregular Muslim cavalry who researched, collated and published the witticisms of West African tribes.

This constant urge for the new, to move outwards to ever fresh experiences, is perhaps even more fully expressed amongst female travellers than male. Dervla Murphy, for example, in addition to her long-established literary career and her status as one of the great female adventurers of our time, has garnered in a host of other parts. As a teenager and young adult she cared for her ailing mother in the traditions of the dutiful Victorian daughter, then became that symbol of modern society, the unmarried mother. In addition to these archetypally feminine rôles, she had penetrated and conquered, during her travels, the conventionally male territories of physical endurance and courage. In the Ethiopian highlands she braved the fleas and the *shifta* bandits and drank her *talla* with the best of them. At times she was obliged to bare her breasts to prove to disbelieving locals that she was not actually a man.[79] It is symptomatic of the experiential bias in the traveller's route to knowledge that when she wanted to understand and write about the Northern Ireland question – in *A Place Apart* – Murphy must go there, meet the protagonists and, as it were, become the troubles herself.

It is interesting, in view of the idea of the traveller's unceasing appetite for new experience, to examine the lifespan of prominent figures over the last two centuries. One of the most striking patterns is that those who wandered Africa tended, by contemporary standards, to die too young: Burton (69), Verney Cameron (50), James Grant (63), Mary Kingsley (38), David Livingstone (60), Mungo Park (35), Frederick Selous (65), John Hanning Speke (37), Henry Morton Stanley (63), Joseph Thomson (37). Of the protagonists in the Nile quest, only Florence and Samuel Baker reached the allotted three score and ten. Only Burton, Grant and Stanley died in their beds. Three of the others fell to the region's formidable arsenal of disease, two to the enemy and one died of a self-inflicted gun wound; though it may be permissible to say that the last six all actually died of Africa. It was almost as if the continent's reputation as a dark maelstrom was an irresistible lure to the self-destructive. Other notable short lives were the speed-addicted T. E. Lawrence, who died at forty-six of his Brough motorbike, and the hard-drinking, chain-smoking Maxwell, who died of inoperable cancer.

This restless passion for new landscapes, both external and internal, expressed most fully in the lives of Burton, Lawrence and Maxwell (though Kingsley, Selous, Stanley and Thomson demonstrated something of the classic centrifugal appetites of the traveller) often carried within it a fatal flaw. Absorbed in the latest enthusiasm, or a multiplicity of enthusiasms, these figures seemed to lose touch with a central point of balance that kept the entire vessel afloat. Without this ballast, this critical point of harmony, their lives could be confused, difficult and, in the case of the last two, tragically brief.

Yet the lives of those travellers, who, in seeking to experience and discover all, were somehow able to keep a grasp of all, have followed a very different course. Another striking pattern amongst twentieth-century travellers is a sometimes remarkable longevity. Philby, at seventy-five, literally wore himself out in relentless activity. Yet three other key Arabists – Wilfrid and Anne Blunt and Charles Doughty – all survived beyond eighty. Of Himalayan explorers, Frank Kingdon Ward was a mere seventy-two, though Younghusband travelled on to seventy-nine and this century's greatest Asiatic explorer, Sven Hedin, to eighty-seven. Frederick Bailey died on 17 April 1967 at eighty-five, and within weeks of his death, his life-long friend, Richard Meinertzhagen, passed away at eighty-nine. An ornithological nomad, Meinertzhagen made the last of his bird voyages just short of his eighty-third birthday. Norman Lewis, Wilfred Thesiger and Laurens van der Post have also all made octagenarian's journeys in the outback. However, women, inevitably, hold the record. At ninety-nine Freya Stark seems immortal, though even she has not yet equalled her great French counterpart, Alexandra David-Neel.[80] David-Neel was three when Stanley met Livingstone at Ujiju, and died, aged 100, in the year that another traveller, US astronaut Neil Armstrong, descended the steps of Apollo 11 to walk on the surface of the moon.

The collective 1,200 years of living enjoyed by the fourteen figures listed above disclose a genius wholly distinct from that of the Romantic artist, blazing into life and consuming himself like a lit firework. Having found a point of equilibrium in all their multifarious activities and interests, travellers, with their ceaseless appetite for experience, can be sustained into a very vigorous old age. In this, they seem to move towards an ideal more fully expressed in the East, where the wise ancient sage is a recurrent figure of religion and philosophy. Otherwise travellers, with their concern for all-round achievement, recall the cultural aspirations of the sixteenth century, and the humanist ideal of the universal man propounded by thinkers like Alberti Leon Battista.

In an era of increasing specialisation and when the divisions between scientific and artistic endeavour become ever more firmly entrenched, the traveller's Renaissance urge to human wholeness seems especially relevant on a number of counts. Firstly, it seems fitting that they should aspire to an ideal which has less and less currency amongst their own society, since it confirms them in their rôle as outsider. The issue also seems to offer one more explanation for the traveller's wish to depart: since it is easy to see why such an individual, brought up in an environment where the all-rounder has no definite ecological niche, should feel himself out of place and obliged, eventually, to undertake constant migrations overseas. In a sense, the natural habitat for this universal being is nowhere in particular. However, the travellers' urge to unity, their refusal to accept the conventional divisions of active and intellectual, scientific and artistic, has an additional importance. It is, in fact, perhaps their major contribution. For travellers keep alive the idea of physical activity as a means and as a type of knowledge in itself; and then the notion that the quest for knowledge can be a physically satisfying, all-absorbing lifelong adventure.

Chapter VIII

Greece – The Dark Crystal

It is one of the curious ironies of travel literature that whenever Robert Byron's admirers write of his achievements there seems to be a persistent undertone that he is in constant need of rediscovery; that their enthusiasm for his work is perhaps in part a response to a general ignorance of it. Jonathan Raban, extolling the brilliance of Byron's final book, *The Road to Oxiana*, for instance, described it as a 'regal lost masterpiece'. Paul Fussell lamented that 'scholars and critics ashamed to own ignorance of the jottings of Wyndham Lewis or William Burroughs are satisfied never to have heard' of Byron at all.[1] It is, perhaps, remarkable that in an age when biographers have assembled the lives of almost every mediocre talent, Byron's life remains uncharted more than fifty years after his death.

Yet in any study of the travel book in the twentieth century it would be impossible to bypass his contribution. This extraordinary man crammed into a brief career spanning only fifteen years a lifetime of travel and nine books, four of them travel works, which have left an indelible mark on the genre. According to Fussell he should be 'venerated as the saint of all those whose imaginations come alight at the thought of travel'.[2] Bruce Chatwin concluded that *The Road to Oxiana* was the work of a genius.[3]

Chatwin went on to confess that in his twenties he followed Byron's routes across Asia and filled notebooks with writing which slavishly aped his hero's own. Even in Chatwin's later work it seems possible to trace Byron's impact. The text of *In Patagonia* is divided into a series of extremely brief, often sharply contrasting chapters, and in his *The Songlines* one finds a long, seemingly informal sequence of extracts from the author's various notebooks. Both of these narrative devices surely owe a good deal to the carefully wrought casualness of *The Road to Oxiana*, which appears to be a compilation of diary jottings.

Another of Byron's major contributions was his pioneering championship of Byzantine art and the rich inheritance that it represented for contemporary Greece. His discovery and adoption of this cause, which remained an important motivating force throughout his brief life, was, appropriately, an accident of travel. He had set out with a group of friends in 1925 on an extensive motor tour across Europe that took him as far as Athens and which was later the subject of his first book, *Europe in the Looking Glass*. Later, Byron recalled that journey and his initial momentous experience of Greece in a 1940 radio broadcast:

> One August morning I set foot in Greece . . . and smelt the
> true Greek smell of hot sweaty dust, and saw the deep blue
> sky and the dried up putty coloured earth and the green
> currant vines and the white box-like houses climbing up
> into the deep blue sky . . . And then as I looked at the
> mountains and the water and the sky, I experienced the kind
> of revelation that only comes to people once or twice in
> their lives. I simply said to myself: now I understand what
> it's all about; this thing, this Greece, I've been learning
> about all these years, isn't dead; it's here; I'm in it; I need it;
> I've found it and I'm going to keep it as long as I live.[4]

If that day in August (according to Byron's own travel diaries it was actually 5 September) was the moment of consummation in his great love affair with Greece, an important emotional source for his championship of the country was deeply rooted in his schooldays. Born in 1905 to a moderately wealthy middle-class family from Wiltshire, Byron attended both Eton and Merton College, Oxford. Although some of his history essays written during his time at the former had been singled out for special praise, he was not a successful student at either institution. His close friend and near contemporary at Oxford, Christopher Sykes, believed that while he loved learning for himself he disliked being taught by others, and on leaving university Byron boasted to a newspaper reporter that he had not attended a single lecture. While this was untrue he departed with only a third-class degree, and his early books contain passionate attacks upon 'professional pedagogues'.

His joyous experiences in Greece and the development of his great passion for Byzantine art had served to reinforce Byron's belief that English academics were peddlers of an immense fallacy concerning European history and civilisation. This shabby false-hood maintained that after the collapse of the western Roman empire in the fifth century AD, its eastern Greek successor based on Constantinople had represented 'the most thoroughly base and despicable form that civilisation has yet assumed'.[5] Sister to this idea was the notion that while the Greek society of the fifth century BC represented a pinnacle of human achievement, ever after it had been swamped and finally obliterated by successive invasions of barbarian Slavs. The contemporary Greeks, therefore, whose forebears had been citizens of the Byzantine empire for almost 1,000 years, bore no relationship to the Greek community of the classical period so cherished by English scholars.

In his one-man defence of the Byzantine inheritance, Byron singled out Edward Gibbon for special blame, seeing *The History of the Decline and Fall of the Roman Empire* as a particularly vicious expression of the 'classico-rationalist' distortion. The other con-spirator that he had sniffed out was the Catholic Church, for its part in the Great Schism and its systematic denigration of its Eastern Orthodox counterpart. Sykes believed that Byron saw 'the Vatican as a sort of ball and chain attached to the West, preventing escape from all that was degrading, uninspired and calamitous in the European past'.[6] Most unforgivable of all the Vatican's crimes, however, was its acquiescence in the Fourth Crusade, whose participants sacked Constantinople in 1204 and plundered its vast historical treasures. 'For humanity in general', lamented Byron, 'history reveals no greater misfortune'.[7]

Most of these themes were adumbrated in his second book *The Station*, an account of his return visit to Greece in 1927 with two friends, Mark Ogilvie-Grant and David Talbot-Rice. Supported by an advance from the publisher Duckworth, he intended to produce a book on the journey, whose principal objective was to study and photograph the Byzantine art treasures held in the monasteries of Mount Athos. The Orthodox community on the Holy Mountain represented for Byron a living articulate expression of the Greeks' great imperial past.

Although claims have been put forward for its status as a minor classic, *The Station* gives notice of the future achievements of an extremely talented writer, rather than confirming their actual attainment. Christopher Sykes concluded that at twenty-two Byron had not yet gained control of his immense cleverness and that the book was about forty pages too long. The precision and economy of his later style were obscured by a ponderous and rather Victorian striving for gravitas. Take, for instance, the opening sentences from two separate chapters:

> The habits of frivolous children of the world were
> powerless against the traditions of half the Christian era.
> And our days assumed a complexion of monastic regularity,
> both in the ordering of their hours and the sobriety with
> which we set each to his avocations.[8]

> It is noticeable, as the visitor's boat is impelled up and down
> the waves by some jocund octogenarian whose peaked
> shade against the glare of the sun on the water resembles the
> helmet of a Spanish trooper . . .[9]

As a consequence of this type of writing the book is slow moving, while his gifts for rendering character and for comic dialogue, though evident, were unrefined. It was in a third book, *The Byzantine Achievement*, that Byron stripped away some of the earlier wordiness and demonstrated his capacity for clear and sustained argument.

The book actually started life as a historical account of the events in the eastern Mediterranean immediately after the First World War – events that occurred during Byron's final years at Eton. These had culminated in the massacre of 13 September 1922, when the Greek quarters in the Ottoman city of Smyrna were razed to the ground and thousands of its inhabitants murdered or literally driven into the sea by the Turks. It was a disaster that finally extinguished

Hellenic dreams of restoring an empire in Asia Minor. It also brought to a close 2,500 years of Greek supremacy in western Anatolia. Byron sensed that the Great Powers, including Britain, had connived in the events that led to the Smyrna massacre and had then done little to avert the tragedy. For him it was a contemporary expression of an unresolved conflict that had bedevilled relations between Western and Eastern Europe and which had led to the Great Schism and the Fourth Crusade.[10] However, in searching for the origins of this problem, Byron gradually shifted his focus from the present to the past. The book accordingly metamorphosed from a contemporary history into a spirited apostrophe to the Christian civilisation centred on Constantinople.

Both *The Station* and *The Byzantine Achievement* were criticised, even by Byron's admirers, for his blistering assaults on those he considered his opponents. In the earlier book, for instance, he had taken revenge on all the tutors who had stood before him and failed to inspire. Academia was dismissed *en bloc* as that 'cobwebbed old man, paid instrument of enormous stagnation':[11]

> ranging himself in opposition to commonsense observation
> and the whole science of anthropology, affirms, with one
> snap of his bitten, ink-stained fingers, that the modern
> Greek is related neither in language, body, nor mind to the
> ancient . . . Not, however, content with this purposeful
> obscurantism, the Anglo-Saxon professor, with the
> nauseating self-sufficiency of his kind, must even blame the
> native for pronouncing his language in the manner it
> demands.[12]

In *The Byzantine Achievement* one of Byron's most vigorous attacks was against the Catholic Church.

> St Peter's, consummate negation of religious inspiration and
> affirmation of the papal ego, breathes empty flesh in every
> joint of its irremediable classicism . . . It sums completely the
> difference between Orthodox and Catholic Europe. The
> existence of St Sophia is atmospheric, that of St Peter's,
> over-poweringly, imminently substantial. One is a church

to God; the other, a salon for his agents. One is consecrated to Reality, the other to illusion. St Sophia, in fact, is large, and St Peter's is vilely, tragically small.[13]

This deeply partisan approach to European history meant that when the book appeared in 1929 it was held in suspicion by professional historians of the period. Even those who agreed with many of Byron's ideas were apparently disconcerted by the book's anti-academic stance and ignored it for that reason. However, the work's extremism was, according to Christopher Sykes, an inevitable function of the author's personality. Byron's mind naturally worked on a system of complete opposites. Those subjects that became the focus of his intellectual and emotional sympathies absorbed his entire energies. Likening these mental processes to the operations of a lighthouse, Sykes suggested that 'the beams struck out in many directions, but between the beams was darkness. He was a curious case of vision and blindness together'.[14] While the civilisation of Constantinople was illuminated by that intense vision, Catholicism, classical Greece and the Western academic obsession with it were all firmly shut out in the dark.

Despite these shortcomings, Sykes, himself a Catholic, described *The Byzantine Achievement* as 'an enduring and beautiful book', while the historian G. M. Young, a biographer of Gibbon, recommended Byron's 'brilliant and forcible' work as a corrective to the bias in the *Decline and Fall*.[15] Even in 1984 John Julius Norwich felt that it deserved republication more than any book he knew.[16] This collective praise was not directed towards its author's occasional and unbalanced tirades but his sustained analysis of what had transformed the Eastern empire of the Romans into one of the world's great civilisations.

Byron opened the book with a consideration of what actually constituted civilisation and defined three essential elements: political and economic stability, the quest for transcendental values and an associated code of ethics, and thirdly a corporate intellectual activity expressed in art and science. Of these three elements – 'the stable, the transcendental and the cultural' – Byron argued that the Western empire possessed only the first. The Pax Romana held the various imperial states and provinces together, but these 'lay passive beneath the heterogeneous vapour of ideas, arts and cults which swirled from Chester to Bagdad . . . ponderous, derivative and fruitless as a herd of mules'.[17] However, with the advent of the Eastern empire a completely new entity emerged. The Emperor Constantine consciously drew together the old political machinery of Rome, the new Christian faith that emanated from the East and 'the great cohesive substructure of Hellenic culture'. In Byron's view this triple fusion was the supreme Byzantine achievement and the source of an enduring, stable, immensely prosperous state that conferred on its subjects a more advanced culture and greater freedom and opportunity than any previous political structure.

When the book was published in 1929 its author, remarkably, was still only twenty-four. For the remaining dozen years of his life Byron's sympathies for Byzantine art and contemporary Greece never diminished. However, he would never return to the country for a prolonged stay, while the account of events in the eastern Mediterranean he had intended to write, and which later metamorphosed a second time – into a projected history of the First World War – was never started. Byron's lighthouse vision had simply touched new horizons and his travels took him further and further afield: Russia, India, Tibet, Persia, Afghanistan, China, America.

It is extremely difficult to calculate exactly the contribution made by a single individual to what amounts almost to a cultural movement; but it is now widely acknowledged that Byron deserves some credit for helping to revise attitudes in academic circles towards the achievements of the Byzantine empire. Admirers like John Julius Norwich have been in no doubt, suggesting that his second book on Greece advanced views that were 'little short of revolutionary'.[18] Byron's friend David Talbot-Rice, himself a claimant to the title of chief revisionist concerning Byzantine art, believed that Byron's 'role in changing our comprehension of an age in the world's history has been very considerable'.[19]

He may in addition have played some part in modifying the views of a more general audience towards the inhabitants of contemporary Greece. Certainly his works marked the starting point of a great wave of enthusiasm for Greek travel and for books about the country, which reached its peak in a twenty-year period after the Second World War. A personal, unsystematic count of these titles has produced a list of over eighty, and an impressive array of writers: Patrick Balfour, Gerald and Lawrence Durrell, Patrick Leigh Fermor, Osbert Lancaster, Robert Liddell, Peter Levi, Compton Mackenzie, Henry Miller, Dilys Powell, Colin Thubron and Rex Warner. Byron's catalytic impact on this literary efflorescence is undoubted, though he is not its only source. The recent preoccupations with Greece originated in a whole range of factors. These include not only the climate, physical environment, the extraordinarily long, rich history and unique temperament of the southern European nation, but also many of the preoccupations current amongst British writers overseas. The deeply fertile interplay of these two elements – traveller and travelled Greek environment – has produced perhaps some of the finest books of place since the war. These in turn disclose themes crucial to any consideration of travel literature.

While it was the case that the rich vein unearthed by Byron in the eastern Mediterranean would be mined to greater profit by subsequent philhellenes, most notably by Durrell and Fermor, it is appropriate to open analysis with the author of *The Station*. Byron's portrait of the Greek landscape and people in this book was largely restricted to Athos and its monastic inhabitants. Here he showed a touching affection and almost reverence for the monks – a response to fellow humans that is extremely noteworthy in the author's canon.

Fussell and Sykes have insisted that Byron was a great humanist, an example of 'the disciplined moral intelligence beleaguered by stupidity, convention, received error, greed, provincialism, nationalism and aggression'.[20] While this might be the case, it seems equally true that Byron ascribed one or more of these defects to many of the people he actually encountered, and he frequently portrayed them in his books with a comic mockery that bordered on scorn. The humanity with which he appears to have felt most comfortable was a dematerialised abstraction found in his books. For these – the Greeks, the Byzantines, the Jews, the Indians, the Afghanis – Byron might fight tooth and nail. Although even when his fellow men were simplified to an idea, he could not always resist his comic jibes: 'Most Persians look like a decayed railway porter';[21] 'The Armenians are a pathetic, pugnacious little people'.[22] From the common press of humankind itself he could recoil with an almost neurotic shiver of disgust. Fellow bathers at a Jerusalem swimming pool, for example, are 'a lot of hairy dwarves who smelt of garlic'.[23]

It is remarkable how one who had travelled so widely, so successfully maintained an upper atmosphere. As Jan Morris has pointed out, on the journeys undertaken by Byron and his companions, 'there is the innate expectation that they will be befriended by consuls, put up by ambassadors, entertained by friends from Oxford or bump into influential acquaintances'.[24] It is typical that when the twenty-two-year-old Byron arrives in Crete he is received and driven round by the greatest Greek politician of his day, Eleutherios Venizelos.[25] While Byron's letters to his mother contain references to ninety-two titled aristocrats, his sense of the lower orders seems to have been based merely on hearsay. 'Those who have moved among the English working classes', he wrote in *The Byzantine Achievement*, 'testify unanimously that their interest in politics is aroused only during the transitory excitement of the elections'.[26] As Morris has also shown, aware of the 'stupendous gulf' between himself and the common man, he and his travel friends felt that they could 'behave everywhere by their own lights. Byron was not above smuggling works of art out of Greece or squabbling with American cops, and when he and an English friend wished to inspect a locked chapel at Monemvasia [in the Peloponnese] they simply threw boulders at its door'.[27]

What, then, did Greece represent to Byron? It is perhaps true to say that when he hoisted his personal flag on Hellenic soil and embarked on the Byronic struggle, the things that he was prepared to die for most were not the living Greek people, for whom he undoubtedly felt great sympathy, nor the keepers of Byzantium, whom he undoubted revered, but Byzantine artworks and Byzantine architecture. For Byron was above everything a great lover of art, and the real subjects of his travel books are not foreign places and their people but buildings and paintings. Born in north-western Europe in the twentieth century, with a burning concern for aesthetic issues, he found himself marooned with a sensibility at odds with the traditions of realism which had prevailed for the last half-millennium. Searching back through history he found in Christian Constantinople a civilisation that best approximated to his idea of artistic utopia.

Greece, however, was more than just a repository for his chosen aesthetic. The battle for Byzantium was part of a larger personal struggle for self-expression and self-definition. The instinctive extremism in Byron's character has already been noted. To be either totally for or totally against was the natural condition of his soul. Just as his passions for art and architecture were essential to Byron, so were the passions aroused by the business of opposition. In this he demonstrates an archetypal impulse amongst British travellers: the feeling that this country is too small and airless for his kind. It should not be surprising that one finds in Byron strong echoes of the great travel rebel of the nineteenth century, Richard Burton. The two men, both failures at Oxford, both brilliant scholars, even fought the same battle. Each sizzled with indignation when their university tutors insisted on a Greek 'pronunciation invented by the ignorant English scholars of the sixteenth century', instead of speaking the language in the manner of the living Greeks themselves.[28] The struggle for Byzantine culture, just like the struggle against English academia, was part of a single process, whose product was the definition of a unique and brilliant personality.

It is interesting to note that when writing of the home country, Lawrence Durrell, like Byron, conflated his sense of disillusionment with a general anti-academic posture. 'That mean, shabby little island up there', he wrote from Corfu to Henry Miller in 1937, 'wrung my guts out of me and tried to destroy anything singular and unique in me . . . The list of schools I've been to would be a yard long. I failed every known civil service exam.'[29] There are further shades of Byron in the first of Durrell's trilogy on Greek islands, *Prospero's Cell*, which was published in 1945. He expressed, for example, dislike of Gibbon's 'podgy prose' and of the 'shabby hirelings' of the Fourth Crusade. He also stressed the continuity between classical and contemporary Greeks. Trailing his coat, perhaps, before conventional scholarship, he considered Homer's *Odyssey* a bore, badly constructed and shapeless. 'Yet with what delightful and poignant accuracy does the poem describe the modern

Greek; it is a portrait of a nation which rings as clear to-day as when it was written.'[30]

Possibly the most significant connection between the work of these two philhellenes is the shared structure of Durrell's first travel book and Byron's last. Christopher Sykes considered *The Road to Oxiana* his friend's masterpiece; Chatwin throught it *the* masterpiece amongst thirties travel works; while Paul Fussell suggested that 'it may not be going too far to say that what *Ulysses* is to the novel between the wars and what *The Waste Land* is to poetry, *The Road to Oxiana* is to the travel book'.[31] The fact that, in common with this work, *Prospero's Cell* appears to be a collection of rather haphazardly arranged diary jottings might perhaps indicate the compelling attraction that Byron's book exercised for anyone then setting out to convey the fleeting experiences, moods and tones engendered by foreign landscapes. Although any theory about Durrell's debt to Byron must take account of the fact that none of Durrell's six works of travel, in all of which Greece and Greek civilisation are an important theme, nor his published collections of letters mention the author of *The Byzantine Achievement*. The similarity between their books may ultimately be just an interesting coincidence.

An aspect of Durrell's work that definitely owes little to Byron is his description of the Greeks themselves. While humour and sympathy play a major part in their respective portraits of Greek character, Durrell is softer, more intimate and more affectionate. While Byron could appear remote and tended to generalise, Durrell was domestic and personal; while one gravitated towards the upper echelons of Greek civil and ecclesiastical society, the other moved amongst a simple rural populace. Durrell's descriptions were also more closely observed – the product of over a decade of residence amongst Greek-speaking communities. And as his friend Richard Aldington remarked, it would be more accurate to describe his Greek trilogy as works of 'foreign residence' rather than travel books.[32]

Prospero's Cell covers two of his four years – 1935–1939 – living on the island of Corfu. Ostensibly it described the pre-war life of the young writer and his artist wife, Nancy, supported comfortably by an allowance of four pounds a week, at leisure to explore their respective talents, while enjoying the company of a group of artistic and intellectual friends. The series of informal journal entries are arranged non-chronologically in seven loosely associated chapters, each suggested by aspects of their island environment.

However, operating as a continuous background in his evocation of this idyllic lifestyle, and one of the book's major cohesive themes, is the island's wider human community. This is presented as a kind of eternal society. It is typical of his sense of the wholeness of Corfiot life that on the second page Durrell writes: 'This is become our unregretted home. A world. Corcyra.'[33] The world invoked is of a rustic peasantry indefatigable in the face of poverty. Their food and few utilitarian possessions are literally hewn from the resistant, rock-strewn landscape. Hands and feet 'are blunt and hideous: mere spades grown upon their members through a long battle with soil, ropes, and wood'.[34] The diet is basic and unvarying – 'coarse peasant bread . . . dense and foul', black olives and their oil, whose taste is 'older than meat, older than wine. A taste as old as cold water'.[35] Hardship, even brutality is endemic. Durrell describes fishing excursions in which struggling octopus are bitten through the head to dispatch them; and an enormous eel, 'with the ferocity and determination of Satan', is left tò thrash itself into extinction on the beach, while tridents protrude from its brains.

These actions however, carry no moral valency: they are inherent in the natural order. And for all the exigent simplicity of their lives, the Corfiots possess an instinctive dignity. 'Hands as horny as oaks', wrote Durrell, 'faces lined like druids, but with the fine manners of kings'.[36] Noting the 'chastened, ageless quality' in their faces, he thought of 'the Byzantine faces which stare at one out of the ikons in Salonika, Athens, Ravenna . . . And behind this front rank, so to speak, the calm profiles of ancient Greek statues'.[37] The Corfiots also know a profound contentment. Unlike the Sicilian peasantry, described in Gavin Maxwell's *The Ten Pains of Death*, who seem confined to a joyless stoicism by social and religious tradition, Durrell's Greeks are actually liberated by their determinism from guilt and a sense of ultimate responsibility. And while they show a deep piety and superstition, they have shaped their gods to their own human ends. Durrell suggests that the psychological attitude to the saints is one of rough familiarity, while 'prayer is a form of bargaining . . . There is no question of humble pleading, and a foregone acceptance of refusal; the petitioner, whatever his request . . . assumes that it is most likely to be granted'.[38] In equilibrium with the ultimate forces in the universe, the Greeks have evolved a rich and salty humour, profound tenderness towards their own and an instinctive hospitality towards outsiders like the Durrells.

The immense, enduring genius of Greek society is expressed not only through what is actually given in *Prospero's Cell*, but also, curiously, by what Durrell omits to say. Half a century later it is perhaps less easy to appreciate how deeply anomalous it is that a book published in 1945, describing European life in the late thirties, should almost entirely avoid the momentous political turmoil on that continent. Only in the final five pages does Durrell draw the world of Corfu into its wider European context. Yet as one encounters the sequence of dated diary entries in *Prospero's Cell* – dates that have the tragic inevitability of a death march – it is virtually impossible not to supply a parallel, undisclosed sequence of events.

On 29 April 1937, for instance, Durrell notes 'all the charms of seclusion' enjoyed by their old fisherman's cottage, twenty miles from the nearest town. And two days after he settles down at his cypress-shaded desk to add 'This is become our unregretted home. A world. Corcyra', nine waves of Heinkels, piloted by Germans dressed in Spanish uniform, release their 550-pound bombs on the northern Iberian town of Guernica. Many of the 1,654 killed are women and children. Adolf Hitler, deflecting blame, denounces the raid as *bolschewistische* – the work of Stalin. 'You wake one morning in the late autumn', runs Durrell's entry for 15 November 1937, 'and notice that the tone of everything has changed'. At Berchtesgaden in Bavaria only forty-eight hours earlier the Austrian chancellor makes those concessions that lead to his imprisonment and the Nazi annexation of his country. 'The tone of everything has changed', runs Durrell, 'the sky shines more deeply pearl, and the sun rises like a ball of blood – for the peaks of the Albanian hills are touched with snow'.[39] While Durrell attends a country dance under the stars of April 1938, the professors of Vienna university scrub the streets with their bare hands. Later in the year, on almost the same heavenly September day that Durrell and his friends 'retire to the arbours by the house to drink coffee and pass the long morning in idle talk', Harold Nicolson accompanies Winston Churchill in the lift to the latter's flat.[40] Nicolson says, 'This is hell.' The other man replies, 'It is the end of the British Empire.'[41] Eight days later Czechoslovakia falls effortlessly into the hands of Nazidom and Neville Chamberlain stands at the window of 10 Downing Street announcing, 'I believe it is peace in our time.'

If *Prospero's Cell* could be rendered in paint then it might be represented as a small disc of intense white surrounded by an immense black canvas. It is only in relation to that encircling darkness that one can fully appreciate the brilliance of the central sphere. It is only with a background awareness of the boiling anarchy loose on the European continent that one can understand Durrell's sense of the enduring qualities and sheer sanity of demotic Greek life.

For Durrell, one of the areas in which that continuity in Hellenic civilisation was most apparent was in the Greek love of communal dance. Coming upon the Bacchanalia under the April stars of 1938, he describes it almost as if it were a mystical re-enactment of cosmic order. The men's faces are 'devout and abstract'; the entire body of dancers, a 'multi-coloured wheel', that 'spins and reverses, spins and reverses, while the lone-moving satellites plot out their intricate measures'.[42] The dance theme, picked out in *Prospero's Cell* and resumed and enlarged in the second of Durrell's island trilogy, is only one of many continuities between the two works. In fact, *Reflections on a Marine Venus*, while exploring a completely different island setting – Rhodes in the Dodecanese – and published eight years later, in 1953, seems at times almost an extension of *Prospero's Cell*. Certainly it resumes his meditation on the interrelations of Greek landscape and people.

This is most fully expressed in a prolonged description of the island festivities that accompanied the panagyri for Saint Soulas of Soroni. The chapter, some of Durrell's finest writing on Greece, expresses his capacity to marry the almost scientific exactness of his observations to a richly poetic prose, whose exquisiteness is perhaps a factor in the current ebb-tide of Durrell's reputation. It is, however, a sustained *tour de force*, particularly for the enormous range of moods created: from the slapstick farce of a holiday bus, double-booked then assaulted by a crowd twice its capacity, to the dramatic pathos of a near-fatal accident involving a child crushed beneath the wheels of a lorry and rushed away for emergency surgery.

Durrell situates amongst this his long passage on the dance, setting the tone through a succession of images stressing the deep Greek affinity with the natural world. The milling crowds suggest the ebb and flow of the tide, a wafting shelf of seaweed, the shapeless clotting of bees at the entrance to a hive. The many circles of dancers whirling throughout the festival grounds have the symbolic resonance of mandalas, expressing the Greeks' autochthonous origins, their deep unity amongst themselves, and their abiding intimacy with the Greek earth.

> The whole dance-floor has become one swelling cloud of reddish dust by now in the centre of which (their faces preoccupied and remote) ride the dancers, their flower-like bodies carried forward on the music like river-narcissus. The warm dust-cloud has risen to the height of their top-boots, giving them the ghostly appearance of goddesses being born from the earth itself, and aided only by their struggles, and the unearthly music of the fiddles which torment them. The young dance-leader alone raises his feet above the dust-cloud, capering and shaking his tambourine, proudly showing his twinkling heels. His goat-like eyes glitter.
>
> I am reminded, as so often in Greece, that dancing is never a performance so much as a communal rite – the transmission of an enigmatic knowledge which the musician has summoned up from below the earth. It flows outward through the dancing feet which are building the dusty circle, stitch by stitch, like a fabric being woven: step by step like a city being built: and the darker circle outside, the lookers-on, gradually absorb the rhythm which triumphs over them by sheer repetition – being laid down on their consciousness like successive coats of a thrilling colour. One can watch the crowd being drawn into such a dance man by man,

impelled by something like that gravitational law which
decrees that autumn windfalls should plunge towards the
centre of the earth when they are ripe. The vivid circle of the
dancers is the centre towards which the audience leans, its
blood quickened by the notation of the music – itself (who
knows?) a transcription in terms of cat-gut and wind of
profounder melodies which the musician has quarried from
his native disenchantments and the earth.[43]

The dance, however, is more than just a celebration of the
Greeks' organic primitiveness. This profound sensuality is the
bedrock of what remains a deeply cultured society, whose dazzling
achievements stretch back to the very origins of civilisation. Part of
that immense heritage is the classical marble statuary that has
inspired the world for two and a half millennia, typified by the
marine Venus of the book's title. Hauled out of Rhodes harbour in
fishermen's nets, the statue was concealed in a dark crypt at the time
of Nazi occupation, and only retrieved from its hiding place and
restored to the museum during Durrell's post-war residence on the
island. The marble goddess is a leitmotif in his evocation of Rhodes.
He sees her as the 'presiding genius of the place'. However, the
statue also has a wider resonance: 'Behind and through her the
whole idea of Greece glows sadly'. Her survival symbolises the
persistence of the people that gave rise to her.

In Rhodes we have been the willing bondsmen of the
marine Venus – the figure that sits up there alone in the
Museum, disregarded, sightless; yet somehow we have
learned to share that timeless, exact musical contemplation –
the secret of her self-sufficiency – which has helped her to
outlive the savage noise of wars and change, to maintain
unbroken the fine thread of her thoughts through the
centuries past. Yes, and through her we have learned to see
Greece with the inner eyes – not as a collection of battered
vestiges left over from cultures long since abandoned – but
as something ever-present and ever-renewed.[44]

Like Byron, Durrell found in Greece the grounds for his revolt against England and the time and space in which to exercise his own literary personality. But whereas for the former the crucial issue had been the Greek artistic inheritance from the Byzantine past, for Durrell the key element was the sheer genius of the contemporary Greeks for living life passionately. Their achievement, which boiled down partly to a matter of enjoying sex, was a yardstick with which to beat fellow countrymen. 'The central dramas of life here', Durrell wrote from Rhodes to T. S. Eliot, 'come out of sex; and sex informs and warms everything. One is saturated and exhausted and bored to death with sex; consequently it is only here that one is ever *free* of it'.[45]

Another area in which Britain showed to disadvantage was in the false and petty superiorities of its colonial administration, when set against the instinctive hospitality and egalitarianism of the Greeks. 'The people here! My God the people!' Durrell fumed in a letter to a friend. 'No greater collection of defrocked priests, ex-jockeys, haberdashers, and ruined boxers was ever gathered together to lord it over an innocent and peaceful people'.[46] Five years before, Durrell's great friend and early literary mentor, the American novelist Henry Miller, had felt exactly the same: 'The English in Greece . . . are torpid, unimaginative, lacking in resiliency . . . The Englishman is a farce and an eyesore: he isn't worth the dirt between a poor Greek's toes'.[47]

However, it was not just Britain that was found wanting in comparison with Greece. The Italian landscapes which had so inspired those earlier British pagans, Norman Douglas and D. H. Lawrence, were rejected for their 'finickyness', their lack of the Panic spirit so evident in the montane peninsula to the east. And in the same wartime letter that Durrell extolled 'the marvellous chivalry of the Greek air force', he wrote of the 'lying crawling meanness' of the Italians.[48] Nor was it just Durrell who sensed that Hellas was the final repository in Europe for an ancient and authentic wisdom. Visiting the Catholic Spain beloved of Gerald Brenan and Norman Lewis, Henry Miller found the country 'dark, morose, sinister, brutal'.[49] The American novelist went on to propose that 'Greece is now . . . the only Paradise in Europe';[50] and Fermor seconded the idea, adding that a 'stubbornly incorruptible innocence is a quality that . . . has vanished from the whole of

Europe except Greece',[51] and that 'Greek manners towards strangers are . . . a hundred times better and more friendly than anywhere else'.[52]

For these partisans there was also a common perception that the Greeks were destined to play an important part in the development of the continent. As early as 1929 Robert Byron had felt that on the shorelines of the eastern Mediterranean 'may lie the future of Europe and then the future of the earth'.[53] A dozen years on Miller wondered 'What a place it will be when it is restored to its pristine verdure . . . A revivified Greece can very conceivably alter the whole destiny of Europe';[54] while Fermor thought that 'the restless, dispersed and unharnessable but indestructible Greek genius, released at last, will produce something which will astonish and enrich the world again beyond all our imagination'.[55]

The idea that a foreign land and its people have much to teach the country of their own birth is, as we have seen, common currency amongst travellers. However, there were factors in citing Greece as a model society that made the comparative process much more significant. While Thesiger, say, in the Bedu of Arabia or van der Post in the San of the Kalahari had found societies against which they could measure deficiencies in the home country, these places and their peoples were alien utopias, with an environment and cultural history totally inapplicable to the British context. But how much more appropriate to gauge the soullessness of Blackburn or Tunbridge Wells by reference to a society that was both European and Christian? Laying rural Greece side by side with smokestacked Britain was the nearest thing, both geographically and culturally, to a before and after of the industrial age. It was the smallest distance one had to travel in order to appreciate where we had gone wrong.

For all Durrell's unfavourable comparisons of Britain with Greece, he also seems to have had a sense of the affinities that existed between the two nations, which was perhaps most apparent in times of conflict. With the Balkans facing invasion in 1940, for instance, he wrote to Miller from Athens, 'I am so happy that England and Greece are in this together; with all their faults they both stand for something great'.[56] Behind this remark is a longstanding political association that goes back to the Greek war of independence in the 1820s, to Codrington's triumph at the Battle of Navarino and, above all, to the championship of the Hellenic cause by Lord Byron. In fact, Fermor has suggested that such is the Greek regard for the poet that, even today, every English traveller in that country, 'however humble or unimpressive . . . is the beneficiary of some reflected fragment of [Byron's] glory'.[57] Following his death at Missolonghi the bonds of friendship were expressed in Britain's cession, however reluctantly, of the Ionian islands to Greek control. After the First World War it was in part the friendship between Lloyd George and Venizelos that had licensed the Greek premier's pursuit of the *Megali Idhea*, the Great Idea – the restoration of empire in Asia Minor. During the Second World War Churchill squeezed Britain's army in the Middle East to move reinforcements to the Greek northern passes and to garrison Crete in the face of German and Italian invasions. Whatever the wider strategic purpose behind the actions of British leaders, the fact that Anglo-Saxon lives and gold were spent in defence of Greek soil established a genuine fraternity that makes the 600-year-old Anglo-Portuguese association seem a mere historical curiosity. In fact, it is a link that has no parallel in modern British relations with any other country of the Mediterranean. And a link felt on both sides: 'England "sent her greatest poet to help them raise the flag. He died for Greece and England – they are both not countries, but symbols of liberty incarnate" '.[58] This nugget was quarried by Durrell from a Cypriot school essay.

It is undoubtedly the case that this background history of political and military co-operation between the two nations has played a significant part in the strong tradition of travel in the Greek peninsula. It is a country in which Britons have instinctively felt at home. However, it was the shattering of these apparent bonds of friendship that was the subject of Durrell's third island book, *Bitter Lemons*.

Following his post in Rhodes, Durrell had held a number of overseas government positions, latterly that of press attaché in the Yugoslavian capital, Belgrade. In 1952 he resigned from this office and moved to Cyprus with his daughter, in order to devote himself to writing full-time. Shortly after he had bought, restored and settled into an old Turkish house close to the northern coastal town of Kyrenia, the political situation in the island deteriorated.

Britain's decision to withdraw from Egypt, announced in 1954, and to make Cyprus its principal base in the eastern Mediterranean, triggered increased Cypriot calls for independence and Enosis, union with Greece. Refusal to negotiate with local leaders simply intensified demands for self-determination and gave rise to the terrorist attacks of EOKA, a Cypriot guerilla organisation. With his savings exhausted by family commitments and by his work on the house at Bellapaix, Durrell was drawn back into government service, as director of public relations to the British administration.

Bitter Lemons is an expression of the author's deeply divided loyalties. On one side was Durrell's obvious sensitivity towards the Greeks and their aspirations, expressed in his fluency in their language, his years of political service on their behalf and more than a decade of residence amongst them. On the other side was his loyalty to the British administration. This was not just professional duty to the institution that paid him. At times the post he occupied brought with it threats even to his own life. And Durrell felt genuine admiration for the work of some of his fellow Britons in extremely difficult circumstances. Sir John Harding, for example, the last governor he was to serve, was described as a 'patient and tidy lion-hearted little man' who combined 'the graces of a courtier . . . with the repose and mildness of a family sage'.[59]

Bitter Lemons, which went through five impressions in almost as many months and which earned its author the Duff Cooper Memorial Prize, is perhaps the finest of Durrell's island trilogy. It is significant for its atmosphere of tolerance and its capacity to render successfully the wider historical and political events largely through their impact on individual lives. However, it never manages to reaffirm that triumph of the domestic over the political, wherein lay, for Durrell, the very secret of survival of Hellenic society. Despite the comedy of village and tavern lowlife recreated in early chapters, the book's dominant tone is one of elegiac regret. This rises to its climax in the penultimate chapter entitled 'The Vanishing Landmarks', which is also memorable for Durrell's inferential approach to his central subject, so powerfully deployed in *Prospero's Cell*.

Appearing at the end of a book that documents an inexorable slide from sleepy co-existence to bloody crisis, punctuated by murder and bomb-blast, the chapter is almost entirely without dramatic content. The single sound of gunshot comes from a local farmer taking aim at jackdaws. It describes an excursion undertaken by Durrell and his schoolteacher friend Panos, with whom he had lodged shortly after his arrival in Cyprus. The object of their picnic outing was to gather the wild flowers of early spring and to inspect the layout of a friend's garden. Durrell's description of his companion suggests a man deeply sensitive to natural beauty, who shrinks from the current violence. When he and Durrell take their lunch Panos proposes the day's toast: ' "That we may pass beyond [i.e. the present troubles] and that we might emerge once more in the forgotten Cyprus – as if through a looking-glass" '.[60] Approaching sixty, he announces with Socratic profundity: 'what a pleasure it is to get old'. Yet in order to savour views of the landscape he clambers child-like into the branches of a tree. It is the peace-loving Panos who offers a final and penetrating commentary on the origins and course of the political crisis. 'O Lord! . . . sometimes you ask such silly questions', he admonishes his friend gently. It is appropriate that in giving weight to his exegesis, Panos has recourse to Cypriot proverb – 'He thought he could beat his wife without the neighbours hearing'; 'He can't gather the honey without killing the bees' – which represents the distilled wisdom of an ancient, peasant community.[61]

In many ways the chapter recalls the gentle idyll evoked by Durrell's earlier works on Greece and the happier times of the first part of the book, before the violence erupted. Together he and Panos had delighted in the cyclamens and anemones. They filled baskets with the super-abundant blooms. They shared the simple picnic with a near-stranger. A story is recounted of a rural village where children shout abuse at an English couple, then gather flowers for the lady in an urge to make amends. At a roadblock manned by good-natured English soldiers, Panos burdens one with great handfuls of flowers. Later he studies the arrangement of trees in the friend's garden, while Durrell goes swimming, before taking final leave of a gentle old Muslim holy man at a remote mosque. All this would amount to a portrait of tranquillity and beauty, except that Durrell had stated before his description of the excursion:

And then Panos was shot dead. He had walked out for a breath of air at dusk, through the winding narrow streets near the harbour. The walls around wore the familiar autograph of Dighenis though I doubt if Dighenis himself pressed the trigger of the pistol which killed him.[62]

He makes no further comment. However, the information invests his account of their idyllic outing and the many small beauties of soul revealed in his friend with a new and tragic significance. These are the bitter, intolerable forfeits exacted by the political unrest. Obliquely Durrell conveys the senseless brutality of the Greek terrorists, and may also indicate, perhaps, that the Greek gift for right living, while now dormant in the wider community, survives in individuals like his murdered friend. For he makes clear that Panos's death had been as a direct consequence of his association with himself – an officer of the British administration. The schoolteacher had even received a death threat before his day out with Durrell, but had chosen to ignore it: 'Life . . . would be unendurable if one had to obey the dictates of the hotheads'.[63] In effect, Panos had valued an excursion to appreciate and gather wild flowers with a friend from another country – activities that express those human sensitivities which are perhaps the very essence of a civilisation – as highly as life itself. Despite this veiled assertion, the closing lines of the chapter are true to the book's larger atmosphere of loss: 'My footsteps echoed softly upon the sea-wall. I was, I realized, very tired after this two years' spell as a servant of the Crown; and I had achieved nothing. It was good to be leaving.'[64]

For Durrell, Greece 'was changed out of all recognition by the Enosis problem' and his departure from Cyprus in 1956 marked a final break in his years of Greek residence, which had extended over three decades.[65] His government post and nominal obedience to British policy on the island had forced him to see himself increasingly as an outsider. From this new perspective he noted not only the deep Mediterranean loyalty to the life of the emotions, but also its flipside – an inability to interpret life in anything but emotional and personal terms. This realisation and the long wearying months of violence informed his descriptions of Cypriot society with a reserve, even impatience, that was totally absent from *Prospero's Cell*: 'They thought like Persian women, capriciously, waywardly, moving from impulse to impulse, completely under the domination of mood' was one of Durrell's shriller conclusions.[66]

Not that he had ever suggested he should have found in Cyprus what he had known in other parts of Greece. Very soon after his arrival in 1952 the poet's antennae, which had showed such sensitivity to the atmosphere of Corfu or Rhodes, were soon registering a very different set of signals. 'It's a bit of Asia Minor washed out to sea', he wrote to Miller. 'It's Middle East – taste of Turkey and Egypt';[67] 'I think it is a weird and rather malefic sort of island – not at *all* like Greek islands'. The Cypriots too, with their 'listless Outer Mongolian looks', were quite unlike the people on the mainland.[68]

It was clear that Cyprus was different in other ways. Without a university, theatre, bookshop or even swimming pool, the capital, Nicosia, was compared in terms of its amenities to 'some fly-blown Anatolian township, bemused and forgotten on the central steppes'.[69] And while Durrell had always enjoyed the lowlife camaraderie of the taverna or *kafenio*, and while his friend Panos had shared his botanical interests, Cyprus never supplied the supportive community of intellectuals and artists that he had enjoyed on Corfu or Rhodes. The life of 'blameless monotony' amongst the British community was relieved only by a tiny number of congenial expatriates and the regular arrival of itinerant friends like Patrick Balfour, Patrick Leigh Fermor, John Lehmann, Sir Harry Luke, Rose Macaulay and Freya Stark. Though Durrell suggests the relief and stimulation of these visitors – 'bringing with them the conversations of the great capitals' – in *Bitter Lemons* there is very little of the unhurried philosophical banter, the leisured intellectual enquiries that are such a feature of *Prospero's Cell* and *Reflections on a Marine Venus*. This scholarship is one of the major themes of the earlier two books, in fact, one of the main themes of travel literature in Greece.

However, it is a scholarship of a very specific brand. It is a private, untested, unrestricted expression of intellectual vigour and originality. It has less to do with any formal conventions of learning than with the tavern, good food, good wine and congenial

company. It is part of the business of right and healthy living. On
Corfu its natural locale is an inn called 'The Partridge'. The diverse
personnel at these gatherings seem apiece with Durrell's deep sense
of Corfiot self-sufficiency. The 'grey, eminent and imposing'
Zarian is an Armenian poet and journalist who writes for a number
of new world newspapers. Fluent in Russian, Italian, German and
French, he is also, appropriately, engaged in 'an exhaustive study of
the island wines'.[70] Theodore Stephanides is a Greek scholar,
physician and expert in all aspects of Corfiot natural history, with
'the driest and most fastidious styles of exposition ever seen'. On
his first visit to the Durrells' cottage, he stalks off mid conversation
to trap a sandfly landed on the wall, and announces triumphantly:
'Got it. Four hundred and second'.[71] The coterie of epicureans is
completed by a Polish aristocrat, Max Nimiec, and the unidentified
Count D. – a character based on the real-life figure of Dr
Palatioano, who had kept the skull of his mistress on a velvet square
on his writing desk.[72] On Rhodes, Durrell had enjoyed a similar
circle of friends: a monocled Indian army regular 'of culture and
comparatively wide reading', a consular official with nine
languages and a heart condition, and a medical doctor.

The meetings at 'The Partridge' in *Prospero's Cell* and their
elaborate intellectual speculations are totally removed from the
basic blood consciousness of his Corfiot peasants and their mystical
oneness with the earth. Yet they are activities deeply appropriate to
the Greek environment, and Durrell's description of them seems to
draw some of its resonance from the country's classical past and that
period's legend as an unattainable peak of intellectual achievement.
In his evocations of leisured contemplation, of the group's hypo-
thetical questions to Socrates, its speculations on lost references in
Shakespearian plays or of arcane disquisition on landscape and art,
he seems to wish to echo a philosophical world represented perhaps
by the shaded groves of Aristotle's Lyceum or the Academy of
Plato. This atmosphere of 'endless conversations' also underscores,
incidentally, the deep sense of Corfu's separateness suggested in
Prospero's Cell. For if the Corfiot peasantry are a bulwark for sanity
amidst the madness of late-thirties Europe, 'The Partridge' school
of contemplation is a final citadel.

Greece's historical role as formidable powerhouse of civilisation has escaped the attention of few of its visitors. In fact, most of the travel books on the country in the mid twentieth century describe a predictable circuit of classical ruins, temples and ancient battle-fields, liberally interspersed with the legends and stories that attach to each site. Though in Greece of all places there is least excuse for repetition. As Fermor has pointed out, 'There is hardly a rock or a stream without a battle or a myth, a miracle or a peasant anecdote or a superstition'.[73] It is the extraordinary depth and density of the country's cultural life, and the inexhaustible range of intellectual, historical, artistic and mythological associations to which the localities give rise, important to the development of Europe and even the world, which make Greece the ultimate hunting ground for an intellectual freebooter like the traveller.

There are additional dimensions to travel scholarship deserving consideration, one of which is perhaps personified by Durrell's friend, George Katsimbalis. This extraordinary character was an Athenian sophisticate fully at home in Paris or London, whose family's fortune was based on a grandfather's property specula-tions. These had shown brilliant insight into Greek character. When he learnt that the city planners wanted to expand Athens in a southerly direction towards Piraeus harbour, Katsimbalis senior immediately snapped up all the land he could to the north. Once the public were also told that they were intended to dwell in the south they too started to buy property, in the opposite direction. The business psychologist thus reaped his rewards.[74]

Katsimbalis himself was editor of the Greek journal *Ta Nea Grammata, New Letters*, that had published Breton, Lawrence, Lorca and Rimbaud. Amongst a distinguished group of Athenian intellectuals, which included Nobel-prize-winning poet George Seferis, he was the towering personality. Durrell called him 'the truest Greek I know'.[75] A Katsimbalis anecdote is the source of one of the most memorable passages in Fermor's *Mani*, and he is the eponymous hero in Miller's *The Colossus of Maroussi*.[76] When the American novelist visited Greece before the outbreak of the Second World War, he was captivated by Katsimbalis's Falstaffian bragga-docio and his gift for converting personal incident or adventure into a 'Wagnerian cycle of stories'.[77] In a sustained portrait of his Greek friend, Miller likened him to a bull, a vulture, a leopard, a dove, gorilla, snake, goat, dog, falcon, bird, bear, whale, fish and great starfish. It is a description that gives some sense of the protean nature of the Katsimbalis monologue and the volcanic energies of its performer. This massive raconteur dramatised in the most extreme fashion a key aspect of the intellectual life of travellers in Greece.

It was a process not only of thought and imagination, but of emotion and even physical activity. It involved total expression. To employ the word *scholarship* to describe their mental pursuits is perhaps misleading, since anything like footnoted academia would be the kiss of death to their interests. It is surely significant that none of the four major writers on Greece – Byron, Durrell, Fermor, Miller – enjoyed a conventionally successful academic career.

Byron's scholarship is absolutely typical. He had formidable intellectual gifts and took great pains in the preparation of a work like *The Byzantine Achievement*, but there was little concern for retaining any objectivity. The book, as we have seen, was full of the deep passions, even the private malice one might encounter in a letter to an individual. Byron could hate Catholicism as if it were a personal enemy or a malign factor in his own family's affairs. And his attacks upon it suggest a conception of scholarship as a type of mental warfare. Fermor hit the mark perfectly when he suggested that Byron's approach to intellectual obstacles was that of a cavalryman to the enemy: 'Instead of evading or dismantling them he points the target out, as it were with a sabre, and then, with dazzling bravura . . . slashes and kicks it to matchwood and rides on'.[78] *The Byzantine Achievement* can be considered a work of history, but it is also a vigorous assault upon the idea of the past as a received and inaccessible province, and upon those historians who might wish to peddle it as such. Byron, so typical of the twentieth-century travel writer, seemed to be reclaiming history for himself, at times almost shaping it to suit individual ends. In *The Station*, for instance, he wrote of Mount Athos as 'one fragment, one living articulate community of *my chosen past*' [my italics].[79]

The very language he used also seemed to indicate an urge to recreate history, not as a great impersonal force, but as simple human lives, interconnecting and touching one another even unto the author himself; and it is perhaps in this context that he appears most like a humanist. Here is how he sought to convey one particular historical era.

> The fifteenth century had passed its middle year. Donatello
> was an old man. Caxton middle-aged, Columbus and
> Botticelli were boys. Thirty years more and the earth should
> bear the small feet of Erasmus, Michelangelo and Martin
> Luther. Joan of Arc was dead and the Middle Ages with
> her.[80]

Thirty years on, exactly the same type of sentence, suggesting the same process of connectedness, was used by Fermor after his meeting with a Greek, reputedly 127 years old: 'He was born two years before Byron died in Missolonghi. George IV, Charles X, and Alexander II were on their thrones, Wellington, Metternich and Talleyrand scarcely more than middle-aged'.[81]

It is typical of this totality of expression that a number of the key British travellers in Greece not only wrote on the country, but struggled for it in wartime service. Early in 1941 Byron left the BBC for a post as a 'special correspondent' at an undisclosed eastern location. Sadly, he would never even reach the first port of call in Egypt: his transport ship was torpedoed off northern Scotland and he drowned. Sykes, however, believed that his friend's ultimate destination was 'so blatantly obvious. His name was Byron and the battle of Greece was drawing near.'[82]

Durrell saw this struggle at first hand, initially in Athens then Kalamata. After fleeing by caique to Crete and on to Egypt, he found his knowledge of the Greek language and people continued to determine the nature of his work. During the remaining four years of conflict he was first foreign press officer in Cairo with responsibility for the Greek press, then press attaché in Alexandria, with its huge Greek population.

Of the three Britons, Patrick Leigh Fermor played the most active military role, initially as a British liaison officer with the Greek army in Albania. He then fought in the battles for both Greece and Crete, returning to the latter to organise an efficient guerilla force. For two years he lived with Cretan fighters in caves and mountain hideouts disguised as a shepherd.

The impulse so widely found amongst travellers to keep a foot in the conventionally opposed camps of the active and the intellectual, reaches its apotheosis in Fermor. He is the Sir Philip Sidney of his age and enjoys the Elizabethan's dual reputation. The name, 'always surrounded with the aura of romance', immediately invokes two outstanding legends.[83] One of these, implying a largeness of design and physical persistence that is perhaps more Medieval than Renaissance, concerns Fermor's two-year tramp across the European continent from London to Constantinople, undertaken while still in his teens. The second involves the kidnap of General Karl Kreipe, the commanding officer of the German garrison in Crete.

Fermor, together with his friend William Stanley Moss and a small band of Cretan guerillas, held up Kreipe's car during its routine journey to the general's quarters. The driver was coshed and removed and Kreipe held at knife-point in the back, while Fermor assumed the general's seat and hat, coolly posing as his captive through twenty-two roadblocks in German-occupied Heraklion.[84] The kidnap probably has few contenders as the war's most daring episode.

Fermor's legend as a man of action is more than equalled by his reputation in the sphere of letters. In a literary age consumed with the literary prize, four of his works have been honoured with six awards. He is the most obvious heir to Byron's pre-war mantle as leading philhellene amongst British writers and as the travel book's great stylist. In fact he is considered one of the major stylists in any genre, creating 'English prose as few have written it . . . this century'.[85]

Greece, once again, is a deeply appropriate landscape for a Renaissance figure equally at ease, as it were, with an automatic rifle or a volume of C. P. Cavafy. For the Greek borders contain not just the entire world of human ideas, but some of the last montane wilderness in Europe. Where England is a mosaic of ploughland, pasture and coppice, choked by car fumes or chimney smoke, Greece retains the authentic whiff of adventure. Until mid century it harboured Europe's last nomads and highland shepherds armed to the teeth and given to robbery and rustling. Today it is a final European lair for the wolf, the bear, the vulture, the nose-horned viper. It is the kind of place an Anglo-Irish war hero might settle down. And it is highly characteristic that Fermor chose as home a region traditionally considered the most rugged and lawless on the mainland. The southernmost Peloponnese is the focus of Fermor's *Mani*, the finest book in an outstanding canon. Like its sequel *Roumeli* it could not be considered a conventional travel work. Although the first does describe a journey, neither is truly an account of a simple linear transect through the country. Both are a distillation of many years' study, experience and observation of the Hellenic environment.

Fermor's contribution to the development of the genre is substantial. In particular he has sustained the concern, expressed in *The Road to Oxiana* or *Prospero's Cell*, to establish that sense of immediate contact between reader and travelled environment; perhaps the hallmark of a great travel book. However, Fermor's route to this effect was completely different. Where Byron and Durrell conveyed, through works cleverly disguised as diaries, the impression of a mind revealed in its moment of flight, Fermor presents his travel experiences with the informality almost of a personal letter. And as in a letter the author moves constantly in his narrative from his one past and present, to the anticipated future moment of the reader. The impact of the two formats – letter and diary – is much the same. Both suggest freedom from the discipline of more formal writings, and the pleasures of composing by and for oneself; and if not exactly for oneself in Fermor's case, then for somebody very like-minded. Both devices also create the illusion of intimacy, of direct access to the writer's most private and unguarded disclosures.

Fermor reinforces the atmosphere of immediate and personal contact between reader and author by his frequent asides and digressions. At one point in a detailed analysis of a puzzling coat of arms, found above the door of a Maniot cathedral, he steps out from behind the narrative, makes a drawing of the emblem, then asks his reader for help with identification.[86] Solicitous footnotes gently direct the audience to other works of reference: 'In this context, I would like to recommend most strongly Mr Philip Sherrard's remarkable book'.[87] Perhaps implicit in these asides is the possibility that the author/reader relationship will exceed the confines of *Mani*'s covers.

Fermor's footnotes deserve further analysis. In fact, they are almost a literary form in themselves. They have the courteous and informal tone of an eighteenth-century gentleman-scholar, and suggest a writer for whom a single linear narrative is never quite adequate to contain the burning multiplicity of ideas exercising him at any one moment. One can almost hear in these notes the great private enthusiasms with which he points out other lines of enquiry, recalls his earlier works, or apologises for past errors. Others disclose autobiographical titbits, announce stop-press the death of a friend, the name of a castle, or they enlarge on theses too erudite for the principal text. Occasionally, they turn aside to make a joke. One memorable footnote in *Roumeli* elaborates on the distinction between the classical written Greek language, *Katharévousa*, and the common idiom of the people, *Demotiki*.

> *Katharévousa* is an expensive faded leather case stamped with a tarnished monogram, holding a set of geometrical instruments: stiff jointed dividers and compasses neatly slotted into their plush beds. *Demotiki* is an everyday instrument – a spade, an adze or a sickle – the edge thinned and keen with honing and bright from the whetstone; and the wooden shaft, mellow with sweat and smooth with the patina of generations of handling, lies in the palm with an easy balance. Partisanship for the two idioms has led to rioting in the Athens streets, to bloodshed and even death.[88]

Here is the scholarly footnote that aspires to the condition of poetry.

The narrative device by which Fermor creates the illusion of our personal access to him as narrator, also permits him to suggest almost our participation in the traveller's adventures. This is classically illustrated in *Mani* by a Fermor aside appearing after a long discursive passage which ranges over a whole spectrum of subjects, including vanished items of Greek life and costume. The entire digression is carefully disguised as merely random thoughts that have been inspired by his immediate surroundings and experiences in a fortified tower in a Maniot village, to which the author has retired with the intention of writing. Fermor then breaks

into this passage, with apparent spontaneity, to announce: 'The
sound of feet coming up the ladder put to flight these musings on
obsolete headgear and their sociological implications ("and about
time too", I can hear the reader murmuring)'.[89]

In this moment Fermor achieves a double sleight of hand. It is the
imagined readers and their drumming fingers of impatience, as
much as his Greek host mounting the ladder to check on his guest,
that have interrupted the train of thought. At a stroke Fermor's
narrative abolishes the divisions of time and space which inevitably
separate reader from author, and then the author himself from the
travel experiences he describes. It is as if reader, author and Greek
host are all simultaneously present at that precise moment of airy
speculation.

These described flights of fancy are the great set-pieces of
Fermor's Greek books. In the context of the travel genre they are
the equivalent of Joyce's interior monologue. And their effect is
much the same, investing life's neglected and seemingly meaningless off-moments with a psychological significance, even drama.
None of these daydreams is more finely recreated, nor richer in
implications for the travel genre than that in chapter three of *Mani*;
though in order to do full justice to the cumulative impact of
Fermor's magnificent rhetoric, the entire seven-page passage
should really be reproduced verbatim.

Its narrative setting is Kardamyli, a small coastal town in which
Fermor subsequently designed and built his own house. The flight
of fancy is triggered by the author's enquiries into the fate of
surviving members of the Palaeologi, the dynasty that ruled the
Byzantine empire at its fall in the fifteenth century. On learning that
one of these reputed descendants actually lives in Kardamyli,
Fermor, in obedience to his insatiable curiosity, visits the man.
Strati Mourtzinos is a humble fisherman consumed, less with his
500-year-old dynastic claims, than the need to find a market for his
produce. As his Greek host enlarges on these domestic problems,
Fermor describes the parallel workings of his own imagination –
assisted, significantly, by generous rounds of ouzo – as he
speculates on what it might mean if:

this modest and distinguished looking fisherman were really

heir of the Palaeologi, descendant of Constantine XI and of
Michael VIII the Liberator, successor to Alexis Comnene and
Basil the Bulgar-Slayer and Leo the Isaurian and Justinian and
Theodosius and St. Constantine the Great? And, for that
matter, to Diocletian and Heliogabalus . . . all the way back to
the Throne of Augustus Caesar on the Palatine.[90]

As the influence of the potent spirits increases, so fantasy comes to
triumph increasingly over reality. He envisions the Turks, 'in token
of friendship and historical appropriateness', retiring to the Central
Asian steppes and returning the Byzantine Empire to the Greeks.
Strati the fisherman, as the rightful heir, is returned to Constantinople to be enthroned as Emperor of Byzantium. Fermor continues
with an extravagant accumulation of detail.

> The fifth ouzo carried us, in a ruffle of white foam, across
> the Aegean archipelago and at every island a score of vessels
> joined the convoy. By the time we entered the Hellespont,
> it stretched from Troy to Sestos and Abydos . . . on we
> went, past the islands of the shining Propontis until, like a
> magical city hanging in mid-air, Constantinople appeared
> beyond our bows, its towers and bastions glittering, its
> countless domes and cupolas bubbling among pinnacles and
> dark sheaves of cypresses, all of them climbing to the single
> great dome topped with the flashing cross that Constantine
> had seen in a vision on the Milvian bridge. There, by the
> Golden Gate, in the heart of a mighty concourse, waited the
> lords of Byzantium: the lesser Caesars and Despots and
> Sebastocrators, the Grand Logothete in his globular
> headgear, the Counts of the Palace, the Sword Bearer, the
> Chartophylax, the Great Duke, the thalassocrats and
> polemarchs, the Strateges of the Cretan archers, of the
> hoplites and the peltasts and the cataphracts; the Silentiaries,
> the Count of the Excubitors, the governors of the Asian
> Themes, the Clissourarchs, the Grand Eunuch, and (for by
> now all Byzantine history had melted into a single
> anachronistic maelstrom) the Prefects of Sicily and Nubia
> and Ethiopia and Egypt and Armenia, the Exarchs of

Ravenna and Carthage, the Nomarch of Tarentum, the Catapan of Bari, the Abbot of Studium.[91]

After two further pages of similar exoticism, the enthronement moves to its climax. Yet as he goes, Fermor weaves amongst the gorgeous fabric of his daydream an account of Strati's actual conversation: the size of a fish, the inferior dyes obtained from pine cones that he uses on his nets, and the difficulties of finding an alternative. The fisherman's tale then rises to its own crescendo as Strati narrates the story of a storm and shipwreck off a cape close to Kardamyli. The two strands of narrative are at last drawn to a final consummation.

> The whole City was shaken by an unending, ear-splitting roar. Entwined in whorls of incense, the pillars turned in their sockets, and tears of felicity ran down the mosaic Virgin's and the cold ikon's cheeks . . .
>
> Leaning forward urgently, Strati crossed himself. '*Holy Virgin and all the Saints!*' he said. 'I was never in a worse situation! It was pitch dark and pouring with rain, the mast and the rudder were broken, the bung was lost, and the waves were the size of a house . . .'
>
> . . . the whole of Constantinople seemed to be rising on a dazzling golden cloud and the central dome began to revolve as the redoubled clamour of the Byzantines hoisted it aloft. Loud with bells and gongs, with cannon flashing from the walls and a cloud-borne fleet firing long crimson radii of Greek fire, the entire visionary city, turning in faster and faster spirals, sailed to a blinding and unconjecturable zenith . . . The rain had turned to hail, the wind had risen to a scream; the boat had broken and sunk and, through the ink-black storm, Strati was swimming for life towards the thunderous rocks of Laconia . . .
>
> . . . The bottle was empty.[92]

This whole passage operates on a number of levels. It is firstly, exactly as it seems, a light and inconsequential daydream, an episode of rich bathetic comedy as the author's overblown imaginings are punctured by bald and prosaic realities.

The passage is also a delightful expression of the traveller's great liberation from the restraints of time, responsibility, and even reality itself. This complex of freedoms is of particular importance to Fermor. They offer him an inner space in which he frequently luxuriates. Warm, detailed, approving descriptions of the sensations released by daydreaming, swimming, smoking and drinking probably feature more regularly in his works than in any other travel writer's. These experiences are essentially of a metaphysical nature, yet they appear so real and palpable to him that they should almost be indexed in his books like any town, person, building or monastery. Moreover, the appropriateness of celebrating such leisure in a book about Greece will be apparent to anyone who has observed the life of the *kafenion*, and their solitary customers seated for hours absorbed in a glass of water or a thimbleful of coffee.

This travel leisure, like travel scholarship, to which it is closely allied, requires further definition. It is not merely the absence of activity, though this can be a part of it. It is the one great, vital commodity so often lacking in modern industrial societies, which measure its scarcity in the hands of the clock. From the perspective of a traveller like Fermor, 'numberless dawdling afternoons in museums',[93] or the 'unnumbered hours' spent in dark halls studying voodoo in Haiti are not profligate wastes of energy.[94] These periods of leisure and the unhurried activities that fill them are an essential part of the creative traveller's life. They are, however, important to more than just the traveller. Since leisure is the free ground out of which all works of imagination or art, or thought, ultimately emerge. Travel leisure is thus one confirmation and precondition of civilisation.

The Kardamyli passage, then, is a celebration not only of the freedom travel offers, but also of the creative processes which travel can liberate. In particular, it expresses the capacity of the traveller to annihilate time and space – if only temporarily – through imagination; and to reinhabit and enjoy the past as a living and contemporary experience. This is the magical power that so many travel books in the mid twentieth century have quested for and proclaimed. Durrell, for example, while watching the dance at the festival for Saint Soulas of Soroni on Rhodes, seemed to see not merely an echo of the ancient Bacchanalian rites, but the very enactment of that most remote Greek past. Colin Thubron, in *The Hills of Adonis*, revivified the pre-Christian cults of Aphrodite and Adonis along the Lebanese coast. In *A Dragon Apparent* Norman Lewis documented his route back to prehistory through his encounter with the Moï people of Indochina, whose oral traditions still included names and descriptions of the mammoth and megatherium. Wilfred Thesiger, equally, sensed 'that nowhere in the world was there such continuity as in the Arabian desert'.

> Here Semitic nomads, resembling my companions, must
> have herded their flocks before the Pyramids were built or
> the Flood wiped out all trace of man in the Euphrates
> valley. Successive civilizations rose and fell around the
> desert's edge . . . but in the desert the nomad tribes live
> on, the pattern of their lives but little changed over this
> enormous span of time.[95]

In the hands of each of these writers – as well as others like Chatwin, Douglas, Maxwell, Stark and van der Post – the travel book can be a journey not only to another place but another time. Fermor also suggests this possibility, though the comedy in the passage above never quite permits the idea to be taken too categorically. Travellers can both summon up the past and they cannot. The traveller might rebuild the great imperial age of Greece out of a fisherman's life in his seaside shack, it might be a vision that has great clarity and personal significance, but it is without permanent foundation and cannot last. The humour in Fermor's passage is a defence against the possibility of self-deception.

Yet the humour may simultaneously disguise from the reader an important aspect of Fermor's writing. It would be easy, for instance, to enjoy the fleeting insubstantiality of the alcohol-induced daydream, without ever reflecting on the efforts by which that leisured atmosphere was re-created. We may confuse the 'vacuous and Olympian sloth' of the traveller with the immense exertions of the travel writer. This is a fundamental paradox in Fermor's books: it has cost almost a lifetime's travail to suggest what joy there can be where work is absent. A writing career of over forty years has produced, in addition to two translations, only a novella and seven travel books. Three of these are only about a hundred pages long. Between the appearance of any two of the four major works, the shortest period is eight years; while composition of Fermor's trilogy concerning his two-year trudge to Constaninople has extended over three decades. The arboreal slowness of this production – 'often three transcripts, myriad alterations, inversions, additions, subtractions, interpolations and supplements' – has resulted in a prose of such associative complexity and lyrical concision that it often more closely approximates to poetry.[96] To rip through a travel book by Fermor as if it were an adventure-filled romp and nothing more is to miss the point entirely.

The style of this prose in *Mani* and *Roumeli* is worth examining in some detail. For the writing itself seems to embody, in its very structure, in its imagery and the devices it employs, a philosophical and even spiritual message about the Greek environment that Fermor shares with other writers on the country.

Most immediately apparent is the sheer size of Fermor's vocabulary – there are probably few larger amongst twentieth-century writers of English. Here are just a few Fermor gems from a vast hoard: iod, caul, aulic, agora, snark, skete, thews, coign, fanes, neumes, soffit, imberb, ogival, rugous, pavane, plastron, hidalgo, celesta, bourdon, boojums, epigone, cicerone, narthex, melopee, caduceus, falchion, nepenthean, anabasis, gambado, skeyning, dittany, voivodes, doxology, dalmatics, iconodules, gibnut, gibbous, gallooned, spandrel, speluncar, triforium, apostropaic, coryphaeus, unfissile, semantron, saraband, stomacher, rambraced, terebinth, tramontana, heteroclite, Phlegethontic, chryselephantine. This extraordinary collection suggests an antiquarian's delight in the rare, neglected and forgotten. It also reveals a concern for words not merely as the means to ratiocination, but for their visual impact and audible quantity. When threaded on to a single line – 'corkscrew-snouted swine gimble and gyre in gloomy equinoctial wabes' – these words can elicit the primitive responses in a reader akin to those generated by an incomprehensible language.[97]

Constantly one senses behind the fabric of Fermor's prose the idea that language has material properties that can almost be

sculptured. 'I often have the impression', he wrote in the penultimate chapter of *Mani*, 'listening to a Greek argument, that I can
actually see the words spin from their mouths like the long balloons
in comic strips;'

> the noble shapes of the Greek letters, complete with their
> hard and soft breathings, the flicker of accents with the
> change of enclitic and proclitic and the hovering
> boomerangs of perispomena sail through the air and, if a
> piece of high flown language or a fragment of the liturgy
> should be embedded in the demotic flux, which it often is,
> iota subscripts dangle.[98]

Here is how he describes the voices at High Mass in a Benedictine
monastery:

> The antiphonal singing from the stall continued to build its
> invisible architecture of music: a scaffolding that sent
> columns of plain-song soaring upwards, to be completed by
> an anthem from the choir that roofed it like a canopy. The
> anthem was followed by a long stillness which seemed to be
> scooped out of the very heart of sound.[99]

It is perhaps natural that one then finds the reverse process in
Fermor's writing. Instead of the immaterial being described as if it
existed on a physical plane, one finds that concrete objects can
assume startlingly unfamiliar appearances or values. Successive
images make this idea an almost constant undertone in *Mani* and
Roumeli. So, for instance, one has 'a scattered plague of stunted
Christmas trees', an 'intervening ossuary of hillside', an 'insurrec-
tion of pink and white oleander', a 'cataract of derision and
clanking', 'an anarchy of landslides and chasms'. Their cumulative
effect is unsettling. It is as if, in Greece, the conventional parameters
of experience begin to dissolve. One often finds that those objects
that usually exist on a micro-scale become fantastically enlarged: 'a
black pyramid of olives', 'pyramids of severed heads', 'tangled
cataracts of white and black grapes'; while on an improvised plate of
fig-leaves Fermor tucks into a meal comprising 'puddles of oil' and

'detached fragments of bread' that 'look like nothing so much as the brown, treeless islets scattered round the coasts'. In Greece standard empiricism ceases to be a guide to reality. Miller echoed this idea when he wrote: 'Greece is *not* a small country – it is impressively vast'.

> No country I have visited has given me such a sense of
> grandeur. Size is not created by mileage always. In a way
> which it is beyond the comprehension of my fellow
> countrymen to grasp Greece is infinitely larger than the
> United States. Greece could swallow both the United States
> and Europe. Greece is a little like China or India. It is a
> world of illusion.[100]

It is part of that world of illusion that the physical, inanimate landscape itself assumes independent and dynamic life. A wild fig tree, for example, can gesticulate and olive trees whizz past in the dark. The sun declares a truce, tramples overhead, comes stampeding down to the attack. Mountains also rush down, the road unwinds, peaks roll, gentle foothills wave softly seawards and subside, and 'a tall thin tower silvered by the moon along one of its rectangular flanks' rises into the boiling night. In such a kaleidoscopic landscape, ironically, it is the nomadic and ever restless traveller who becomes the one still point of the turning world. However, it is not just the inanimate that has the power of transubstantiation, but also the air itself. For Fermor it 'is not merely a negative void between solids;'

> the sea itself, the houses and rocks and trees . . . are
> embedded in it; it is alive and positive and volatile and one
> is as aware of its contact as if it could . . . be grasped in
> handfuls, tapped for electricity, bottled, used for blasting,
> set fire to, sliced into sparkling cubes . . . pounded down
> with pestle and mortar for cocaine, drunk from a ballet
> shoe, or spun, woven and worn on solemn feasts.[101]

And in Greece there is yet one further factor subverting the traveller's ordinary perceptions – the light. Durrell believed the 'magnesium-flare quality' of the sunlight was the key factor separating Greece from Italy or Spain, and called it 'the naked eyeball of God' with the power to blind;[102] for Fermor 'it acts like an X-ray, giving mineral and tree and masonry an air of transparence'.[103] Its impact was to re-order the values of solid object and that object's shadow, so that the outline cast by a tree-trunk or passing bird becomes more real than the physical items themselves, which 'the light, by comparison, has immaterialized'. Miller also sensed its extraordinary qualities: 'it is not the light of the Mediterranean alone,' he wrote, 'it is something more, something unfathomable, something holy. Here the light penetrates directly to the soul, opens the doors and windows of the heart, makes one naked, exposed, isolated in a metaphysical bliss'.[104]

At times these three authors, whose ideas and language have perhaps ricocheted off each other's, have described their experiences of Greece, not in terms of mere physical activity. For them, movement through the Greek environment impelled a sort of sannyasin's pilgrimage, where the conventional route-markers, the simple quotidian realities on which they might have relied, could disintegrate entirely. The standard divisions between interior and external worlds begin to blur, and physical, immanent landscapes are revealed as simply veils of illusion, demanding penetration. On the first page of his first book on Greece, Lawrence Durrell summed up the impact of these experiences in only six lines:

> You enter Greece as one might enter a dark crystal; the
> form of things becomes irregular, refracted. Mirages
> suddenly swallow islands, and wherever you look the
> trembling curtain of atmosphere deceives.
>   Other countries may offer you discoveries in manner or
> lore or landscape; Greece offers you something harder – the
> discovery of yourself.

Perhaps only one country this century has inspired more books of place and travel. No country – not even Arabia, India or China – has given rise to a richer collection of works, or played a more important part in the genre in the last fifty years. No country could. In Greece, mid century, there existed an extraordinary constellation of circumstances to inspire recent British travellers. By the time industrial society reached the blinding terminus at Hiroshima, many of these felt that there was only one direction to go – backwards. Other parts of the world offered that possibility, but in Greece, both Christian and European, one could make pilgrimage all the way back to something like the origins of the home country itself, which is perhaps these travellers' real destination. Parts of Spain or Italy might still inspire those same rich nostalgias, but in Hellas there were other key factors. In a history of human civilisation, for instance, where Greece would absorb several chapters, Spain might appear on a page or two. While in the Eastern Mediterranean the air was still alive with the rank odour of goat and the scent of wild thyme, in the west any imaginative space was being trampled flat by the Falangist jackboot or the tourist's flip-flop. Greeks had, in addition, what Durrell called that 'quixotic irrational love of England which no other nation' seemed to have.[105] And who knows? Possibly there is something in the Greek air and light, in its wine-dark seas and myth-darkened mountains, that points the way to deeper experiences. Certainly it inspired one American and four Anglo-Irish works of exceptional quality, one of which, in this author's opinion, is as near to perfection as a travel book has come.

Chapter IX
The Real Tibet of my Imagination

The only place that might challenge Greece, in terms of the sheer volume of British travel books it has inspired this century, is Tibet. Yet, ironically, it remains even today amongst those countries least visited by Western travellers. At the turn of the century there were probably fewer than fifty living Europeans or North Americans who had crossed its borders. Not one of these had seen its capital. The last Briton to have done so was Thomas Manning, nearly ninety years earlier; and when he arrived in Lhasa in December 1811, he was also the first. Curiously, it was those geographical and political circumstances so restricting access to Tibet which have contributed to the country being so frequently described, since almost every person fortunate to have got there felt that he or she had something valuable to say.

One of the most significant facets of these Tibetan travel books, separating them from those on almost all other places, is that for a period they were the principal source of information on the country. While there might have been a similar abundance of travel writing on Greece, it did not determine the foreigner's perception of Hellenic life. It was simply one portion of an immense literature by and about Greeks. Moreover, Greece projected its own image overseas through a worldwide network of embassies, through its newspapers and other organs of international representation. It also had a large expatriate population – a globally dispersed diaspora that Patrick Leigh Fermor has celebrated in one of the most extravagant sentences in all travel literature.[1]

Tibet was different. Until its invasion and military occupation by the Chinese in 1950, which eventually brought about a large-scale exodus of refugees, the country and its people had been extraordinarily self-contained. They had no diplomats overseas, nor accepted foreign representation in their capital except from immediate neighbours – Bhutan, China, Nepal, and, later, from British then independent India. Only a minute number of Tibetans had ever left the national borders, let alone the Asian continent. Their deep isolation was further confirmed by the absence, even until the late 1940s, of any airport, any roads, and all but the most basic telecommunications. Although Tibetan Buddhist monks and saints had produced an extensive religious literature, little of it was widely known outside Central Asia before 1900. Until the mid 1920s and the detailed studies of the British diplomat, Sir Charles Bell, and scholars like the Italian Professor Guiseppe Tucci, there were virtually no general accounts of its history or culture. For the first five decades of the twentieth century, Tibet was quite literally the domain of the travel book. Even today acquaintance with Tibetan life is most usually obtained through the pages of works like Heinrich Harrer's bestselling *Seven Years in Tibet.*

Not only was this trans-Himalayan region the preserve of the travel book, but these works were the vehicle for a set of Western ideas, in fact, an entire mythology that was perhaps more extraordinary than that attaching to any other country. It was a myth that persisted even beyond the date when Tibet ceased to exist as an independent or even coherent political and cultural entity. By overlaying and obscuring a no less remarkable reality, the legend served sometimes to distort international understanding of Tibet; and in many ways it revealed more about the fantasies and aspirations of Western industrial society than it did about the country that it was meant to explain. The nature and function of the myth about Tibet, as expressed through the travel book, is one of the most significant themes of the genre in the twentieth century.

It is a legend that had its origins in a number of interlocking background factors, one of which concerned the state of affairs in the obsessively competitive game of exploration at the end of the nineteenth century. By that period, Africa, so long the focus of European overseas attention, was largely exhausted as a theatre of operation. The basic division of territorial spoils had been agreed by the colonial powers, while most of the burning questions of African geography had been answered. The Congo, the Nile and Niger had been mapped to their source, Livingstone had been found, the previously forbidden cities of Timbuktu and Harar had been penetrated and described. Discounting the two poles, of the three major blank spaces on the globe – Amazonia, Arabia and Central Asia – only the last two were of any real geopolitical importance to the British.

The Arabian interior was theoretically close to the lines of communication with Britain's imperial possessions in Africa and the East. Moreover, it bordered a whole host of British outposts on the shores of the Persian Gulf and Indian Ocean. However, the Arabian deserts were marginal to British political interests and they remained economically backward. By the time of the discovery of Arabian oil, Arabian exploration had largely become the personal fiefdom of a single individual – Sheikh Abdullah Philby.

Tibet was in a different category. It was an immense region, covering an area equal to three-quarters of Europe, and stood at the meeting point of three competing empires – the British, the Chinese and the Russian. With the exception of 800 kilometres represented by the independent kingdom of Nepal, British India and Tibet enjoyed a border that stretched almost the entire length of the Himalaya. Largely consisting of barren mountains and high-altitude desert, when viewed through the lens of imperial paranoia, Tibet's wastelands assumed considerable strategic significance. These were one of the playing fields of the Great Game – that curiously nineteenth-century version of the Cold War, in which the English and the Russians sought to out-manoeuvre their rival from Persia to the borders of Assam. 'As a student of Russian aspirations and methods for fifteen years', wrote George Curzon, first Indian Viceroy of the twentieth century and a principal player in the Great Game, 'I assert with confidence what I do not think any of her own statesmen would deny – that her ultimate ambition is the dominion of Asia'.[2] Exercised by a vision of Russian hordes streaming through Himalayan passes onto the plains of India, the British thought of Tibet as a crucial buffer state between the two empires.

Unfortunately, British attempts to influence Tibetan politics had been singularly unsuccessful. Apart from diplomatic missions sent by the Governor of Bengal, Warren Hastings, in 1774 and again in 1783, there had been almost no official contact between the two countries. China, the nominal suzerain power in Lhasa since the eighteenth century, had long worked on Tibetan suspicions concerning the great power on their southern frontier. Eventually, foreign policy in Lhasa expressed only a single national impulse – a desire to exclude all Europeans. Successive attempts to enter the Tibetan capital by American, British, Canadian, French, Russian and Swedish explorers had all been halted and turned back. From the 1860s onwards British intelligence officers had used another strategy to fill some of the political and geographical blanks on the map of their northern borders. Agents, drawn from the Himalayan communities under Indian control and resembling Tibetans in appearance, crossed the mountains disguised as pilgrims. These Asian spies, known collectively as the Pundits, were able to travel extensively in trans-Himalayan regions, even as far as Mongolia, and brought back an enormous quantity of intelligence.

The Pundits' work involved enormous risks. Exposure might easily have meant execution; while at least one of the European adventurers, a Frenchman, had been killed and a Briton repeatedly tortured.[3] The Tibetan officials who failed to recognise and halt foreign visitors were also severely punished. Despite these dangers, almost because of them, there was no shortage of willing explorers. Such was the political sensitivity of the region that anyone completing a successful visit could be sure of the plaudits of the home country. Eric Bailey's second expedition in eastern Tibet during 1913 was a typical example. Prior to departure he had known of a forthcoming conference between Britain, China and Tibet that was intended to settle outstanding political problems. By exploring previously unmapped border areas, Bailey and Morshead were able to contribute substantially to the conference's efforts to delimit an Indo-Tibetan frontier. In doing so, the two men could count on the gratitude of their superiors, and in 1915 Bailey was made a Companion of the Order of the Indian Empire.

Although the geopolitical spin-offs could often explain a British or Russian preoccupation with trans-Himalayan exploration, clearly they were a less relevant motive for a French, a Swedish or an American traveller. One of the other key factors stimulating the Western obsession with Tibet was the extraordinary geographical richness of the area. At an average altitude of 5,000 metres it is the highest country in the world. Even the most straightforward route from British India to Lhasa involved the crossing of passes higher than the tallest mountain in Europe. Tibet's borders enclosed much of the greatest mountain chain on earth and the tallest mountain on earth. Even those who felt contempt for its people were happy to admit that they had never faced a more sublime or terrible landscape.

The Northern Plateau, known as the Chang Tang, was the ultimate challenge. For almost a million square kilometres, sparsely vegetated grasslands and internally draining marshes sweep upwards to smooth-topped peaks, then fall away in apparently endless succession. At a distance, in panorama, the soft, cumulative folds in this landscape have an almost feminine sinuosity. Yet it is utterly desolate. The Chang Tang could swallow both France and the United Kingdom comfortably, and it has one of the harshest climates on the planet. To indicate the austerity of their crossing, the nineteenth-century French missionaries, Evariste-Régis Huc and Joseph Gabet, described how they lived off barley flour moistened in yak-butter tea for two months. This bland mixture was rolled into balls, which the Frenchmen held in warmed pouches next to their bodies. This was then kept inside a thick sheepskin robe, inside a lambskin jacket, inside a foxskin cloak, inside a great woollen overall. Despite these measures their flour balls froze.[4]

Another of Tibet's compelling attractions was the complexity of its drainage systems. The relationship between the country's principal river, the Tsangpo, and the three major tributaries of the Brahmaputra, discussed earlier in Chapter 2, had been a great puzzle for nineteenth-century geographers. One of the most remarkable of all the episodes in the story of the Pundits concerns the efforts of Kintup – a Sikkimese agent codenamed K.P. – to fix which of the three tributaries the Tsangpo joined. The method of identification involved sending 500 specially marked logs down the Tsangpo. In order to alert the British authorities to look out for his logs he had to walk from the Tsangpo to Lhasa, send a letter and then return. This involved a trek of more than 800 kilometres. After four years away, two of which had been spent in servitude after his fellow-agent had sold him as a slave, Kintup returned to find that the logs had floated down to the Bay of Bengal completely unnoticed. His letter to alert the British authorities had never reached them.[5]

The Tsangpo/Brahmaputra relationship was only one of a number of riddles. The putative existence of great Tibetan falls rivalling Niagara, the fabled Tsangpo Falls, was, according to Kingdon Ward, 'the great romance of geography'; but then Ward was himself a famous Tibetan traveller, and perhaps partisan when it came to awarding such titles.[6] However, six more of Asia's great rivers – the Ganges, Indus, Mekong, Salween, Sutlej and Yangtze – had their sources in Tibet, and none of them had been completely mapped by the turn of the century.

Perhaps most remarkable of all Tibet's geographical conundrums concerned Mount Kailas and the holy lake at its base – Manasarowar. To people of the Buddhist and Hindu faiths, Kailas was the traditional centre of the universe and the most sacred place of pilgrimage. Even today it remains a deeply holy site. Hindus believed it to be Mount Meru, the home of their god Siva, and it was celebrated in their sacred texts, the *Puranas*, as the source of four mighty rivers that flowed outwards to the four corners of the earth. Behind this myth was actually a substantial amount of truth. For the Tsangpo/Brahmaputra, the Indus, Sutlej and the Karnali, one of the principal tributaries of the Ganges, all rose virtually within sight of Mount Kailas. As we have seen, the desire to be the first to follow the world's great rivers to their source had always been one of the most powerful motivating forces amongst nineteenth-century explorers. Here, at Mount Kailas, the ambitions of Western geography mingled inextricably with the emotions aroused by Oriental cosmology. It was a heady mixture, and for decades the area drew one traveller after another.

In addition to the wide spectrum of unresolved political and geographical issues associated with the trans-Himalayan region, there was one further dimension to the Tibetan landscape that made it such a compelling attraction for Western travellers. This concerned the remarkable condition of its cultural and political life, which was almost entirely dominated by Buddhism. By the early

1950s, when the first British nuclear bombs had been exploded off the Monte Bello Islands near Australia, Tibet was still a feudal theocracy arranged along lines that approximated to those in the early medieval states of Europe. Its temporal leader, the Dalai Lama, was also its spiritual head and worshipped by the Buddhist communities of Central Asia as a living deity – a reincarnation of the Tibetan god of mercy, Chenrezi. Apart from those filled by its feudal aristocracy, most Tibetan high political offices were occupied by the country's spiritual élite. In many spheres, state affairs and religious ritual were indivisible. National policy, for instance, could be decided by omens or horoscopes or the utterance of state oracles during a condition of trance.

Even well away from Lhasa and all its national ecclesiastical institutions, pious observance was a constant in ordinary Tibetan life. Monasteries, often rising eerily from crags and mountain tops, commanded the skyline in almost every human settlement. Their religious communities represented perhaps as much as a quarter of Tibet's entire male population. Each village had its chortens – whitewashed, decorated structures whose design embodied a complex spiritual symbolism. There were also huge prayer wheels which were thought to send out positive energies when turned by passers-by. Religious texts were carved into suitable rockfaces and other natural features, and most of the rough roads in the country were punctuated by cairns built entirely of stones inscribed with prayers and deposited by travellers. Above individual houses, on poles, rose lengths of cloth completely covered with scriptural verse, which Tibetans believed to be carried to the heavens on each gust of wind. Pilgrims and pilgrimage were a feature of daily life. Many people, even in the course of domestic chores, fingered rosaries or whirled personal prayer wheels, whose revolutions were accompanied by the constant muttering of Tibet's all-embracing mantra – 'Om Mani Padme Hum'.

The quotidian life of a simple Tibetan village expressed a *Weltanschauung* fundamentally alien to the mind of the white colonial people living south of the Himalayan range. Yet these everyday expressions of their faith demanded only a small leap of the sympathetic imagination in order for the average British rationalist to comprehend them, particularly when compared with the more esoteric practices that were found in Tibet. Some of the most difficult sacred texts of Mahayana Buddhism, for example, like the Tantras, were known only to lamas of high spiritual attainment, and they would only communicate their learning to a select band of disciples. Without such personal initiation the content and meaning of these scriptures remained hidden behind an impenetrably symbolic language. Only when initiates had bound themselves to their guru by vows of obedience would the dark screen be lifted. Such secretive religious traditions were fertile ground for speculation, and it was widely believed that some of these holy men were endowed with extraordinary psychic and physical powers. Tibetan religious literature was filled with tales of lamas who had lived in isolated caves and, in the course of retreats lasting several years, had survived with almost no food. By various yogic practices they had also been able to generate bodily heat spontaneously, and could continue their meditations in the absence of fire and even clothes. Other fantastic stories featured monks with the power of levitation, or of flight, or to move immense weights. The Dalai Lama himself was credited by Tibetans with the capacity to be in two places simultaneously.

The inscrutable ways of the Orient were a commonplace amongst Victorians. Writing of the British expedition to Lhasa which Eric Bailey had accompanied in 1903, the traveller Peter Fleming wrote:

> The men and women of their generation regarded the East
> as mysterious. They saw Asia as possessing – they almost
> willed it to possess – some inner, hidden quality which
> Europe lacked. Of what this quality consisted they were not
> sure. Wisdom? Spirituality? Ripeness? They could not say;
> they knew only that there was *something* there, something of
> which the proudest among them was prepared to stand in
> awe.[7]

Even the most hard-boiled adept of Asian *realpolitik*, George Curzon, announced: 'The East . . . is a temple where the suppliant adores but never catches sight of the object of his devotion. It is a journey the goal of which is always in sight but is never attained.'[8]

Views like these were almost certainly linked to the scientific and

technological thrust of intellectual life in eighteenth- and nineteenth-century Europe. The Victorians' burning desire to know,
for instance, had brought them face to face with the fact that they
had not been fashioned in God's image, but with a striking
resemblance to a monkey. Such a mundane genealogy was deeply
disorienting. Moreover, geography, like all the other empirical
systems of enquiry, had established whole continents of knowledge
but at the expense of a different province – the unknown. Yet it
seemed the second was as important to the human spirit as the first.
Or why else would the West have believed in, and become
increasingly obsessed with, the mysteries of the East? It was
because the Orient held out the last hope of those magical
possibilities, the transcendence of a grinding, inexorable predetermined machinery, to which materialist Europeans had confined all
life.

Amongst the countries of the Orient, Tibet seemed to represent
the final domain of that magic. The dark spaces in the Western
psyche found their most fitting correlative in the eerie, wind-
tormented uplands of Central Asia. It was a vast region, most of it
was unknown and unvisited, and to the European mind its cultural
life appeared inexplicable. Unwittingly perhaps, it was the
Tibetans themselves who had provided the West with that final
confirmation that their land did hold the planet's last great secrets.
By systematically blocking all attempts at exploration, or any form
of international intercourse, they seemed to behave as if there was
something to hide. Certainly, they fuelled the fascination, and to
the peculiarly masculine psyche of colonial Europe, being spurned
in this way became itself a justification for penetrating Tibet's
forbidden valleys. It was exactly this complex of ideas that Austine
Waddell, Buddhist scholar and member of the British expedition to
Tibet, expressed in the opening lines of his book, *Lhasa and Its
Mysteries*:

> Wreathed in the romance of centuries . . . the secret citadel
> of the 'undying' Grand Lama, has stood shrouded in
> impenetrable mystery on the Roof-of-the-World, alluring
> yet defying our most adventurous travellers to enter her
> closed gates. With all the fascination of an unsolved enigma,

the mysterious city has held the imagination captive, as one of
the last of the secret places of the earth, as the Mecca of East
Asia.[9]

Thinking along much the same lines, George Curzon wrote: 'In the
heart of Asia lasts to this day the one mystery which the nineteenth
century has still left to the twentieth to explore – the Tibetan oracle
of Lhasa'.[10]

It was undoubtedly the case that Tibet and the extraordinary
cultural life of its people were rich, complex and fundamentally
different, but the mystery existed nowhere so much as in the
preconceived mental images of the foreigners who went there.
These ideas were so firmly in place by the start of the twentieth
century that it was an almost ineradicable portion of their
experience north of the Himalaya. The ideas persist even today.
The efforts of Western travellers to come to terms with them
resulted in writings that can seem, in retrospect, highly comical and
at times deeply hypocritical. For what they were attempting to do
was the intellectual equivalent of catching their own shadow. The
mountaineer and explorer Frederick Spencer Chapman expressed it
perfectly when he wrote, without any apparent awareness of his
solecism, 'Gradually the country became transformed, and we
entered the real Tibet of my imagination.'[11]

The *annus mirabilis* for British travel writing on the country was
1905 – the year after Sir Francis Younghusband's successful
expedition to Lhasa, which resulted in the signing of an Anglo-
Tibetan convention. Viceroy Curzon, wishing to pre-empt what
he saw as a Russian manoeuvre to gain ascendancy in the Tibetan
capital, had championed the idea of a diplomatic mission and
selected his old friend to lead it. However, with one side unwilling
to negotiate and deeply resentful of foreign intrusion, the diplomatic mission eventually became a military invasion. Small-scale
battles punctuated British progress to Lhasa, which was occupied in
August 1904. The fighting, however, was a strikingly one-sided
affair. The Tibetans, equipped with primitive matchlocks or
weapons typical of the Middle Ages, were faced with an efficient
well-armed modern force and the difference showed in their
respective casualty figures. The Tibetans lost about 1,500 men for a

dozen on the British side. Peter Fleming, author of a penetrating account of the 1903–1904 mission, *Bayonets To Lhasa*, described it as 'a campaign scarcely matched in the annals of war either for its administrative difficulties or for the combination of audacity and humanity with which it was conducted.'[12]

Perhaps one of the incidents Fleming had in mind, when he made this judgement, was the engagement at Guru which took place on 31 March 1904. During this grotesque débâcle the British surrounded a Tibetan force huddled behind a low defensive wall, and attempted to disarm it. This was a signal for pandemonium, shots rang out and an Indian sepoy was hit in the face. The order of the commanding British officer was 'to make as big a bag as possible', and only ninety seconds after the Maxim guns had opened up, 500 Tibetans were dead or dying.[13] The British then quickly set about the medical care of the 200 Tibetan wounded. Their own casualties numbered six, none fatal. Younghusband called it a 'terrible and ghastly business'.[14]

The immediate consequences of the mission were not those for which its principal sponsor and its participants had hoped. Younghusband was to be ceremoniously insulted, while the home government quickly abandoned a number of the concessions he had won from Tibet in the convention. Moreover, the nation that most increased its influence in Lhasa in the short term was not Britain, nor Russia, but China. Yet the expedition did initiate a period of increased contact between the British and Tibetans and paved the way for cordial relations that lasted almost half a century. It also led to a flurry of books about the place, by the British officers and newspaper correspondents who had gone there.

Lhasa and Its Mysteries, The Opening of Tibet, The Unveiling of Lhasa, To Lhasa At Last, The Truth About Tibet – these were the works that appeared in the months after the mission's return. Collectively, the titles suggest the extent to which the mission participants felt that it was their journey that had at last put Tibet on the record. It was no longer a matter for conjecture; the place had been done, and here were the facts once and for all. It was, of course, the classic sales pitch of the publishing world, but there lay behind it a genuine belief that the mysteries were largely cleared up. And indeed the journalists and officers did bring back an enormous amount of information, and their books were long and detailed.

However, what these authors seemed unwilling to take account of was the fact that there already existed a fairly substantial literature about Tibet. At least, it was a substantial as the literature that the British might have had on, say, the parts of Indochina that now form Cambodia, or the Philippine island of Mindanao, and neither of these would have retained any claims to mystery. Moreover, in the last half of the nineteenth century the number of Tibetan books published had been gathering pace. There were even works by or about people who had got to Lhasa – Manning in 1811, Gabet and Huc in 1846 and one of the Pundits, Sarat Chandra Das, in 1882. Most of the various European adventurers who had attempted to equal Gabet and Huc's feat, in the 1870s, 1880s and 1890s, also produced books about Tibet if not about its capital. The experiences of all these pioneers, even those of the later British expedition members, were basically the same. They were out-siders, they were officially unwelcome, as a travelling party they were usually fairly self-contained, and their relations with Tibetans were no deeper (nor more superficial) than those of anyone travelling fairly quickly through a foreign country. What was so ironic about the batch of books that appeared in 1905 was that, while they were billed as the great exposé on Tibet, and while there was, indeed, an enormous amount still to be discovered about life beyond the Himalaya, they largely revealed the very things that had already been said.

The other object that these books failed to achieve was to extinguish the myth of mysteriousness. The idea rolled on down the decades, helping to sell each new addition to the growing Tibetan library. Even in 1953 the blurb to Harrer's multi-million-selling *Seven Years in Tibet* could announce: 'Now and then, very infrequently, a European or an American has made his way into mysterious Tibet for a short stay on a specific mission. But no man has ever gone into that strange land in the same circumstance . . . or stayed there anything like so long'. Like all blurbs, this one took liberties with the truth, especially in view of the fact that Harrer's book would take its place on the library shelf where one could already find a volume entitled *Twenty Years in Tibet*, by David Macdonald.

As late as 1982 the author of a highly competent book on the country still felt it appropriate to write: 'Even with the arrival of satellite photography it remains to this day the least known, least explored country on earth, rich in mysteries, still beckoning us with its secrets and still denying us the answer – a vacuum at the centre of the world.'[15] While it might be true that there are Tibetan areas unvisited by Europeans, there are probably still portions of Australia or Canada that would fall in much the same category or, at least, that have been visited by only a minuscule number. Yet how many would suggest that they too were 'rich in mysteries' or that they beckon us with their secrets? Moreover, like vast areas of Canadian and Australian territory, major portions of Tibet consist of only a single biome. While large areas of this might be unmapped, equally large areas have been; and to have seen and experienced one stretch of high-altitude grassland is to be able to predict almost exactly what the other unvisited portions will look like and consist of. More important than this, all of the country will have been seen by the people who have lived there for millennia – the Tibetans. By these processes of association all of Tibet is familiar now. Yet this situation seems insufficient to rob the region of its mystery tag. In fact, the reverse would seem to be the case. Until every last square centimetre of these unseen areas has been tramped over and logged down by white men, Tibet as a whole will retain for them the allure of *terra incognita*.

Perhaps another by-product of the country's Forbidden-Land legend is an issue raised earlier – the willingness of travellers, particularly the British, to repeat the information provided by their forebears. The similarities between one account of Tibet and the next, as previously observed, derived partly from the similarities in the experiences of the travellers. They were also a product of the closeness in training and outlook of the personnel who gained access to the country. They were usually soldiers or political officers of the Raj. Even the most sympathetic amongst them, like Younghusband, were accustomed to see the Asiatic client states or neighbours on their northern frontiers – the Bhutanese, Sikkimese, Nepalese and Tibetans – as cultural and technological inferiors. In addition, because they were dignitaries of a foreign government, they were treated by the Tibetans and expected to be treated by them according to prescribed diplomatic rules. This official status thus largely determined the nature and level of their social relations.

There were also other factors at work. Their time in the country was often relatively brief, and their knowledge of the language was restricted, if only because Tibetan is particularly complex. Frederick O'Connor, interpreter for Younghusband during 1903–1904, explained how he could make a perfectly intelligible sentence out of thirteen words all of which sounded like 'ta'.[16] Moreover, there were certain fixtures in the Tibetan physical and human landscape that in particular seemed to galvanise the European imagination. The theory of reincarnation was one of these. Tibetan cultural life is unintelligible without even a cursory awareness of its function, and virtually every book on the country has described how the temporal and spiritual leader, the Dalai Lama, is believed to be a reincarnation of the last incumbent, that shortly after the latter's death, a delegation of monks goes in search of the successor, that the discovery and selection of the new god-child depends firstly on the infant having certain physical attributes and secondly on his response to a number of the last ruler's possessions. Another of the fixtures that all felt obliged to record was the Tibetan system of disposing of the dead. Because the ground was often too frozen to dig a grave and wood too scarce for cremation, the people cut up their deceased relatives to feed to the vultures and dogs.

Aspects of Tibetan life like these obviously made a profound impression on foreigners. Their very strangeness commanded attention and then their appearance in any subsequent written account, even if virtually every previous book had already mentioned it. But there was almost certainly another factor at work, which is particularly apparent when one considers another ubiquitous feature of Tibetan life – their method for preparing tea.

In his book *Black River of Tibet*, John Hanbury-Tracy, an explorer who had attempted to map the upper reaches of the Salween, explained that the Tibetan drink was a mixture of tea, salt, butter and water.

This startling but invigorating brew formed a staple part of our diet in Tibet. The butter should be of a certain vintage if the mixture is to be up to standard. To appreciate it you should banish your preconceived notions of tea and reflect that you are drinking rich salty soup. Then it is excellent.[17]

What makes his comment particularly interesting is that Hanbury-Tracy's companion on his two-year expedition during 1935–6 was a man called Ronald Kaulback. The latter had himself already made a journey in Tibet in 1933 and had written a book on these experiences, entitled *Tibetan Trek*, which Hanbury-Tracy would certainly have read. Early on in this work, Kaulback had explained that tea in Tibet was made in 'a cylindrical churn . . . violently mixed with rancid butter, salt, and soda . . . The result is not much like tea in our sense of the word. It tastes something like soup, and is very warming and sustaining'.[18]

What makes Kaulback's statement doubly interesting is that his companion on the earlier 1933 expedition was Frank Kingdon Ward, author of a 1913 travel work, *The Land of the Blue Poppy*. Kaulback, and even Hanbury-Tracy, would certainly have read Ward's classic account of his experiences in the Sino-Tibetan borderlands. Yet in Ward's book, when he was already echoing a whole host of predecessors right back to Abbé Huc in 1851, he himself had written about the Tibetan brew:

Taken hot from a cup, as tea, the Englishman is apt to find it nauseating, particularly when there are yak hairs from the butter generously distributed throughout it; but taken hot with a spoon, as soup, it is quite palatable. Such is the power of the association of ideas.[19]

There seem to be two, in many ways opposing, strands of thought operating behind these extraordinary repetitions. On the one hand, there is internal evidence in Kaulback's and then Hanbury-Tracy's books that the authors had some impression of the type of people who would read them. For example, when introducing British personnel that a man like Kaulback met en route, there was no attempt to give context to the name Tom Farrell – other than to indicate he was the Assistant Commandant at Sadiya – or to identify H. Clutterbuck, except to say he had been an earlier companion of Kingdon Ward. Conversely, when mentioning an uncle living in Calcutta, Kaulback felt it might be helpful to add to the reference '(H. P. V. Townend of the I.C.S.)'. These names are surely inserted and left to stand on their own by Kaulback because there was a presumption that the reader was someone like himself – one who would recognise these names, because they had either read about them before or even knew the characters personally, or at least had friends of friends who knew them. They were also, therefore, part of that community already familiar with travel books on Tibet. There is even a good indication that the later authors thought their own readers were exactly the people who would have already read Kingdon Ward's many book of Tibetan travel. This is surely the reason behind Kingdon Ward's introduction to Kaulback's *Tibetan Trek*: a recommendation by the old hand for one who was ploughing exactly the same furrow.

Yet despite all this the authors still persisted in their repetitions, down sometimes to the smallest nuance or detail. The other strand of the author's thinking that may explain this has to do with the myth of Tibet as the great unknown. Just as each traveller felt that the country and its ways were always mysterious virgin soils, so the audience he or she later addressed was always a clean slate. Just as everything the traveller encountered in Tibet was a startling discovery for him- or herself, so it would come as a startling revelation to his or her readers. The myth of mystery had spawned its associated myth of ignorance. There was no possibility of a reader acquiring a cumulative understanding of the subject. Each time it was necessary to start from scratch, revealing in detail every aspect of the author's personal experiences in Tibet. Not only did this myth of ignorance license repetition, but, more insidious, also error and misrepresentation. It was possible to say anything because no one knew any better. Even these seemingly innocuous passages about tea confirm the point. As Professor Goldstein, author of the monumental *A History of Modern Tibet: 1913–1951*, has pointed out: 'The oft-repeated comment that Tibetans particularly appreciate rancid butter in their tea is one of the ridiculously untrue myths about Tibet.'[20]

An even worse consequence of the Tibetan legend was the deep sense of anticlimax that some European travellers could experience when they discovered the real thing was not quite as they had imagined. This was largely true of the members of the British 1903–1904 mission, which, once it had got to the Forbidden City and completed its sightseeing, filled the boredom with gymkhanas, race-meetings, shooting contests and football matches.[21] Not that a sense of disappointment was entirely beyond comprehension. Although Tibet could have been utterly absorbing for anyone with the inclination to plumb its depths, it was also an extraordinarily difficult environment. Just simply getting there demanded enormous physical stamina. The altitude strained foreigners unaccustomed to operating five kilometres above sea-level, and many suffered from headaches, nausea, sleeplessness and irritability. Not only was Tibet high, it was cold. When the British were obliged to over-winter they experienced the most severe conditions. At night, even when fully clothed and covered with blankets from head to toe, it was impossible to sleep for hours. A stray arm or hand uncovered during the hours of darkness might mean frostbite or pneumonia by the morning. Ink solidified in its pen, boiled eggs cracked and splintered in the mouth, oil froze in rifles. The comparatively large number of troops and transport staff placed large burdens on local supplies of food and fuel. Much of it had to be brought up from India by over 10,000 porters and nearly 20,000 pack animals. Casualties amongst the former numbered eighty-eight, while losses of the latter amounted to more than 7,000.[22] This plethora of elemental difficulties delayed them considerably. It should also have exorcised for all the time the vision of Russian armies pouring effortlessly across the Tibetan tableland to ravage lowland India.

If the mission had expected Tibet to be populated with white-robed monks serene in the knowledge of the earth's ancient secrets and capable of pyrotechnical displays of magic like something out of the Arabian Nights, they were rapidly disabused. The ordinary Tibetan people were, in fact, immensely resilient and were able to find in their austere lives a constant source of humour, if not hilarity. They were, even in the face of military invasion, humble, affectionate, helpful and inquisitive. They were also flea-ridden and incredibly dirty and lived amongst considerable domestic squalor. Men like Austine Waddell, who had served for a decade as the assistant sanitary commissioner in the Indian medical service, found this intolerable. He thought one place en route, Phari, 'possibly the dirtiest and foulest town on earth'.

> The people . . . are sunk in almost the lowest depths of savagery. Clothed in greasy rags and sheepskins, their ugly flat features scourged by the cold and seared by the frost, begrimed and blackened like a chimney-sweep's with the deeply ingrained dirt and smoke of years, they were indeed repulsively hideous. [23]

Finding that things were not as he had dreamed, Waddell wrote as if his exposé of actual conditions were a triumph of realism. 'Now', he wrote of the country, '. . . her closed doors are broken down, her dark veil of mystery is lifted up, and the long-sealed shrine, with its grotesque cults and idolised Grand Lama, shorn of his sham nimbus, have yielded up their secrets, and lie disenchanted before our Western eyes'. [24] This was a classic case of projection. In Waddell's mind it was not the West which had given rise to the idea of a land of magic and mystery beyond the Himalaya, it was the Tibetans themselves. It was they who had tried to suggest that Tibet was wonderful, when in fact, it was incredibly tough and grimy. It was they who tried to deceive the world. For had they not been 'alluring yet defying our most adventurous travellers to enter her closed gates'? When the British invaded with the shining light of science and exposed Tibet for the dirty fake she was, she had got no more than was already coming to her.

In Waddell's presentation of affairs one finds the standard thought processes of the anti-Semite or the rapist. What is so fascinating and repugnant about his book, which is shot through with a post-coital disappointment, are the bizarre distortions that his mind could encompass. At one point he claimed that 'notwith-standing the magnificent defence which the Himalayas afforded to India on the east, it is not the Himalayas but the vast and lofty plateau to the north of them and of Tibet, the great desert wall of the Kuen Lun plateau which forms India's scientific frontier'. [25] This is an extraordinary statement. An equivalent would be for the Greeks to claim the Caucasus as their natural frontier, or the Portuguese to define the Alps as a 'scientific' border. However, this unreason reached its climax when Waddell suggested that while the Tibetans 'were entitled to the credit which belongs to brave men defending their homes against odds', it must be qualified by the fact that they were enemies, 'not only of ourselves, but in some sense, by reason of their savagery and superstition, of the human race'.[26] Thus, the invasion of a foreign country and occupation of its capital – for which a modern equivalent, in certain respects, would be the Soviet tanks rumbling into Prague – have metamorphosed into the high-altitude defence of humankind.[27]

The response of the early British visitors to the monastic communities of Tibet could be equally ambivalent and at times deeply hostile. The lamas played a multiple rôle in Tibetan society, as guardians of the spiritual flame and arbiters of the country's cultural life, and also as the main power élite in the government. They were the sector of the population that most vociferously opposed European penetration, and it was their unwillingness to accommodate Younghusband's mission that largely determined the British response to them. Waddell referred to 'hosts of vampire priests', and spoke of their 'exasperating hostility and insolence'.[28] Even more than thirty years later, Spencer Chapman, accompanying another delegation as secretary to the political officer Basil Gould, called them 'unwashed insolent parasites'.[29] 'I wish I could like these hostile inscrutable monks, but I cannot see what good they do either to themselves or anybody else.'[30]

The monks themselves justified their antagonism as the defence of their own unique culture and religion against expansionist foreigners. Abbé Huc, as long ago as the 1840s, thought it 'probable that the English would not be excluded more than any other nation, had not their invasive march into Hindoostan inspired the [Dalai] Lama with a natural terror'.[31] However, men like Chapman and Waddell felt there was a more selfish motive for the monks' aggression. 'Only occasionally does a monk gaze at one with sullen malevolence', wrote the former, 'perhaps realizing that we represent progress, and that progress spells the end of the unquestioned and unquestioning power of Lamaism'.[32] In short, Tibet's priesthood was a privileged class defending its own material interests. What Chapman seemed unwilling to allow was that the monks held a position in Tibet in some ways analogous to his own in British

India. In both countries there existed a rigidly stratified society governed by a minority, and in each that oligarchy would have justified its control of power with the same arguments: that they were ruling in the interests of the entire community and they were the ones best fitted to do so.

However much this might have vitiated the moral stance of an Indian Civil Service man or a British officer, it did not lessen the accuracy of some of the comments made by visitors like Chapman and Waddell. There was deep injustice in Tibet. The monasteries and the aristocracy held huge estates and commanded much of the country's wealth, while large numbers of serfs lived in conditions of near slavery. The justice meted out to these peasants could be arbitrary and medieval by the usual standards of British India. One visitor to Tibet in the 1960s came across a serf who had worked for one of the great monasteries near Lhasa. When he was caught stealing two sheep belonging to a minor official his punishment was swift and brutal. One of his eyes was gouged out with a knife and the other sucked from its socket by a half-hollowed ball. His left hand was then bound in a rope which was twisted and pulled until two fingers dropped off. The mangled stumps were wrapped in salted yak hide that was left to shrink.[33]

More than fifty years earlier, brutality of this kind had been brought to the attention of the Younghusband mission, and it simply confirmed their anti-clericism. Although there was perhaps a further dimension to the vitriolic assaults of some of the British, which was to do with their own national history. Tibet resembled very closely a feudal state of the European and Catholic Middle Ages. Beyond the Himalaya, Victorians like Waddell could look on the abuses of greedy barons and fat abbots and it filled them with anger. In reviling Tibet's inequalities and proposing change they were righting wrongs done, not to the cheerful, grubby and impoverished peasantry, but perhaps to themselves, or at least to their own ancestors. Tibet revealed the grimmer aspects of their own past and they were incensed by that realisation.[34]

The deep-seated opposition felt by imperial servants like Waddell led to one of the most curious allegiances in travel literature on Tibet. Half a century after the Younghusband mission had occupied Lhasa, Stuart and Roma Gelder, in an attempt to give weight to their contention that pre-1950 Tibet was a cruel and barbarous tyranny, cited the writings of the earlier British visitors as supportive evidence. The Gelders and someone like Waddell might have been in complete agreement in condemning the Tibetan state, but not with regard to motives. For while the old colonel's criticisms were in part justifying the invasion of a foreign country by his imperial government, the Gelders had been invited to Tibet by the Chinese after they had assumed control of the country. The later couple, perhaps discreetly guided towards their conclusions by their hosts, vilified the feudal Buddhist system in an attempt to bring to the fore the infinite virtues of communist China – an ideology and a nation that Waddell would have hated even more than the vanished regime of the lamas.

It was perhaps inevitable that those who despised the monks in their rôle as Tibet's political overlords would find similar fault with their particular form of Buddhist worship. What was so interesting is that a man like Austine Waddell, a student of the religion, author of *The Buddhism of Tibet or Lamaism*, and later professor of Tibetan at University College London, in 1905 reserved for their faith a special sort of scorn. There was a profound irony in this. For, if the myth of mysterious Tibet had any validity whatsoever, it was because of the country's remarkable religious life.

No doubt Tibetan Buddhism appeared radically different to the non-theistic doctrine originally taught by Gautama Buddha in the sixth century BC, with which the British travellers would have become acquainted in India. Certainly the visual language of the Tibetan faith, expressed in its ubiquitous idols and temples, and in the scriptural paintings, known as *thangkas*, or their religious dramas and rituals, suggested a religion populated with an incomprehensible assembly of gods, saints, devils and spirits. These visual images of the deities were presented in the gaudiest colours and often in the most lurid postures. Some paintings showed divine beings in orgasmic union with their consorts, or black, fanged devils breathing fire and wearing human skulls in their hair. An American visitor to Lhasa in the 1950s may have shown greater insight than he realised, when he wrote: 'There is a touch of Superman in some of these ancient Tibetan religious dramas.'[35] This fantastic iconography presented in the most dramatic fashion, to an often illiterate agricultural people, the Buddhist vision of moral order in the universe. Yet beneath the spectacular outer ritual and pageant, the Tibetans held to the fundamental principle of transcendence common to all forms of Buddhism.

The individual soul was caught in a cycle of birth and rebirth, called samsara, and in each successive reincarnation experienced suffering or happiness according to the person's moral behaviour in the last life. The ultimate goal was the attainment of enlightenment or nirvana, which meant liberation from the unending chain of existence. The complex of Buddhist yogic and meditational practices used by Tibetan lamas, such as those contained in the Tantras, was a kind of metaphysical scaffolding by which a soul might climb towards enlightenment. Another fundamental element of the spiritual path was the retreat – long periods, often years, spent in constant and solitary meditation. It has been a part of Asiatic spiritual life for millennia. It was only through this absolute submission to the impacts of loneliness and time that consciousness could be so radically transformed. Gautama Buddha himself was reputed to have spent six years in the forest. The eleventh-century Milarepa, one of Tibet's greatest saints, spent many years isolated in a cave.

It was the mythical stories associated with yogis like Milarepa and their super-normal powers that had excited such a sense of wonder amongst Europeans. A measure, for example, of the curious fantasies that some of Waddell's contemporaries, if not he himself, had entertained are the questions he put to one of Tibet's leading spiritual figures during an interview. When the lama claimed no knowledge of these enlightened miracle-performing sages, Waddell explained to his audience:

> There is then, I am sorry to say, little hope to hold out to those who fondly fancied that the last secrets of the beginnings of the earliest civilisation of the world, anterior to that of Ancient Egypt and Assyria, which perished with the sinking of Atlantis in the Western Ocean, might still be preserved in that land.[36]

The secrets of the earliest civilisations, Ancient Egypt, Assyria,

Atlantis – it was as if the entire encyclopaedia of unsolved mysteries might be cleared up once and for all in Tibet. What they seemed to have hoped for was confirmation of everything they had heard in some empirically verifiable form, like a conjuring show. When the Tibetans refused to perform, Waddell felt 'the ring fence of mysticism has been penetrated and the full glare of Reality has dispelled the mirage of spurious marvels'.[37]

If anything could have convinced Waddell of a richness and sophistication in Tibetan culture, it was an examination of their religious life. But for him, hurrying through on a military expedition, this was beyond his means or his inclination. Instead he projected onto it part of that wider disillusionment, which was itself largely a consequence of preconceived expectations. Where he might have discovered the Tibetans' complex science of the soul, he found only a 'ring fence of mysticism' – a mere defence for the bogus, something to be broken down in the course of progress. And if it was not an incitement to attack, the word 'mysticism' served to ward off Waddell's readers, like a 'No Entry' sign. It suggested that further enquiry was worthless, since all that lay beyond was vague and nebulous – 'silly . . . puerilities' which vaporised on contact with the adult senses.[38] There was also perhaps a mildly cautionary note in Waddell's usage: mysticism was merely a hollow sham, but if there was ever anything in these matters, it might possibly be threatening.

This was certainly his response when he was confronted with the physical reality of a lama in retreat – a devotee confined to his anchorite's cell for a staggering twenty-one years. The sight of the man's gloved hand drawing in his daily food through a small hatch was a profound imaginative experience for Waddell. 'The whole action', he wrote, 'was muffled like a dream, so slow, so stealthy, so silent and creepy. In the daylight it was unearthly and horrible to a degree. Only a gloved hand!'[39] This experience was one of the bases for concluding that the Tibetan religion was an 'absurd perversion of the original' Buddhism, and called the retreat a 'repulsive . . . form of religious observance'.[40] Thirty-two years later, Spencer Chapman had an experience of a similar order. Entering a complex of religious buildings inside the fort of Gyantse, Tibet's third largest town, Chapman wrote:

The dzong [fort], which is half ruined, is built tier upon tier to the summit of the steep rock; not unlike Mont St Michel. Went right up to the top. There are no staircases, so we had to pull the ladder up from roof to roof. In a tiny dark room at the very top sat a monk, muffled up in a heavy red cape, beating a huge gong and praying to the spirit of the dzong. He seemed to be in a trance and appeared quite oblivious of our presence. I felt an unaccountable terror as if in the presence of something deeply sinister.[41]

It is perhaps not surprising that these Britons, confronted with Tibetan spiritual practices, whose ultimate aim was the extinction of the ego, would react in this way. For men like Waddell and Chapman such an apparently passive display of renunciation was a negation of the entire complex of progressive, rational, dynamic and purposeful emotions and ideas which formed their mental lives. The lama's behaviour, in expressing beliefs diametrically opposed to their own, seemed no less than evil. Indeed, Waddell repeatedly referred to monks as 'wizards' and 'wizard priests'.[42] He even apologised that he had 'brought so prominently before the reader' so much 'devil worship and superstition'.[43]

Fortunately, these deeply negative views of Tibetan life were not the only reaction to the country. There were other British travellers who were prepared to acknowledge that the land beyond the Himalaya had been a source of some satisfaction. This was particularly the case in the years after the Younghusband mission, reflecting, in part, the changed political relations between the two countries. In 1910 the Dalai Lama, fleeing from invading Chinese forces, took refuge in Darjeeling and remained a guest of the Raj until his return to Tibet in June 1912. With the easing of trade restrictions and the establishment of British trade agents, like Eric Bailey, at Yatung, Gyantse and Gartok, relations gradually improved further. There was, therefore, less political incentive to condemn Tibetans as savage brutes.

Not that many visitors wished to. On the contrary, as Fosco Mariani observed in *Secret Tibet*:

The Tibetans are really xenophobes of a most curious kind.

Their xenophobia is exclusively abstract and theoretical. They close their country to foreigners, and the most rigorous laws are issued from Lhasa to keep them out, but when a white man arrives in their midst they greet him with enthusiasm and make a tremendous fuss of him.[44]

Most of those so greeted were at least willing to concede with Francis Younghusband that the Tibetans were 'very pleasant, cheery people'.[45] Others went further, particularly when they were judging them against other Asiatics. In the 1840s Abbé Huc had found them 'so generous, so hospitable, so fraternal towards strangers'. He had contrasted these qualities with the dominant characteristics of the Chinese – 'that thorough nation of shop-keepers, with hearts dry as a ship-biscuit, and grasping as a monkey'.[46] In 1913 Frank Kingdon Ward had similar feelings. 'Personally', he wrote, 'my sympathies are all with the Tibetans . . . [they] always strike me as being so much more jolly and irresponsible than the Chinese, who are . . . sedate and gloomy'.[47] By the 1930s the praise had risen to new heights. Basil Gould suggested that 'at the present time it is in Tibet, more than any other country of which I have knowledge, that the Britisher who has the good fortune to serve there finds himself made welcome'.[48] In 1938 John Hanbury-Tracy, expressing a new mainstream view and reversing the verdict of critics like Waddell, proposed the Tibetans as 'surely the most religion loving people in the world, and the most contented'.[49]

It became a central condition of his or her enjoyment of Tibet that the traveller be around its people, whose average individual was apparently:

a simple life-loving soul; revelling in broad humour of a schoolboy nature; unwashed, unkempt, working always in the open with simple tools; gay, sad or frightened with the simplicity of a child, and like a child believing in spirits, hobgoblins, and demons all round him, in the trees, in the rivers, and in his towering awe-inspiring mountains.[50]

John Hanbury-Tracy's perception of their child-like nature was also a constant amongst British travellers. Younghusband, for example, thought them 'excessively childish'.[51] Spencer Chapman felt they had 'all the charm and many of the faults of children'.[52] For Peter Fleming, 'Logic was a concept wholly alien to the Tibetan mind. A small child, ordered to do something which it does not want to do, will enquire, over and over again. "But why must I?" The Tibetans' power of reasoning did not extend even thus far.'[53] Stuart and Roma Gelder described their first excursion into a Tibetan landscape as 'stepping into a child's dream world of gods and demons, where good and evil spirits lived in stones and trees'.[54]

Being amongst those they deemed to be children, some European travellers felt at liberty to divest themselves of many of the regulations that constrained adult behaviour at home. Hanbury-Tracy made the point perfectly when he noted, in relation to table manners, that 'Good behaviour in Europe inevitably means uncomfortable behaviour; now we let ourselves go, and rejoiced in the freedom of Asia'.[55] Part of what Tibet meant to them was being able to fart and belch and slurp their food with a schoolboy's relish.

Even the dirtiness of the Tibetans, which had been such a barrier to close relations for Waddell, became a perverse source of satisfaction amongst later visitors. Since the locals did not wash – a consequence of the extreme cold and sometimes the lack of water – nor need the visitor. Lowell Thomas Jr. and his father (the journalist who had converted another British traveller into a household legend – Lawrence of Arabia) were amongst the first Americans to visit Lhasa. In his 1952 account of their journey the son declared with a somewhat excessive sense of drama: 'We had been on the trail more than a week since our last tub in Gyantse!'[56] This was decidedly puny in comparison with some of the unwashed greats. In *Tibetan Trek*, for example, Ronald Kaulback disclosed that he had not bathed for 154 days, while on his second journey he and Hanbury-Tracy had not done so for ten months.[57] When the latter did eventually take a soak, it fulfilled a different sort of child-like fantasy. The vessel he used was 'actually the monastery tea-kettle' and, doubled up in a copper cauldron 'in a cloud of steam, with the fire close by, the bather looked like an unfortunate missionary being stewed for a cannibal feast'.[58]

Even experiences that would have been deeply unpleasant at

home, in Tibet, where they were both novel and temporary, were discussed almost as if they were amusing entertainments. The country's multitude of parasitic nasties were a classic case. In Kaulback's *Tibetan Trek*, blood-sucking ticks were anthropomorphised and castigated playfully as 'varmints';[59] sandflies that inflicted an irritating bite became 'our old friends';[60] mosquitoes kept him 'amused and diverted',[61] while fleas – 'Tibet is the fleas' paradise' – were 'gentlemanly pests and playful in their habits'.[62] He and his companion had a kind of competition to see who could remove the most leeches; Kaulback's count for those he pulled off his chest was 186.[63]

With the classic British instinct for domestication, he also captured wild animals and cherished them as pets. A species of parrot was christened Timothy; a rat that ran over their sleeping bodies at night and stole left-over scraps of chapatti was called Rupert. However, Kaulback's wonderfully eccentric speciality was snakes, to which he ascribed various comic names – Sally, Cuthbert, Cuthberta, Bertram and Robert. Sally, the first of his serpents, was 'a green viper of sorts, about three feet long, with glittering dark brown eyes', and probably venomous. Having nowhere to put it, Kaulback stuffed it inside his shirt, where 'she grew to be the friend of my bosom in very truth'.[64]

> Moreover, even when she became frisky and energetic
> again, she never once struck at me. B. C. [his companion]
> could not bring himself to love her as I did, though he
> became more or less used to her after a time, and as for the
> coolies, they were struck all of a heap by my carrying her
> around. They went about with their eyes fixed fearfully on
> my shirt, dreading to see her head appear for a moment's
> breath of air, and chattering like monkeys if it ever did.[65]

The last of Kaulback's catch was a Russell's viper, one of Asia's most poisonous snakes. While being deposited in a length of bamboo, the creature, inevitably renamed as Christabel, bit him on his finger, which left his arm 'swollen up like a huge sausage as far as the elbow, and very painful'.[66]

Kaulback's book is full of dangerous incidents of this kind and, while they were worn as marks of distinction, they were also presented with a self-deprecating humour. This was not just the seemly modesty of the traveller, it was in keeping with the Tibetan environment. As Kingdon Ward had remarked more than twenty years earlier, the Tibetans could 'stand pain such as would make the European gasp'.[67] Hanbury-Tracy agreed: 'The hardiness of the peasant is something utterly beyond mere fitness acquired by means of artificial exercises and organised games'.[68] On meeting a group of Ladakhi merchants, he noted with considerable insight:

> these little men hurried about the heart of Asia as nonchalantly as though it were the Surrey hills! They had crossed the Karakoram half a dozen times in the ordinary course of business, much as a City worker might catch the morning train. They had moved quietly in and out of Srinagar, Darjeeling and Calcutta . . . What a pother we Europeans make about our own puny travels![69]

For some Britons travel in Tibet was not just the means to impressing one's neighbour at a dinner party on return, it was the challenge of living up to standards set by the Tibetans themselves. The country thus bred a cult of toughness. Spencer Chapman, a mountaineer who had scaled the Tibetan peak Chomo Lhari to its 7,313-metre summit, felt that 'Our sensibilities and characters were made to be sharpened against the hard forces of Nature'.

> But how few people nowadays get any chance to test their physical endurance to breaking-point, to feel cold fear gnawing at their hearts, or to have to make decisions that hold life and death in the balance? That is why men flock so easily to war; to test a manhood that is perverted by the present state of civilization.[70]

In Tibet, where these lines were written, that challenge was simply a precondition of being there. It was one of the ultimate physical environments, and its rigours became a measure of Western softness, even decadence. This was a point Hanbury-Tracy moved towards when he wrote:

In many ways Tibet is a crude country, but you never meet a man there with neurasthenia, heartburn, cancer or a complex of any kind. Nor do you meet drug-fiends, sharepushers, pseudo-intellectuals, pole-squatters, crooners, or any other such fungoid growths of modern civilization. There are no new-fangled '-isms', and no political shirts, either black, brown or red . . . the fevered mass mentality of big cities could not long survive in the rarefied air of the great hills. At those heights man is subdued by his surroundings, and much that is mere froth has a way of vanishing like breath on a windowpane.[71]

From Waddell's time, the argument was now coming full circle. Instead of Tibetans being filthy, barbarous and savage, 'enemies . . . of the human race', they were seen increasingly as essential members – final guardians of a portion of the human spirit that had been extinguished everywhere else.

What had been scorned as criminal backwardness was now one of their greatest virtues – their extraordinary conservatism. They were the most unchanging and enduring people on the planet. Reflecting on what might happen to them after the Chinese invasion of 1950, Peter Fleming thought it unlikely that 'their conquerors will be able to alter the Tibetan character, so curiously compounded of mysticism and jollity, of shrewdness and superstition, of tolerance and strict convention'.[72] Paul Theroux described them simply as 'indestructible'.[73] Such views paid testimony to the fact that they had preserved a way of life that had changed in little but the tiniest details since the Dark Ages. Instead of seeking to impose the new, by breaking open the closed doors and hammering down the 'ring fence of mysticism', European travellers wanted increasingly to keep it as it was. They were often appalled by signs of change. Finding that cheap Japanese goods were replacing handmade Tibetan items, Ronald Kaulback complained that the imported trash looked 'perfectly awful and horribly out of place'.[74] When Hanbury-Tracy came across merchants using recently printed paper money, instead of lumps of silver in the shape of a pony's hooves, he was 'depressed to think that the country might be "going modern" '.[75] It was now realised that by completely excluding the outside world, Tibetans had kept alive not only their own way of life but something for all of us. 'If ever Western civilization really penetrates into Tibet', warned Hanbury-Tracy, 'it will be yet another Fall of Man'.[76]

One of the things the Tibetans had conserved that could affect Europeans profoundly was their sense of time. It ceased to press on the traveller as it did in the West. Time became a void, unfolding endlessly like the landscape itself. 'As the weeks went by', wrote Hanbury-Tracy, 'and telegraphs and news retreated to a vague sub-existence . . . we became gradually attuned to a new sense of time – or a very old one'.

> Time was now reckoned in months, and distance in days
> . . . we treated time with respect, as people do in high Asia,
> and time, reacting kindly, never harassed us. I never knew if
> it was Wednesday or Friday. It was immaterial.[77]

Taking in for the first occasion the Lhasan atmosphere – 'the ragged, dirty, malodorous, sinister, handsome, crippled, sturdy, colourful crowd' – the Gelders likened it to 'a dream, when all sense of waking time is a confusion where we meet and talk with the dead and living in a spaceless, timeless present'.[78]

One of the other facets of Tibet that had always generated a sense of excitement, even from the time of the very earliest visitors, was the opportunities it offered for a simple one-upmanship. What made it so fantastic was the thought that so few had done what you were doing. It was why Hanbury-Tracy, setting off on his trek up the Salween, delighted in the idea that 'In a few weeks we would cross rivers and passes now marked on the map with those fascinating queries, and others unheard of in the western world'.[79] It was why, reaching one idyllic spot, he 'envied Colonel [Eric] Bailey, the first Englishman to have seen that monastery and the quiet lake'.[80] It seemed that, for Hanbury-Tracy, the experience of that monastery and that quiet lake was not a limitless thing open for all time, it was like an apportioned cake, which was dished out on a first-come first-served basis. After a while there would be nothing left for latecomers. It was by this logic that in 1935 he could judge a pass called the Ata Kang La – 'crossed by the Indian pundit A-k in

1882, and by Kingdon Ward in 1933' – 'a well-trodden route'.[81] Fortunately, as the number of visitors increased over the course of the twentieth century, so the standards tended to slip. And the Lowell Thomases could still get high on the idea that they were the seventh and eighth Americans to visit Lhasa, and only the fourth and fifth to be received officially.[82] For those lucky enough to have got there first it was an ecstasy that seemed tinged with the sexual. The Swede Sven Hedin, perhaps the most outstanding European explorer in Tibet, rowed out over Lake Manasarowar at the foot of Mount Kailas and, believing himself to be the first westerner on its waters (actually he was the second), wrote:

> Leaning on the gunwale I enjoy the voyage to the full, for nothing I remember in my long wanderings in Asia can compare with the overpowering beauty of this nocturnal sail. I seem to hear the gentle but powerful beat of the great heart of Nature, its pulsation growing weaker in the arms of night, and gaining fresh vigour in the glow of the morning red. The scene, gradually changing as the hours go by, seems to belong not to earth but to the outermost boundary of unattainable space, as though it lay much nearer heaven, the misty fairyland of dreams and imagination, of hope and yearning, than to the earth with its mortals, its cares, its sins and its vanity. The moon describes its arch in the sky, its restless reflexion quivering on the water . . .
> The queen of night and her robe become paler.[83]

This erotic dimension to the Tibetan traveller's experience was classically conveyed by Lord Curzon in a letter to Hedin. Referring to the recently returned Younghusband mission that the viceroy had authorised, he said: 'I hope . . . in the interests of the world that you will perform one more big journey before you settle down. From this point of view I am almost ashamed of having destroyed the virginity of the bride to whom you aspired, viz. Lhasa'.[84] Typical of a latent violence evident amongst Tibetan travellers was Kingdon Ward's description of one of his own expedition's objectives. Referring to his attempt to visit the last few unsurveyed kilometres of the Tsangpo valleys, he wrote, 'We would, if possible, go right through the gorge, and tear this last secret from its heart'.[85]

Clearly there were aggressive urges to dominance as well as deeply acquisitive and competitive aspects mingled with the travellers' joys in Tibet. Their testimonials to the country were also, inevitably, those of visitors and full, therefore, of the partialities and inaccuracies of all holiday romances. Moreover the things that inspired them were often not those elements of Tibetan life that Tibetans themselves might even have recognised or valued. European fulfilment was often in the context of European aspirations. Yet it is impossible to dismiss all they said of the country as transient illusion. Men like Hedin, Hanbury-Tracy and Kaulback had spent literally years in the country and had certainly not made snap decisions. In fact, the longer they had been there the more positive was the judgement. Heinrich Harrer stayed seven years and never wished to leave, until obliged to do so by the Chinese invasion. For Harrer, Tibet was 'the country that supplied me with my dreams and furnished me with a goal for my life'.[86]

Perhaps the acid test for the positive judgements made by visitors were the experiences to which Alexandra David-Neel subjected herself. This extraordinary Parisian traveller had spent several years studying Buddhism in various Tibetan monasteries. She spoke the language fluently, had adopted a young Sikkimese monk as her son and had made numerous journeys in the country. In 1923, however, baulked of her ambition to visit Lhasa by British officialdom, she decided to attempt to reach it disguised as an impoverished mendicant. She was not, therefore, the archetypal European traveller, riding through and expecting and receiving automatic entry, on a honorary basis, to Tibet's privileged classes. She walked all the way in the depths of winter on the footing of a serf. Frequently she and her companion were obliged to camp out in the open or take their place amongst other pilgrims in Tibetan hovels. Yet she described her time as 'the most blessed existence one can dream of, and I consider as the happiest in my life those days when . . . I wandered as one of the countless tribe of Thibetan beggar pilgrims'.[87] 'I cannot say often enough', she added, 'that Tibet is a land of wonder which changes everything for the best'.[88]

Both psychologically and physiographically Tibet was utterly removed from Western experience. In its incomparable landscapes, travellers felt bathed in the other. The word that kept recurring to David-Neel, as it had occurred to Hedin, was 'fairyland'.[89] Tibet was like an immense secret garden, or adventure playground, it was Shangri La, a place where dreams and magic actually came true. 'I would not have been very startled had I suddenly surprised some elfs seated on sun rays', wrote David-Neel, 'or come upon the Enchanted Palace of Sleeping Beauty'.[90] Even old campaigners like Hanbury-Tracy and Kaulback said they felt like 'Martians arriving on the Earth',[91] and on seeing his first monastery, the former had 'the sensation of entering a lost world'.[92] This sentiment was echoed in 1940 – 'we have entered another world' – by Spencer Chapman.[93] Lowell Thomas Jr. thought his invitation to see Lhasa 'the once-in-three-lifetimes opportunity to travel into the heart of an incredible, fabulous, story-book country'.[94] On seeing the capital itself he felt he had 'come as close as ever I would to finding that pot of gold at the end of the rainbow'.[95] Even cynical old Waddell, despite all he had said and done, wrote of the 'world of dreams and magic which may be said to be ever with us in the mystic Land of the Lamas'.[96] Reaching Lhasa, he too experienced 'heartfelt exultation'.[97]

By the mid twentieth century if Tibet was no longer a *fantasy* to Europeans, if the physical realities had been substantiated by witnesses and some of the most excessive myths dispelled, it still remained the place *for their fantasies*, however they might be expressed. It was a region that gave licence to all imaginings, to the idea of the impossible, and those who went there loved it. Tibet was a place apart, insulated from the modern world by colossal walls, and its visitors hoped it could remain that way. From the occidental perspective there now seemed little reason why it should not. Politically and militarily it was insignificant. The Russian threat, that had so exercised men like Curzon, had evaporated by 1917. True, Tibet was a large country, but it was high, difficult and barren, *Lebensraum* for yaks only. Moreover, its population was small, its army was minuscule and its people pacific. For Westerners it could be a zone of peace and happiness, left to its own devices. However, it was another type of foreigner, the inhabitants of the Middle Kingdom, that had always looked upon the Tibetans as hairy, barbarian and savage, who would determine the method of Tibet's assimilation into the modern world.

On 7 October 1950 the People's Liberation Army invaded Tibet at several points along its eastern and western borders, and quickly turned aside the spirited, though ill-armed local resistance. For nine years, the Dalai Lama was permitted to remain as the head of his government and Tibet was spared full-scale integration into the communist state. However, what had started out as a policy of conciliation gradually hardened as the Chinese failed to have any impact on Tibetan society, and as the Tibetans themselves came increasingly to resent foreign occupation. As widespread rebellion was brutally suppressed in 1959, the Dalai Lama fled to India. Transformation of the feudal Buddhist society was then begun in earnest.

By 1983 the Tibetan government in exile had compiled and cross-checked a list of the names of 1,207,487 people. This represented more than a sixth of Tibet's entire population – a higher percentage of society than that which had once made up its monastic community. The government-in-exile's list, however, referred not to monks and nuns but to the Tibetans killed by the Chinese.[98] Communist policy in Tibet has been likened to that of the Nazis against Jews. It has been an assault not only on what they saw as the exploitative members of the old feudal regime, but on the entire Tibetan culture.

The religion was a principal target. Of an estimated 6,259 original monasteries there were only thirteen still functioning by the end of the Cultural Revolution.[99] The fate of the Sera Monastery close to Lhasa was a typical story. Together with the other two great Lhasan monasteries, the Drepung and the Gunden, the Sera was once known as the *Densa* – the three pillars of wisdom. The Chinese, viewing it as a hotbed of rebellion, turfed out the monks and stripped it of its frescoes, some of which were 500 years old. The buildings were then used to quarter troops, to stable donkeys, as a grain store and for the incarceration and torture of prisoners. Most of Tibet's Buddhist treasures have been gathered up and sold on the art market or melted down for bullion. Approximately eighty-five per cent of Tibetan literature has been destroyed. In some places the scriptures were used for toilet paper.

In one incident, where a monk asked the Red Guards to refrain from such desecration, they cut his arm off above the elbow, and told him that God would restore it for him. Many were crucified with nails and left to die.[100] Those less fortunate went to prison. One monk, jailed for twenty-two years, recalled how they were forced to work for twelve hours every day. Sometimes it was so cold their flesh came off on the shovels. The Chinese policy of systematic starvation obliged them to eat flies, or rats, or dogs, or to sift their own shit for pieces of vegetable. Eventually they ate each other. Many committed suicide rather than betray their fellows and those accused of plotting against the Chinese were knifed in the testicles, dying slowly. Many more were simply rounded up and shot, then buried in mass graves. At the close of his interview with Vanya Kewley, the first Western journalist to get eye-witness accounts of Chinese atrocities, the monk said: 'I saw so many people die. I would think about 99 per cent of the prisoners I saw in my twenty-two years in prison are dead. Many died in front of me. Many died around me. Many died close by. I am a left over from death'.[101]

It was not just the lamas who suffered. It was also the oppressive classes amongst the laity, like the simple farmer who could read. This 'intellectual' was made to kneel in front of his family and shot through the back of the head. His family was then asked for the price of the bullet.[102] Tibetans were forbidden to use their own language on pain of imprisonment. Most of the official posts are still occupied by Han Chinese. These are now thought to out-number Tibetans in their own country, over which the Chinese have operated a policy of forcible sterilisation.

When confronted with religious paintings that gave visual expression to aspects of Tibetan Buddhist belief, such as the wrathful deities or terrible scenes from the various types of hell, many European travellers were totally baffled or offended. A man like Hanbury-Tracy called it 'rank ju-juism!'.[103] The no doubt well-intentioned but gullible Gelders thought it 'supernatural hocus pocus'.[104] For the Tibetans themselves, however, under Chinese control, their horrific representations of the fate of the damned must seem a living, indubitable reality.

Chapter X

The Coca-Cola Age

Amongst many of those travel writers prominent in the fifteen years after the Second World War one finds, repeatedly, expressions of a belief that their own lives have spanned a watershed in the travel experience. Within that time the world beyond British shores had changed utterly, and what they had known and encountered themselves during their journeys would very shortly disappear for ever.

Norman Lewis explained that even prior to his 1950 visit to Indochina he had been motivated by an intuition that it 'would have to be seen now, or never again in its present form'. On his return he sensed that he had been a privileged witness to the final act in a momentous Asian drama: that 'when the curtain went up again', as he put it, 'it would be upon something as unrecognizable to an old China hand as to Marco Polo'.[1] Thirty years later, in a fresh preface for *A Dragon Apparent*, his outstanding account of that Indochinese venture, the author described some of the calamitous changes he had predicted. The villages of the tribal Moï, who 'were living as their ancestors had probably lived for thousands of years' when Lewis had visited them, 'had been bombed to nothingness by the B.52s in the Vietnam war'.[2] The gentle and tolerant people of Laos or Cambodia, who, in accordance with the non-violent traditions of their Buddhist faith, had handled leeches tenderly when they fastened on them in the rice paddies, or permitted mosquitoes to feast on their blood, had been 'delivered to the greatest holocaust ever to be visited on the East'.

It consumed not only the present, but the past; an
obliteration of cultures and values as much as physical
things. From the ashes that remained no phoenix would
ever rise. Not enough survived even to recreate the memory
of what the world has lost.[3]

Wilfred Thesiger, in his introduction to *Arabian Sands*, expressed
the same sense of an ending. 'I went to Southern Arabia only just in
time', he wrote. 'If anyone goes there now looking for the life I led
they will not find it, for technicians have been there since,
prospecting for oil'.

Today the desert where I travelled is scarred with the tracks
of lorries and littered with discarded junk imported from
Europe and America. But this material desecration is
unimportant compared with the demoralization which has
resulted among the Bedu themselves.[4]

In a postscript written a generation and a half later, Thesiger
concluded that his book had become 'a memorial to a vanished past,
a tribute to a once magnificent people'.[5]

The Second World War itself seemed to lie behind at least some of
these alterations to the travel scene. It had ushered in an atomic age
and the Cold War. Simultaneously Europe, for so long the centre of
world events, was in decline and ultimate power had ridden
outwards in opposing directions to the East and West. It was not,
however, the change in political circumstances that so impinged on
the traveller, though this, as Norman Lewis had noted in the Far
East, was a factor. The real issue was the increasing homogeneity
amongst the global human family. The post-war period and the rise
of two pre-eminently materialist empires had brought immense
social change. It was the universal advance of a technological
mass-produced culture, originating chiefly in the West, that was
cutting off those last avenues of escape for the authentic traveller.
There was nowhere in the world where one could go without
meeting exactly those things that had been left behind. Travel was
steadily being drained of all its meaning. At the end of his
autobiography, Eric Newby blamed much of it on the bulldozer

and its rôle in constructing roads 'through the wilderness and over mountain ranges'. By 1973 the combined impact of 'dozer and road had wrecked the author's beloved Apennines. 'Even worse', he lamented in the book's valedictory sentence, 'will be the day . . . when the desire to be alone has finally been extinguished from the human heart'.[6]

The physical object which travellers have used again and again almost like a motif for this new, overcrowded and uniformly dull landscape was not, as might be expected, the epoch-making inventions of the last war, the atomic bomb or the jet engine. It was something they themselves encountered far more frequently and which was also much more innocent-seeming and thus, perhaps, more devastating in its ultimate impact.

Lawrence Durrell, analysing the travel writer's purpose in an article entitled 'Landscape and Character', felt that the key objective was 'to isolate the germ in the people which is expressed by their landscape', an investigation that demanded of the author a type of mental submission to the foreign locality.[7] 'The secret', he suggested, 'is identification'. However, in the very essay that gave us the core of his travel philosophy, Durrell named, almost incidentally, those objects that might ultimately render his theory worthless. Selecting Egypt as his example, Durrell wrote:

> If you sit on the top of the Mena House pyramid at sunset
> . . . (forgetting the noise of the donkey-boys, and all the
> filthy litter of other travellers – old cartons and Coca-Cola
> bottles): if you sit quite still in the landscape-diviner's pose
> . . . the whole rhythm of ancient Egypt rises up from the
> damp cold sand. You can hear its very pulse tick.[8]

Elsewhere Durrell, striving to convey the immense vacuity he sensed in Argentina, described it as a country 'full of stale air, blue featureless sierras, and businessmen drinking Coca-Cola'. 'I'd give a lifetime of Argentina for three weeks of Greece', he concluded.[9] Yet another philhellene would shortly declare that 'between the butt of a Coca-Cola bottle and the Iron Curtain, much that is precious and venerable, many living mementoes of Greece's past are being hammered to powder'.[10]

With the poet's gift for locating the deeper cultural significance in surface matter, Fermor had named eight years earlier his candidate as the great symbol of the non-travel era. Describing Coke's advertising campaign in the Caribbean, he wrote that it

> has been so intensive and so ruthlessly efficient in its execution, that never for a second are the words Coca-Cola out of one's sight. It is on a scale that nobody who has not crossed the Atlantic can hope to grasp. They are printed on almost everything you touch . . . It becomes the air you breathe, a way of life, an entire civilization – the Coca-Cola age.[11]

Eventually, Fermor mused, the crimped-edged tin tops that were discarded when the bottles were opened would form a 'metal humus' covering the entire Western hemisphere. Then, after nuclear holocaust had eliminated all visible traces of our own civilisation, archaeologists would be able to date 'our buried remains with the help of this stratum of small round lids'.[12]

Coca-Cola's suitability as an emblem of the modern epoch was not just its universal abundance. The brown, effervescent fluid had other properties that made its choice eminently appropriate. It was synthetic, corrosive, mildly addictive and mass-produced; but above all else it was American. It stood therefore for the new world order. The USA was the dominant political entity on the face of the planet. It was also the newest, wealthiest and most advanced expression of industrial society; culturally it was the shallowest and most emulated of nations. And if Coca-Cola held for British travellers all the sinister resonance of an inverted swastika, its human analogue was a garishly clad, camera-strapped, whistle-stopping American tourist.

Colin Thubron's account of his experience in Jerusalem's Dome of the Rock could almost serve as a moment of epiphany for modern British travellers. Invited by a old Muslim sheikh to enter the Well of Spirits, Thubron was asked if he knew ' "that in this rock is a cave where all prayers are answered?" '

We descended to a soft-lit chamber, its walls unfissured, but here and there washed dark.

'Listen to the voices,' he said.

I listened to the stone for its voice; but only heard American tourists.[13]

When Dervla Murphy announced, 'I find it peculiarly irritating to be mistaken for an American', was she perhaps expressing her own fears that the great silences known to the likes of Gertrude Bell or Freya Stark were rapidly being obliterated by this same human sub-species?[14]

The identification of the American people with the end of *real* travel was a British tradition that actually predated the Second World War. In *The Road to Oxiana* Robert Byron had devoted three and a half pages to the verbal assassination of a man named Farquharson, who was heir to a business empire in Memphis, Tennessee ('an unattractive countenance, prognathous, yet weedy with . . . a whining monotone' voice).[15] The American, aped and ridiculed for his insistence that he was on 'a *vurry* hurried trip' and for his obsessive reference to money, was made to represent all that was most meaningless in travel.[16] Buried, of course, beneath Byron's defence of true travel values were the complex snobbery felt by old for new wealth, and the deep insecurities that afflicted a waning power when confronted by one in the ascendant. Yet sometimes there could be, together with a characteristic openness, spontaneity and loud enthusiasm, a curious money-mindedness amongst Americans abroad that tended to justify Old World travel pretensions.

John Gunther was a case in point. Author of the *Inside* series published between 1936 and 1960, he covered most of the globe in just seven books and thousands of pages of facts and statistics. *Inside Africa* is typical of the set. It is symptomatic of the culture which gave birth to such an author that in his preface Gunther attempts almost to break down his African experiences into a column of figures: 105 African towns visited, forty-four different air trips, a total of 64,000 African kilometres ('which is sixteen times the air distance across the United States') and then 1,503 people interviewed and recorded.[17] The exactitude of his lists is the key to

Gunther's experience of abroad. Not for him to plumb the savage depths of 1950s Morocco in the manner of a Gavin Maxwell. Gunther gives us the percentage of the population with venereal disease, or the number of radios and cinemas in the country.[18] Nor would the pyramids serve him as a meditational aid to resurrect the exotic, feline people of the ancient Nile. Gunther dismantles the Great Pyramid of Cheops into 2.5 million blocks and calculates the tonnage of stone required to build it.[19] It also seems significant that when wishing to communicate North Africa's 'groping movement towards fulfilment and change', he should write:

> Formerly the [Moroccan serfs] got no wages – what would they need money for? – but this is changing now. People do want money. They want to buy Coca-Cola and chewing gum and take trips into town. They want radios, better food and education for their children.[20]

As Gunther himself acknowledged, his *Inside Africa* was not travel writing; it was a kind of travel accountancy.[21] The object was not to assume the 'landscape-diviner's pose' and tap into the otherness of a foreign landscape, but the reverse. Everything was converted into a shape and idiom that made Africa homely to the folks States-side. So Rabat is described as 'Morocco's Washington, the great city of Casablanca is its New York'; a *souk* is a 'department store which manufactures some of the goods on the spot'; the 1954 discovery of the Cheops funeral ship in a sealed corridor near the Great Pyramid is 'like walking into a bank every inch of which is familiar and coming across an unknown and unsuspected vault with a million dollars in it'.[22]

For a whole galaxy of reasons it is totally wrong to suggest that it was the Americans alone who had suburbanised the untamed places. Not least of these was the fact that travel writers themselves were implicated in the process. It was with some misgivings, for example, that Dervla Murphy received the suggestion that her own account of cycling overland to India, *Full Tilt*, had played its part in stimulating 'the great eastward Hippy Migration' of the 1960s.[23] Equally troubled by his own creation was Lawrence Durrell. On his return to Corfu he was shocked to learn of the stream of

248

celebrity-hunting tourists that *Prospero's Cell* had stirred up in its wake. It is a measure of the divide that ultimately separates the romancer from the romanticised that while Durrell squirmed at stories of scantily clad British and French visitors, dancing the twist to blaring radios in the idyllic bay where he once lived, his Corfiot friends delighted in the profits they made from their extra sales of Coca-Cola.[24]

Another migrant who sensed he might have fouled his own nest was Wilfred Thesiger. 'Regretfully', he wrote of his cartographic efforts in southern Arabia, 'I realize that the maps I made helped others, with more material aims, to visit and corrupt a people whose spirit once lit the desert like a flame'.[25] There was also perhaps a hint of irony in Eric Newby's lament for a world in which 'the desire to be alone has finally been extinguished from the human heart'. For as travel editor at *The Observer* for nine years he had no doubt made his own small contribution to the great tourist diaspora.

Just as the triangular relationship between traveller, travel book and tourist might be far more complicated than many of the former would wish to acknowledge, so the whole idea that travel is steadily becoming impossible is itself not as straightforward as some might have us believe. It is perhaps valuable to recapitulate the various assertions made by travel authors on this issue.

Thesiger, for example, felt himself to be 'perhaps the last explorer in the tradition of the past'.[26] He suggested in *Arabian Sands* that while others would follow in his footsteps in the Empty Quarter 'they will move about in cars and keep in touch with the outside world by wireless'.[27] For the great Arabist all the technological aids used by his successors severed the links between them and himself completely. They were travellers, but of a separate order. And those who reverted to camel or pack animal in the age of Land-Rover and jeep would simply be involved in a type of theatrical stunt; at best it would be a 'personal experience' of a highly contrived nature.[28] Yet it is interesting to compare Thesiger's end-of-an-era statements with the words of another, wider-travelled Arabian explorer:

I was I think the very last European to sojourn in *Wahhabi*

Arabia before its desert spaces were desecrated by the advent of the motor-car, which made its first appearance in the territories of Ibn Sa'ud within a twelvemonth of my departure. The invasion was at first tentative and timid, but motor transport is now a recognised factor in the life of the Arabs . . .

The Arabia I saw during this period was in all essentials the Arabia of Doughty and Niebuhr. The Arabia of to-day is a very different country.[29]

There is a striking similarity between the ideas expressed in this extract from Philby's *Arabia of the Wahhabis* and the earlier passages by Thesiger. The crucial difference between them, however, is that Philby's book was published thirty years before *Arabian Sands* was written.

Amongst travellers in Greece one encounters a similar situation. In 1931 Robert Byron had written in *The Station*:

Western civilisation is becoming universal, the race a homogeneous one. And before we die, half the variety of the picture will be gone; as if a showman had sold his swing-boats, his hoop-las, his fat woman, and even his merry-go-round, and invested the proceeds in one superlative chairoplane. The view is enlarged, the motion more poignant. And then: all is dull.[30]

Thirty-five years later Patrick Leigh Fermor was exercised by a similar vision of apocalypse in his beloved Hellas. 'The old is breaking up', he intoned in language reminiscent of Yeats, 'ancient customs are dying in scores, landmarks are vanishing, everything is changing with bewildering speed'.[31]

Another prophet of doom was Evelyn Waugh. In 1946, before Fermor or Newby or Thesiger had even put travel pen to paper, he had resigned himself to the idea that he would not 'see many travel books in the near future . . . Never again, I suppose, shall we land on foreign soil with a letter of credit and passport . . . and feel the world wide open before us'.[32] More than a decade later, however, Eric Newby was to prove him completely wrong with the publication of *A Short Walk in the Hindu Kush*. And Waugh, at the grand old age of fifty-five, would acknowledge in the book's introductory preface that its author had 'delighted the heart of a man whose travelling days are done'.[33] Yet, approaching retirement age himself, Newby in his turn would come round to the idea that 'the time was not far off when there would be no place on earth accessible to ordinary human beings in which they would be able to feel themselves alone under the sky without hearing the noise of machines'.[34]

The picture that emerges from this collection of statements seems in many ways only to make matters even more confusing. On the one hand, there seems to be unanimity on the idea that travel had experienced a critical moment of change, that all was in flux never to be the same again. On the other hand, it is a moment that seems to have dragged on for an inordinately long time, in fact for much of the twentieth century. Each of these authors, from Philby in 1917 to Newby in the mid 1980s, had implied that the kaleidoscopic world of variety which dazzled and captivated them had suddenly stopped revolving. It was as if from their time onwards it would be perpetually fixed on a single pattern. The question is, which of them was right? If Philby was correct then it would seem Thesiger had been thirty years too late in his analysis. If humankind had become homogeneous in Byron's day, it is difficult to see how the same process could recur all over again in Fermor's.

In a sense, to be doubly confusing, they were all wrong and all correct. They were totally wrong because each time one of them stood up to declare *Après moi le déluge* another traveller of courage and enterprise and insight came along to prove them false. There is still, as we approach the twenty-first century, a staggering variety amongst the human family. There are still areas, even in the most populous countries on earth, that are almost or completely without inhabitants. Moreover, there is not only scope for travellers; there are still portions of the globe – in Borneo or Papua New Guinea, in the Antarctic or Arctic Canada and Russia – so little visited that those who go there can call themselves 'explorers' even today. There are still communities with rich ancient traditions barely touched by Western influence. There are areas in Iran, Afghanistan or northern Burma that have been 'lost' to the travel fraternity, the last beyond the reach of Western visitors for half a century, if not since the time of Eric Bailey. Then, of course, there is always the eternal mystery of Tibet. In short, travellers today can feel as exhilarated by their solitude as they did a hundred years ago; equally, there are travel books as rich and satisfying as there were then.

At the same time, this century has been an indisputable era of destruction. The Mediterranean coastlines that were the delight of Lewis or Durrell have steadily metamorphosed into Fussell's pseudo-places – crowded, sterile zones of that classic modern oxymoron, the leisure industry. Those portions of inner Asia or Africa that sustained solitaries like Newby and Thesiger are now all one region, the developing world, whose urban populations have more than quadrupled in the thirty-five years from 1950. On its remaining spaces the effects of what Alan Moorehead called 'the dead hand of men and domestic animals' has caused a desertification problem that currently threatens a third of the world's land surface;[35] while tropical forests disappear at a rate of up to 10,000,000 hectares a year – an area equivalent to the size of Austria. For reasons not unconnected, two-thirds of Africa now faces a high risk of prolonged drought every decade, and the entire developing world has seen, since 1950, a fall in grain production per capita from 163 to 130 kg. All this momentous environmental ruin has incalculable human consequences. Ancient, discrete communities are drawn into downward cycles of political confusion, war, drought, then further environmental degradation, to become finally the statistics of famine relief or UN reports on refugees.

When the imagination attempts to grapple with the processes that have brought this to pass, it can become numbed by the slow, glacial inevitability and ice-age scale of it all. And it is surely, in part, this situation which lies at the bottom of the travel fraternity's prophecies of destruction. Each time one of them has taken a sounding of the global scene, whether in 1917, or 1931 or 1946, 1968, or 1982, they have paid testimony to the same ongoing process. Each traveller, therefore, has painted the picture exactly as they saw it.

There is another crucial sense in which the traveller's vision of great change is absolutely accurate. However, it is important not so much for its revelations about the condition of an external reality, but for what it tells us about the travel experience itself. Always known, but sometimes overlooked, is the extent to which journeys take place on an inward level. Travel books express, in terms of landscape and foreign communities, the interior lives of travellers. They narrate discoveries of self through their experiences of place. They are also, unavoidably, a literature of change and of transformation. That psychological process is inherent in any journey. For the desires and undisclosed urges that motivated a particular venture are either purged or modified by its completion. The self that set out is never quite the one that returns. Equally, the insights and revelations inspired by a journey were unique to it. They can neither be repeated identically on a second visit, nor inherited by the next generation of travellers. They are a deeply private, life-limited category of wealth. For all of these reasons, when travellers start to discuss the idea that the travel scene has evolved out of all recognition, it is likely they are referring as much to changes in themselves as to any alterations in the exterior landscape.

Few things better demonstrate the way in which the travel book is a means of encoding changed states of mind than the travel book title. These express again and again, either directly or by implication, the idea of entry or immersion in alien states of consciousness, then return (e.g. *Through the Dark Continent*, *A Year Among the Circassians*). Otherwise they suggest how the mind has been oriented towards or against certain inward experiences (e.g. *The Fearful Void*, *Out of Africa*). The other striking aspect of travel titles is the extraordinary degree of repetition, as authors search for the formula that accommodates that dual focus – the alien, exotic, often risk-involving geographical landscape and the internal, psychological experience which that external reality imposed. Few things better reveal the way in which authors have constantly returned to the same set of ideas and also borrowed so extensively from their predecessors than when travel titles are encountered *en bloc*. So.

In Darkest Africa, *In Wildest Africa*, *Savage Africa*, *The Curse of Central Africa*, *The Heart of Africa*, *Into Africa*, *Into India*, *Out Of This World*, *Out of Chingford*, *Into The Heart Of Borneo*, *The Heart Of A Continent*, *In The Fiery Continent*, *In the Desert*, *In Morocco*, *In Patagonia*, *In Unknown Arabia*, *In Papua New Guinea*, *In Ethiopia*

With A Mule, Travels With A Donkey, Among The Elephants, Among The Bantu Nomads, Wandering Among South Sea Savages, Among The Indians Of Guiana, Among The Russians, Among The Believers, Among The Hills, Between Desert And Sea, Between The Woods And The Water, Between Two Seas, Twixt Land And Sea, Journey To The Border, To The Frontier, On The Frontier, Borderlines, Crossing The Shadow Line, On The Brink In Bengal, To The Frontier And Beyond, Beyond The Frontiers, Beyond Mexique Bay, Beyond Euphrates, Beyond The River Of The Dead, The Pillars Of Hercules, Beyond The Pillars Of Hercules, Beyond The Dragon's Mouth, Beyond The Ural Mountains, Beyond The Java Sea, Through China's Wall, Behind The Wall, Japan Behind The Fan, Behind God's Back, Last Places, Uttermost Part Of The Earth, Journey In The Centre Of The Earth, The Worst Journey In The World, Journey To Kars, Journey To Java, Journey To The Jade Sea, Journey Into Russia, Journey Into Cyprus, The Journey's Echo, A Sabine Journey, Tibetan Journey, A Journey In The Back Country, Return To The Wild, Return to Tibet, Return to India, Return to the Marshes, Journey Without Return, An Unfinished Journey, Journey Without Maps, Too Late to Turn Back, An Area of Darkness, What Am I Doing Here, In Trouble Again, Alone, Alone in the Wilderness, Alone in the Sleeping Sickness Country, Solo Through The Himalayas, To Lhasa in Disguise, Forbidden Journey, In Forbidden China, In The Forbidden Land, No Passport to Tibet, Captured In Tibet, Secret Tibet, The Truth About Tibet, The Opening of Tibet, The Unveiling of Lhasa, Lhasa and Its Mysteries, Tibet the Mysterious, Forgotten Kingdom, Mustang: A Lost Tibetan Kingdom, Hunza: Lost Kingdom of the Himalayas, Tibet: A Lost World, The Lost World of the Kalahari, The Lost Continent, From The Land of Lost Content, Land of Jade, Land of the Midnight Sun, Land of the Ice King, South to the Pole, North to the Pole, Farthest North, North of North Cape, North of South, South, South From Granada, South From the Red Sea, South of the Sahara, East From Tunis, East of Trebizond, East is West, Orientations, Mirror of the Orient, Mirror to Damascus, Arabia Through the Looking Glass, Visions of a Nomad, Reflections on a Marine Venus, Memoirs of a Bengal Civil Servant, Letters from the Battle-fields of Paraguay, News from Tartary, News from South America, Despatches from the Barricades, Rough Notes Taken During some Rapid Journeys Across the Pampas and Among the Andes, Views from Abroad, A Tramp Abroad, Abroad, At Large, Coasting, Time Off in Southern Italy, Muddling through in Madagascar, Barefoot through Mauretania, On a Shoestring to Coorg, On the Shores of the Mediterranean, The Lycean Shore, The Coast of Incense, The Jade Coast, Coast to Coast, The Road to Santiago, The Road to Oxiana, The Road To Angkor, Tracks Across Alaska: A Dog Sled Journey, On Horseback through Asia Minor, A Ride to Khiva, By Sledge and Horseback to Outcast Siberian Lepers, Wheelbarrow Across The Sahara, Juggernaut Trucking to Saudi Arabia, Round The World On A Wheel, Around The World on a bicycle, On Ancient Central-Asian Tracks, On Alexander's Track To The Indus, Alexander's Path, In Clive's Footsteps, In Stanley's Footsteps, In The Tracks of the Trades, Chasing The Monsoon, A Lull Between Monsoons, A Turn in the South, Italian Hours, Mornings in Mexico, Twilight in Italy, Video Nights in Kathmandu, Siberian Days, Twelve Days, Ninety-Two Days, A Winter With The Finnish Lapps, Last Winter in Algeria, A Winter in Arabia, A Winter In Majorca, A Saudi Arabian Winter, South African Winter, An Indian Summer, A Year In Marrakesh, A Year Amongst The Persians, A Year In Tibet, Two Years Beside the Strait, Three Years in Savage Africa, Three Years in Tibet, Four Years in Paradise, Five Years in the East, Five Years in Damascus, Six Years in the Malay Jungle, Seven Years in Tibet, Ten Years in Sarawak, Twenty Years in Tibet, Forty Years in The Wilderness, A Traveller's Life.

Discussing the travel book's significance as an art form Paul Fussell suggested that 'literary accounts of journeys take us very deeply into the centre of instinctive imaginative life. Like no other kinds of writing, travel books exercise and exploit the fundamental intellectual and emotional figure of thought, by which the past is conceived as back and the future as forward'.[36] One might add that few human experiences – except perhaps dreams and the use of hallucinogenic drugs – are better able to reveal the unconscious mind to the conscious than travel. During the journey the whole processes of repression and accommodation by which the domestic environment was rendered safe and stable have been completely jettisoned. In its place is an unending, unpredictable and random stream of new sensory experiences – a flow of disorienting images which, when chemically induced, is known significantly as a 'trip'.

In these powerfully numinous encounters, the traveller can find the moment and the symbols in which to explore previously unknown areas of the psyche. Travel is, in a sense, the greatest image-association game that a human can play.

Invariably, the more deeply travellers commit themselves to this joyous and dangerous enterprise, the richer their subsequent account of the experience. In fact, it is the level of this commitment and the degree of interior change allowed that are the most important measures of how 'travel' differs from other forms of physical movement. Mere mileage alone is nothing. Those who come home almost exactly as they departed have perhaps not really travelled at all and usually produce the least satisfying travel books. Eric Bailey was the classic example. His stern military education had closed the shutters down on introspection, which left him acutely alert to externals, but almost totally unable to respond to these as a furniture for an inner life. Curiously, however, politico-military figures like Bailey are often those who most fully communicate the sheer disorienting impact of travel, since it is they who are most given to recording the welter of external novelties. This passage by Frederick Spencer Chapman in *Lhasa The Holy City* is typical:

> The low flat-roofed rest-house is surrounded by fields of wonderfully rich barley. Walked down to the lake and watched a man ploughing with two yaks. Followed a winding stream to a lake, and put up a pair of goosanders. There are thousands of animals grazing on the pasture-land here. The lake is very shallow and muddy with sandbanks running far out. Some large fish rippling the surface. Many different kinds of waders and ducks here. Returned by the village. It has turned cold now and is overcast. My face is very sore from the sun. The others returned in the afternoon having seen only one gazelle in the distance.[37]

After reading forty pages of this fragmented stream of consciousness, one feels the presence of a traveller startled by the variety of unfamiliar objects, one who feels he can prevent himself being overwhelmed by the unknown simply by naming all the phenomena. The passage, with its terse, disparate observations piled one on top of the other, is also highly reminiscent of the excited conversation or writings of a young child.

Travel books, in fact, frequently dramatise a return to the innocence and paradise of childhood. By loosening the mental restraints that secure our adult relationship to the world and, in parallel, by liberating the libido, travel often initiates a state of consciousness that is extremely similar to childhood. In journeys we discover all over again the newness of the world. It is also the licence for fun and juvenile adventure associated with a return to innocence which so often gives travel books their great popular appeal. However, it is a process of regression than can have its more sinister side. Few moments in British travel literature more fully reveal the slide from child's paradise to the infant's pristine savagery than one described in Henry Stanley's *How I Met Livingstone*. On his way south from the Arab settlement of Tabora in modern-day Tanzania, the young explorer broke the trek for a spot of hunting. 'I came upon a scene', he wrote, 'which delighted the innermost recesses of my soul;'

> five, six, seven, eight, ten zebras switching their beautiful striped bodies, and biting one another, within about one hundred and fifty yards. The scene was so pretty, so romantic, never did I so thoroughly realize that I was in Central Africa. I felt momentarily proud that I owned such a vast domain, inhabited with such noble beasts. Here I possessed, within reach of a leaden ball, any one I chose of the beautiful animals, the pride of the African forests! It was at my option to shoot any of them! Mine they were without money and without price; yet knowing this, twice I dropped my rifle, loth to wound the royal beasts, but – crack! and a royal one was on his back battling the air with his legs. Ah, it was such a pity! but, hasten, draw the keen sharp-edged knife across the beautiful stripes which fold around the throat; and – what an ugly gash! it is done, and I have a superb animal at my feet. Hurrah![38]

This is a deeply revealing passage. Though Stanley wished to convey a sense of acute internal conflict, there seems a deep inevitability about the final triumph of his urge to destroy. Equally, while the slaughter is intended to appear as highly distasteful to the author, the moment of death is drawn out with great sensual relish; so that what emerges from the passage is not Stanley's Christian decency as intended, but those sado-masochistic tendencies that his biographer, Frank McLynn, has recently documented.[39] In fact, it is difficult to imagine how a dramatic monologue could have more fully or concisely revealed those aspects of the explorer's personality had it been written by Robert Browning. There is, in addition, a wider significance to the passage. Stanley's successive responses to Africa's Eden-like beauty and potential, is firstly a sheer innocent delight in its vibrancy, then a concern for its ownership, next an almost dizzy excitement on recognising the profits its possession could confer, and finally an urge to destroy in order to realise those gains. In dramatising these successive experiences, Stanley has given us in microcosm almost the entire European colonial experiment on that continent.

Few other travel books have revealed so much of the dark side of the wandering spirit as *How I Met Livingstone*; few wanderers, however, had so much darkness to reveal. Nor is Stanley's violent and acquisitive response towards the foreign environment the key-note sounded by the travel book; certainly not by more modern works, whose frequent emotional theme is a sheer delight in the business of living.

Patrick Leigh Fermor's description of an evening in the Peloponnesian town of Kalamata is archetypal. So typically of the author, it is inserted in the travel narrative as a moment of recollection. He, his wife and friend Xan Fielding arrive in the small Maniot fishing village of Kardamyli. They quickly settle into its comfortable little hotel with its 'old and mellow rooms', their wicker chairs and soft mattresses, while the 'civilized and easy-going' host 'induced in all such a lack of hurry that the teeth of time and urgency and haste seemed all to have been pulled'. Uncovering Kardamyli's 'quiet charm' Fermor notes that its isolated position behind a mountain range makes it 'like those Elysian confines of the world where Homer says that life is easiest for men'. Significantly, he points out that it receives only a half-line mention in the *Guide*

Bleu, that it is too remote 'ever to be seriously endangered by tourism. No wonder', he concludes, 'the nereids made it their home'[40] Later the same day, as Fermor and company set to on their evening meal within sight of the sea, the experience recalls an earlier fish supper in Kalamata.

There, oppressed by the intense summer heat, the trio of diners on 'a sudden, silent, decision . . . stepped down fully dressed into the sea carrying the iron table' with them, and continued their meal sat to their waists in the cooling waters. On arriving at their vanished table, the waiter, with 'a quickly masked flicker of pleasure' immediately responded by wading through the shallows himself and, 'with a butler's gravity', served the holiday feast.

> Diverted by this spectacle, the diners on the quay sent us
> can upon can of retsina till the table was crowded. A dozen
> boats soon gathered there, the craft radiating from the
> table's circumference like the petals of a marguerite. Leaning
> from their gently rocking boats, the fishermen helped us out
> with this sudden flux of wine, and by the time the moon
> and the Dog-Star rose over this odd symposium, a
> mandoline had appeared and *manga* songs in praise of
> hashish rose into the swooning night.[41]

In Fermor's evocation of both setting and the memory it invoked one has virtually the entire catalogue of themes pursued by twentieth-century travel writers. In his sense of Kardamyli's status as forgotten land behind the mountains there is the traveller's arch self-consciousness, the feeling and determination to be set apart. In his references to Homer, to Elysium and the nereids one can detect the recurrent concern to resurrect an ancient past and to find those magical points of access to the golden age of myth. In the mellow room's soft mattresses and wicker chairs 'for tired limbs' there is the omnipresent relish for leisure. Then, in the atmosphere of consummate contentment exhaled by the hotel's owner there is the rejection of the modern obsession with haste. Finally, in Fermor's anxious reference to tourism one can sense the traveller's communal fear of modernity's encroachment.

The description of the submerged dinner itself takes us deeper into the meaning of travel writing. We have the organic bond that exists between the rugged but articulate wandering stranger and the simple warm-hearted community of fisherfolk: a relationship as natural as 'the petals of a marguerite'. In their wish for the warm, comforting amniotic embrace of the Mediterranean and in the holiday irrationality of the visitors' behaviour one has the traveller's return to childhood: in fact, the Mad Hatter's tea-party made flesh. In the superfluity of alcohol, the approach of a 'swooning' darkness, the moon, mandoline and *manga* songs in praise of hashish we recognise the classic constituents of the unconscious. Last of all, there is the instantaneous flash of imagination that sets all of this momentarily alight. The cumulative impact of all these elements is twofold. It confirms the idea that travel is one of the great doors to human freedom and that the travel book is a medium through which humans celebrate this freedom. Despite travellers' frequent claims to the contrary, the history of the travel book so far suggests that until the planet is end to end with concrete and plastic it will continue to do so.

Notes

List of Abbreviations

CO   Colonial Office papers in Public Records Office
IOR   India Office Library and Records
PRO   Public Records Office, London
RHL   Rhodes House Library, Oxford
URL   University of Reading Library

Chapter 1: Stiffkey

1   P. Fussell, *Abroad*, page 43.
2   P. Fussell, *Abroad*, page 39.
3   P. Fussell, *Abroad*, page 38.
4   H. St J. Philby, *The Heart of Arabia*, Volume II, pages 117–56.
5   F. Kingdon Ward, *The Riddle of the Tsangpo Gorges*, page 205.
6   F. Stark, *Beyond Euphrates*, Century edition, page 41.
7   R. Byron, *The Road to Oxiana*, Picador edition, page 233.
8   *The Weekend Guardian*, 11–12.11.1989, page 30.
9   *Encyclopaedia Britannica*, Volume 23, page 194.
10   F. Kingdon Ward, *Modern Exploration*, page 41.
11   *Obituaries From The Times 1961–1970*, F. Roberts (Ed.), (London, Newspaper Archive Developments, 1975), pages 43–4.
12   A. Swinson, *Beyond the Frontiers: The Biography of Colonel F. M. Bailey*, page xi.
13   Leonard Moore to FMB, letter dated 1.3.1944, EUR.F.157/309, IOR.
14   *The Observer*, 9.12.1945, EUR.F.157/313, IOR.
15   *News Chronicle*, 27.3.1957, EUR.F.157/313, IOR.
16   A. Swinson, *Beyond the Frontiers*, page ix.
17   Interview with Iris Portal, 21.9.1989.
18   A. Swinson, *Beyond the Frontiers*, pages 232–3.
19   *Eastern Daily Press*, 4.8.1937, article entitled 'Funeral of Mr Harold Davidson'.
20   *Eastern Daily Press*, 29.7.1937, article entitled 'Mr Harold Davidson Mauled By Lion At Skegness'.
21   Tom Cullen, *The Prostitute's Padre* (London, Bodley Head, 1975), page 64.
22   Tom Cullen, *The Prostitute's Padre*, page 104.
23   Tom Cullen, *The Prostitute's Padre*, page 105.
24   F. Brodie, *The Devil Drives*, Eland edition, page 16.

25 J. Raban, *Arabia Through the Looking Glass*, Picador edition, page 15.

Chapter 2: The Hatter

1   F. M. Bailey, *Mission to Tashkent*, page 211.
2   F. M. Bailey, *Mission to Tashkent*, page 224.
3   Meinertzhagen Diaries, Volume I, 9.6.1901, RHL.
4   F. M. Bailey, *China–Tibet–Assam*, page 160.
5   F. M. Bailey, *China–Tibet–Assam*, page 166.
6   F. M. Bailey, *No Passport to Tibet*, page 63.
7   F. M. Bailey, *Mission to Tashkent*, pages 268–9.
8   F. M. Bailey, *China–Tibet–Assam*, page 18.
9   F. M. Bailey, *China–Tibet–Assam*, pages 27–8.
10 Leonard Moore to FMB, letter dated 1.3.1944, EUR.F.157/309, IOR.
11 *Manchester Courier*, 4.4.1912, EUR.F.157/323, IOR.
12 F. M. Bailey, *China–Tibet–Assam*, pages 30–1.
13 F. M. Bailey, *China–Tibet–Assam*, pages 30–4.
14 F. M. Bailey, *Mission to Tashkent*, page 99.
15 F. M. Bailey, *China–Tibet–Assam*, page 35.
16 F. M. Bailey, *China–Tibet–Assam*, pages 65–6.
17 F. M. Bailey, *Mission to Tashkent*, page 124.
18 Lieutenant-Colonel Henry Treves Morshead was born on 23 November 1882 and educated at Winchester College and the Royal Military Academy, Woolwich. When Bailey met him in the Assamese marches he had been employed in the Survey of India for six years. During the First World War he served in France from 1914–1919, and was awarded the DSO. The following year he joined the Waziristan Field Force, and from 1921–1922 he was one of two surveyors with the first British Mount Everest Expedition led by Charles Howard-Bury. Two of the team reached 8,225 metres without oxygen, just 640 metres from the summit. Morshead lost both fingers and toes from frostbite during this period in the Himalaya. Nine years later, on 17 May 1931, while out horse riding in Burma, he was murdered.
19 F. M. Bailey, *No Passport to Tibet*, page 55.
20 F. M. Bailey, *No Passport to Tibet*, page 51.
21 F. M. Bailey, *China–Tibet–Assam*, page 145.
22 F. M. Bailey, *No Passport to Tibet*, page 235.
23 F. M. Bailey, *China–Tibet–Assam*, page 125.
24 F. M. Bailey, *China–Tibet–Assam*, page 37.
25 F. M. Bailey, *China–Tibet–Assam*, page 45.
26 F. M. Bailey, *China–Tibet–Assam*, page 94.
27 F. M. Bailey, *No Passport to Tibet*, page 45.
28 F. M. Bailey, *No Passport to Tibet*, page 45.
29 F. M. Bailey, *China–Tibet–Assam*, page 58.
30 F. M. Bailey, *China–Tibet–Assam*, page 42.
31 F. M. Bailey, *No Passport to Tibet*, pages 113–14; also see Eric Newby's *A Book of Travellers' Tales*, page 331.
32 F. M. Bailey, *No Passport to Tibet*, page 103.
33 F. M. Bailey, *China–Tibet–Assam*, pages 22 and 24.
34 *Overland Mail*, 22.6.1912, EUR.F.157/323, IOR.
35 'The Chinese Frontier of India', Archibald Rose, *Geographical Journal*, volume 39, page 193.
36 F. M. Bailey, 'A Journey Through A Portion of South-Eastern Tibet and The Mishmi

Hills', *Geographical Journal*, volume 39, page 334.
37 Telegram to FMB, dated 16.9.1911, EUR.F.157/274, IOR.
38 Telegram to FMB, dated 6.11.1911, EUR.F.157/274, IOR.
39 F. M. Bailey, *No Passport to Tibet*, pages 31–41.
40 A. Swinson, *Beyond the Frontiers*, page 233.
41 A. Swinson, *Beyond the Frontiers*, page 199.
42 F. M. Bailey, *No Passport to Tibet*, page 70.
43 Interview with Iris Portal, 21.9.1989.
44 A. Swinson, *Beyond the Frontiers*, pages 222–3.

Chapter 3: Lords, Arabian Ladies and Members of the Athenaeum

1 Charles Montagu Doughty (1843–1926) was a poet and traveller, born at Theberton Hall, Suffolk. In 1870, after graduating from Gonville and Caius College, Cambridge, he set out as a poor student across Europe and North Africa. He then went to Palestine, Syria and Egypt, where he developed an interest in geology and Arabia. Having learnt Arabic in Damascus, he joined a caravan on pilgrimage to Mecca. Thus followed twenty-two months of difficult and at times dangerous travel in Central Arabia, during which he gained much new information about the country's geography and the nomadic lifestyle of the Bedu. His account of these adventures, *Travels in Arabia Deserta*, is now considered a classic work on exploration, and strongly influenced a number of other travel writers, particularly T. E. Lawrence. However, in the 1880s it was refused by four publishers before its acceptance by Cambridge University Press. Doughty's emulation of the literary style of the Elizabethans led to a highly complex and poetic book that only became popular after its abridgement by Edward Garnett in 1908 and a subsequent edition in 1921. For the rest of his life Doughty devoted himself to poetry, but this never received the attention of his one prose work.
2 Bertram S. Thomas (1892–1950) was a colonial administrator, explorer and writer, who saw service during the First World War in Belgium, then the Middle East. After six years in Mesopotamia he transferred to Transjordan in 1922, as assistant to the British representative at the court of Emir Abdullah. The British representative at that time was none other than Harry St John Philby. Two years later Thomas became financial adviser to the Sultan of Muscat, and it was in this post that he was able to make a number of exploratory journeys in southern Arabia. Having acquired considerable knowledge of desert travel, he set out in 1930 with a retinue of Bedu to cross from Dhafur in the south to Doha on the Persian Gulf. In so doing he became the first European ever to have explored the Empty Quarter. In later life he became Director of the Middle East Centre of Arabic Studies in Palestine, and later in Lebanon. He wrote several books on Arabia including an account of his crossing of the Rub al Khali, *Arabia Felix*.
3 H. St J. Philby, *Arabian Days*, page 31.
4 E. Monroe, *Philby of Arabia*, page 37.
5 H. St J. Philby, *Arabian Days*, pages 31; also E. Monroe, *Philby of Arabia*, pages 24–5.
6 In the immediate aftermath of the war the Fertile Crescent had been divided into four separate zones each called an Occupied Enemy Territory Administration. Two of these, covering Mesopotamia (later Iraq) and Palestine, were controlled by the British. A third, covering the Lebanon and coastal Syria, went to the French, while the Syrian interior with Damascus as its capital was assigned to the Arabs. At the Paris Peace Conference, however, the British, in order to secure French approval for British control both of the oil-rich areas around Mosul and of Palestine (where they wished to implement a pro-Zionist policy of Jewish settlement), agreed to French occupation of all Syria and Lebanon. In July 1920 French troops seized the formerly Arab-controlled

Occupied Enemy Territory Administration. The following year, in an attempt to give some substance to their pre-war promises to the Arabs, the British conceded the eastern portion of their mandated territory in Palestine to the Hashemite prince Abdullah. This area became known as the fledgling kingdom of Transjordan (later Jordan). Following a fierce revolt in Mesopotamia, the British converted it into the kingdom of Iraq and offered its throne to Abdullah's brother, Feisal. The establishment of both of these 'independent' Arab states was finally agreed at the Cairo Conference in March 1921, presided over by the young Colonial Secretary, Winston Churchill.

7 Wilfrid Scawen Blunt (1840–1922) was a traveller, poet and politician. Following eleven years in the diplomatic service and Blunt's inheritance of his family's Crabbet estates in Sussex, he travelled in the Middle East with his wife Lady Anne. The granddaughter of Byron, she was herself a gifted Arabist and writer, publishing two works on their journeys in Mesopotamia and Central Arabia – *The Bedouin Tribes of the Euphrates* and *A Pilgrimage to Nejd*. Their experiences in Asia, particularly in India and Egypt, convinced Blunt that empire was synonymous with exploitation and that Britain's imperial policies dishonoured his country. He gave vent to these criticisms in his books *The Future of Islam* and *Ideas about India*. His support for Irish independence led eventually to his arrest and imprisonment.

8 E. Monroe, *Philby of Arabia*, page 159.

9 E. Monroe, *Philby of Arabia*, pages 142–4 and 160–1.

10 E. Monroe, *Philby of Arabia*, page 51.

11 H. St J. Philby, *Arabian Days*, page 283.

12 H. St J. Philby, *Forty Years in the Wilderness*, see chapter entitled 'Exile', pages 224–6.

13 In July 1940 Philby fought a by-election for the safe Conservative seat of Hythe as a candidate of the British People's Party.

14 H. St J. Philby, *Arabian Days*, page 281.

15 H. St J. Philby, *Arabian Days*, page 277.

16 H. St J. Philby, *Arabian Days*, page 278.

17 H. St J. Philby, *Arabian Days*, page 281.

18 H. St J. Philby, *The Empty Quarter*, Century edition, pages 109 and 184–5.

19 H. St J. Philby, *Forty Years in the Wilderness*, pages 21–2.

20 H. St J. Philby, 'Rub al Khali: An Account of Exploration In', *Geographical Journal*, volume LXXXI, page 18.

21 H. St J. Philby, *The Empty Quarter*, Century edition, page 261.

22 H. St J. Philby, *Forty Years in the Wilderness*, page 76.

23 H. St J. Philby, *Arabian Days*, preface, page xvi.

24 H. St J. Philby, *The Empty Quarter*, Century edition, page xi.

25 E. Monroe, *Philby of Arabia*, page 152.

26 E. Monroe, *Philby of Arabia*, page 10.

Chapter 4: Old Stone Age

1 E. Monroe, *Philby of Arabia*, pages 15–16.

2 E. Monroe, *Philby of Arabia*, page 270.

3 W. Thesiger, *The Life of My Choice*, page 258.

4 S. Freud, 'Moses and Monotheism', *The Complete Psychological Works of Sigmund Freud*, Volume 22, 1937–9 (London, Hogarth Press, 1964), pages 117–19.

5 G. Maxwell, *A Reed Shaken by the Wind*, Four Square edition, page 8.

6 This claim, first made by Sir John Glubb in the *Sunday Times* review of *Arabian Sands*, appears in the biographical details for the Penguin paperback editions of both the latter book and *The Marsh Arabs*. It also appears in the dust-jacket blurb of *Arabian Sands*.

7   H. St J. Philby, *Forty Years in the Wilderness*, page 78.
8   For a full explanation of why Thesiger was obliged to leave Arabia see the final chapter of *Arabian Sands*, Penguin edition, 'The Closing Door'.
9   Interview with Wilfred Thesiger, 17.5.1989.
10 Interview with Wilfred Thesiger, 17.5.1989.
11 W. Thesiger, *The Life of My Choice*, page 56.
12 Interview with Wilfred Thesiger, 17.5.1989.
13 Interview with Wilfred Thesiger, 17.5.1989.
14 W. Thesiger, *Desert, Marsh and Mountain*, page 31.
15 W. Thesiger, *The Life of My Choice*, page 56.
16 W. Thesiger, *Visions of a Nomad*, page 9.
17 W. Thesiger, *The Life of My Choice*, page 432.
18 W. Thesiger, *Arabian Sands*, Penguin edition, page 50.
19 Interview with Wilfred Thesiger, 17.5.1989.
20 W. Thesiger, *Arabian Sands*, Penguin edition, pages 157–9.
21 W. Thesiger, *Arabian Sands*, Penguin edition, pages 322–5.
22 E. Monroe, *Philby of Arabia*, page 180.
23 H. St J. Philby, *The Empty Quarter*, Century edition, page 219.
24 H. St J. Philby, *The Empty Quarter*, Century edition, page 261.
25 H. St J. Philby, *The Empty Quarter*, Century edition, page 261.
26 H. St J. Philby, *The Empty Quarter*, Century edition, page 216.
27 E. Monroe, *Philby of Arabia*, page 190.
28 H. St J. Philby, *The Empty Quarter*, Century edition, page 200.
29 H. St J. Philby, *The Empty Quarter*, Century edition, page 210.
30 H. St J. Philby, *The Empty Quarter*, Century edition, pages 320–4.
31 E. Monroe, *Philby of Arabia*, page 191.
32 Interview with Wilfred Thesiger, 17.5.1989.
33 W. Thesiger, *Arabian Sands*, Penguin edition, pages 121–2.
34 W. Thesiger, *Arabian Sands*, Penguin edition, page 18.
35 W. Thesiger, *Arabian Sands*, Penguin edition, page 86.
36 W. Thesiger, *Arabian Sands*, Penguin edition, pages 166–7.
37 P. Brent, *Far Arabia*, page 22.
38 W. Thesiger, *Arabian Sands*, Penguin edition, page 38.
39 W. Thesiger, *Arabian Sands*, Penguin edition, page 14.
40 *Geographical Journal*, volume CXI, page 300.
41 W. Thesiger, *Arabian Sands*, Penguin edition, page 142.
42 E. Monroe, *Philby of Arabia*, page 187.
43 H. St J. Philby, *The Empty Quarter*, Century edition, page vii.
44 W. Thesiger, *Arabian Sands*, Penguin edition, page 18.
45 G. Young, *Return to the Marshes*, Penguin edition, page 13.
46 H. St J. Philby, *Forty Years in the Wilderness*, page 78.
47 Interview with Wilfred Thesiger, 17.5.1989.
48 G. Maxwell, *A Reed Shaken by the Wind*, Four Square edition, page 8.
49 W. Thesiger, *Arabian Sands*, Penguin edition, page 8.
50 W. Thesiger, *Desert, Marsh and Mountain*, page 298.
51 Interview with Wilfred Thesiger, 17.5.1989.
52 Interview with Wilfred Thesiger, 17.5.1989.
53 E. Monroe, *Philby of Arabia*, page 296.
54 E. Monroe, *Philby of Arabia*, page 232.
55 Interview with Wilfred Thesiger, 17.5.1989.
56 W. Thesiger, *Arabian Sands*, Penguin edition, pages 92–9.

57   W. Thesiger, *Arabian Sands*, Penguin edition, pages 127–30.
58   W. Thesiger, *Arabian Sands*, Penguin edition, pages 145–6.
59   W. Thesiger, *Arabian Sands*, Penguin edition, page 148.
60   W. Thesiger, *Arabian Sands*, Penguin edition, page 14; also Interview with Wilfred Thesiger, 17.5.1989.
61   W. Thesiger, *Arabian Sands*, Penguin edition, page 38.
62   W. Thesiger, *Arabian Sands*, Penguin edition, page 177.
63   W. Thesiger, *Arabian Sands*, Penguin edition, page 37.
64   J. Raban, *Arabia Through the Looking Glass*, Fontana edition, page 16.
65   W. Thesiger, *Desert, Marsh and Mountain*, page 123.
66   W. Thesiger, *Arabian Sands*, Penguin edition, page 34.
67   G. Young, *Worlds Apart*, Penguin edition, page 277.
68   W. Thesiger, *The Life of My Choice*, page 443.
69   A. Moorehead, *The White Nile*, page 78.

Chapter 5: Truth Stranger than Friction

1   *The Englishman*, 19.9.1920.
2   W. Thesiger, *Arabian Sands*, Penguin edition, pages 227–8.
3   D. Murphy, *In Ethiopia With a Mule*, pages 156–71.
4   Interview with Wilfred Thesiger, 17.5.1989; also see G. Maxwell, *A Reed Shaken by the Wind*, Four Square edition, pages 147–51.
5   F. Stark, *The Southern Gates of Arabia*, pages 270–88.
6   Colonel Gerard Evelyn Leachman, born 27 July 1880, entered the army in 1900, reaching the rank of captain by 1910. He distinguished himself in the Boer War and by the middle years of the First World War had risen to the rank of Brevet Lieutenant-Colonel. For his travels in north-east Arabia, Leachman was awarded the Gill Memorial by the Royal Geographical Society in 1911, the year before it was given to Frederick Bailey. Like the Tibetan explorer he also received the Macgregor Medal from the Royal United Service Institute, in 1910. During his travels Leachman made few concessions to the locals and was known to be a harsh master, contemptuous of most Arabs. His merciless treatment of his servants apparently offended T. E. Lawrence on the occasion that they met. During the Arab uprising in Mesopotamia in 1920 he was serving as political officer in Ramadi. On 12 August he was shot in the back by a sheikh, after having apparently spat in the man's face.
7   Captain William Henry Irving Shakespear was born in India in 1879. After an English education and attendance at Sandhurst, he served as an assistant district officer in Bombay. Joining the Political Department, he was transferred in 1904 to Bushire in Persia, as assistant to the political resident. At only twenty-five he then became consul in Bandar Abbas, the youngest consul appointed by Delhi. In 1908, following other posts in Muscat and Hyderabad, he spent his leave driving a single-cylinder Rover car from Persia to the French coast. His next appointment as political agent in Kuwait permitted his first explorations of Arabia, which culminated in his crossing of the northern peninsula from Kuwait to Egypt in 1914. During his desert travel he stubbornly refused to compromise on issues of costume, behaviour or faith. He was, however, renowned for his courage and sympathetic attitudes to the Arabs. His firm friendship with the young Wahhabi leader, ibn Saud, also smoothed his progress, and was the background to his persistent advocacy of the Arab cause in opposition to Whitehall's support for the Turkish Empire. Shakespear was eventually killed in 1915, when he took part in hostilities between ibn Saud's forces and those of an old adversary, ibn Rashid, the Amir of Hail.

Notes

8 W. Thesiger, *Arabian Sands*, Penguin edition, pages 243–5.

9 W. Thesiger, *The Marsh Arabs*, pages 143–8; also G. Maxwell, *A Reed Shaken by the Wind*, Four Square edition, pages 77–9.

10 *The Bookseller*, 9.2.52.

11 *National Review*, February 1952.

12 *Daily Telegraph*, review by Guy Ramsey entitled 'The Secret Places of Land and Spirit', 25.1.52.

13 *The Observer*, review by Harold Nicolson entitled 'Explorations', 27.1.52.

14 *Sunday Times*, review by Raymond Mortimer entitled 'Into Africa', 27.1.52.

15 *Country Life*, February 1952, review entitled 'A Noble Book of Travel'.

16 *Rhodesia Herald*, 30.1.52, review entitled 'Mission to Nyasaland Yields One of Best Books in Recent Years'.

17 *Cape Argus*, review entitled 'Journey in Two Mediums', 2.2.52.

18 *Rand Daily Mail*, review entitled 'South African Seeks the Essential Africa', 10.2.52.

19 Report entitled 'The Afforestability of the Nyika Plateau', by Dr Ian Craib, PRO CO 1015/479/82/41/01.

20 L. van der Post, *Venture to the Interior*, page 141. In van der Post's version of the trek during which the accident occurred there is a curious 'loss' of a whole day. The group apparently departed on Monday 23 May and Vance was killed on Saturday 28 May, though the author gives an account of only five days of walking. See pages 123–46.

21 L. van der Post, *Yet Being Someone Other*, page 31.

22 L. van der Post, *Venture to the Interior*, page 28.

23 Van der Post has included a brief portrait of his childhood in *Venture to the Interior*, *The Lost World of the Kalahari* and *Jung and the Story of Our Time*. From these it appears that his parents and grandparents operated a highly tolerant regime, their black workers living in very close relations with the van der Post family.

24 F. I. Carpenter, *Laurens van der Post*, page 35.

25 L. van der Post, *The Lost World of the Kalahari*, page 62.

26 L. van der Post, *Venture to the Interior*, Preface, page xiii.

27 Van der Post has given the fullest and most direct account of his interpretation of European history in *Jung and the Story of Our Time*. See the chapter entitled 'The Time and the Space'.

28 L. van der Post, *Journey Into Russia*, page 284.

29 L. van der Post, *Venture to the Interior*, page 109.

30 L. van der Post, *Venture to the Interior*, page 230.

31 L. van der Post, *Venture to the Interior*, pages 94–5.

32 L. van der Post, *Venture to the Interior*, page 160.

33 L. van der Post, *Venture to the Interior*, page 211.

34 L. van der Post, *Venture to the Interior*, pages 212–13.

35 L. van der Post, *A Walk with a White Bushman*, Penguin edition, page 26.

36 L. van der Post, *The Lost World of the Kalahari*, page 10.

37 L. van der Post, *The Lost World of the Kalahari*, page 12.

38 L. van der Post, *The Lost World of the Kalahari*, page 12.

39 L. van der Post, *The Lost World of the Kalahari*, page 69.

40 L. van der Post, *The Lost World of the Kalahari*, page 9.

41 L. van der Post, *The Lost World of the Kalahari*, page 26.

42 L. van der Post, *The Lost World of the Kalahari*, page 26.

43 L. van der Post, *A Walk with a White Bushman*, Penguin edition, page 28.

44 *The Economist*, review entitled 'In Search of the Bushmen', 15.11.58.

45 *Times Literary Supplement*, review entitled 'Hidden Bushmen', 28.11.58.

46 In his book *The Hero with a Thousand Faces*, Joseph Campbell identified the recurrent

ingredients of the quest mono-myth. Many of these elements are evident in *The Lost World of the Kalahari:*

1. Call to Adventure = prior to the Kalahari expedition van der Post had a dramatic realisation on waking from a deep sleep that he must 'go and find the Bushman'.

2. Wonder journey = the voyage into little known parts of the Okovango and Kalahari.

3. Tests = the feud with Spode; the temporary stranding in the swamp; Spode's resignation; the need to seek out a replacement cameraman; the assault by bees; the failure of their cameras and recording equipment at the Slippery Hills.

4. Helper = Samutchoso – the medicine man.

5. Atonement = written apology to the spirits of the Slippery Hills.

6. Resurrection = the location and filming of the San.

7. Elixir = the film of the San.

See *The Hero with a Thousand Faces*, Paladin edition, page 245.

47 L. van der Post, *The Lost World of the Kalahari*, page 152.
48 L. van der Post, *A Walk with a White Bushman*, Penguin edition, page 31.
49 L. van der Post, *A Walk with a White Bushman*, Penguin edition, page 32.
50 L. van der Post, *The Lost World of the Kalahari*, page 78.
51 L. van der Post, *The Lost World of the Kalahari*, page 171.
52 L. van der Post, *The Lost World of the Kalahari*, pages 93–4.
53 L. van der Post, *The Lost World of the Kalahari*, page 186.
54 L. van der Post, *The Lost World of the Kalahari*, page 198.
55 L. van der Post, *The Lost World of the Kalahari*, page 168.
56 L. van der Post, *The Lost World of the Kalahari*, pages 81–2.
57 L. van der Post, *Venture to the Interior*, page 110.
58 L. van der Post, *Venture to the Interior*, page 123.
59 L. van der Post, *Venture to the Interior*, page 129.
60 L. van der Post, *Venture to the Interior*, page 130.
61 *Daily Worker*, undated review entitled 'Mystery Journey'; see Hogarth Press reviews, album no. 2 pages 123–32, URL.
62 *Times Literary Supplement*, review entitled 'Hidden Bushmen', 28.11.58.
63 *Tatler*, 30.1.52.
64 *Daily Mail*, review entitled 'He Brings Africa Back Alive', 2.2.52.
65 L. van der Post, *The Lost World of the Kalahari*, page 218.
66 L. van der Post, *The Lost World of the Kalahari*, page 20.
67 L. van der Post, *The Lost World of the Kalahari*, page 218.
68 L. van der Post, *The Lost World of the Kalahari*, page 20.
69 L. van der Post, *The Lost World of the Kalahari*, page 219.
70 L. van der Post, *The Lost World of the Kalahari*, page 157.
71 L. van der Post, *The Lost World of the Kalahari*, page 79.
72 L. van der Post, *The Dark Eye in Africa*, page 14.
73 L. van der Post, *The Dark Eye in Africa*, page 88.
74 L. van der Post, *The Lost World of the Kalahari*, page 20.
75 L. van der Post, *The Lost World of the Kalahari*, page 168.
76 L. van der Post, *The Lost World of the Kalahari*, page 150.
77 L. van der Post, *The Heart of the Hunter*, pages 74–6.
78 'A Sting and a Prayer', by John Hatt, *Harpers and Queen*, September 1991, pages 232–8.
79 L. van der Post, *Venture to the Interior*, page 148.
80 L. van der Post, *The Lost World of the Kalahari*, page 9.
81 L. van der Post, *Venture to the Interior*, page 7.
82 L. van der Post, *The Lost World of the Kalahari*, page 12.

Notes

83 L. van der Post, *Venture to the Interior*, pages 96–7.
84 L. van der Post, *Venture to the Interior*, pages 145–6.
85 L. van der Post, *Venture to the Interior*, page 155.
86 *The Listener*, 20.11.58.
87 *New Statesman*, review entitled 'Africa and Her Prodigies', 26.1.52.
88 Letter from Leonard Moore to FMB, 19.10.55, IOR, MSS EUR F157/309.
89 F. I. Carpenter, *Laurens van der Post*, page 8.

Chapter 6: The Overreacher

1   G. Maxwell, *Harpoon at a Venture*, Four Square edition, page 88.
2   G. Maxwell, *Harpoon at a Venture*, Four Square edition, pages 89–90.
3   *Folio*, Summer 1990, page 13.
4   R. Frere, *Maxwell's Ghost*, page 11.
5   R. Frere, *Maxwell's Ghost*, page 11.
6   K. Raine, *The Lion's Mouth*, page 154.
7   R. Frere, *Maxwell's Ghost*, page 19.
8   K. Raine, *The Lion's Mouth*, page 13.
9   G. Maxwell, *The House of Elrig*, pages 157–78.
10 G. Maxwell, *Raven Seek Thy Brother*, page 103.
11 Memorandum by Mark Longman, dated 16.4.1957, Longmans Green Archive, File no. 267/10, URL.
12 Memorandum by Michael Hoare dated 13.8.1965, Longmans Green Archive, File no. 259/21, URL.
13 Memorandum by Mark Longman for John Guest, dated 31.1.1958, Longmans Green Archive File no. 258/3; also memorandum by Mark Longman dated 13.12.1957, File no. 267/10, URL.
14 Interview with Wilfred Thesiger, 17.5.1989.
15 Interview with Douglas Botting, 23.5.1990.
16 The strains of living and travelling in such confined conditions with such a tough companion, combined, no doubt, with Maxwell's overly sensitive personality, meant that his period in the Iraqi marshes was occasionally quite difficult. His linguistic deficiencies also contributed to his inability to establish especially positive relations with the Ma'dan. Interview with Wilfred Thesiger, 17.5.1989.
17 G. Maxwell, *God Protect me from my Friends*, Readers Union edition, page 5.
18 Letter from Maxwell to Mark Longman, dated 6.6.1955, Longmans Green Archive, File no. 267/10, URL.
19 Letter from Maxwell to Mark Longman, dated 6.6.1955, Longmans Green Archive, File no. 267/10, URL.
20 W. Thesiger, *The Marsh Arabs*, Penguin edition, page 13.
21 G. Maxwell, *Lords of the Atlas*, Century edition, page 9.
22 P. Fussell, *Abroad*, pages 202–3.
23 G. Maxwell, *Harpoon at a Venture*, Four Square edition, page 156.
24 Memorandum probably by Michael Longman, dated 24.11.1954, Longmans Green Archive, File no. 259/21, URL.
25 G. Maxwell, *Ring of Bright Water*, page 38.
26 G. Maxwell, *Ring of Bright Water*, page 13.
27 G. Maxwell, *Ring of Bright Water*, pages 17–18.
28 G. Maxwell, *Harpoon at a Venture*, Four Square edition, pages 161–2.
29 G. Maxwell, *Harpoon at a Venture*, Four Square edition, page 161.
30 G. Maxwell, *Harpoon at a Venture*, Four Square edition, page 163.

31 G. Maxwell, *Harpoon at a Venture*, Four Square edition, page 162.

32 G. Maxwell, *Harpoon at a Venture*, Four Square edition, page 165.

33 G. Maxwell, *A Reed Shaken by the Wind*, Four Square edition, page 135; also G. Maxwell, *Harpoon at a Venture*, Four Square edition, pages 124–5.

34 G. Maxwell, *Harpoon at a Venture*, Four Square edition, page 15.

35 G. Maxwell, *Harpoon at a Venture*, Four Square edition, page 186.

36 G. Maxwell, *Harpoon at a Venture*, Four Square edition, page 12.

37 G. Maxwell, *Ring of Bright Water*, page 10.

38 G. Maxwell, *Ring of Bright Water*, page 12.

39 G. Maxwell, *Harpoon at a Venture*, Four Square edition, page 13.

40 G. Maxwell, *Harpoon at a Venture*, Four Square edition, page 162.

41 G. Maxwell, *Ring of Bright Water*, page vii.

42 Interview with Douglas Botting, 23.5.1990.

43 G. Maxwell, *Lords of the Atlas*, Century edition, page 11.

44 G. Maxwell, *Ring of Bright Water*, page vii.

45 G. Maxwell, *Raven Seek Thy Brother*, page 13.

46 *Folio*, Summer 1990, page 13.

47 G. Maxwell, *Harpoon at a Venture*, Four Square edition, page 35.

48 G. Maxwell, *Harpoon at a Venture*, Four Square edition, page 19.

49 G. Maxwell, *Harpoon at a Venture*, Four Square edition, page 177.

50 G. Maxwell, *Harpoon at a Venture*, Four Square edition, page 86.

51 G. Maxwell, *Harpoon at a Venture*, Four Square edition, pages 86–8.

52 It is conceivable that Maxwell's persistent error over the gender of the basking shark offers some insight into the author's own sexuality. According to Frere, his friend was a bisexual. Maxwell's marriage to Lavinia Lascelles in 1962 lasted barely twelve months and was annulled in 1964. Generally he appears to have preferred the company of his own gender, particularly adolescents with whom 'he was gentle in his affections'; these young men, according to Frere, 'gained sophistication and wisdom from his patronage'. In *Harpoon at a Venture*, Maxwell appears to project onto his daily struggle with the sharks elements of the internal discord deriving from his confused sexuality. The sexual symbolism of a giant fish is obvious. Moreover, it seems significant that in *The House of Elrig*, where Maxwell discusses his slow development in adolescence, he refers to his own bisexual urges as 'the phantom serpent' and 'the demon'. This symbolic language is strikingly similar to the dragon images he uses in association with the basking shark. The idea that Maxwell identified his submerged, perhaps troublesome desires with the subaqueous shark meshes fully with the moral tag he attaches to his role as shark fisherman: i.e. he as dragon-slayer is good, the fish he kills is evil.

53 G. Maxwell, *Harpoon at a Venture*, Four Square edition, page 64.

54 G. Maxwell, *Harpoon at a Venture*, Four Square edition, page 67.

55 G. Maxwell, *Harpoon at a Venture*, Four Square edition, page 18.

56 G. Maxwell, *Harpoon at a Venture*, Four Square edition, page 19.

57 G. Maxwell, *Harpoon at a Venture*, Four Square edition, page 25.

58 G. Maxwell, *Harpoon at a Venture*, Four Square edition, page 64.

59 G. Maxwell, *Harpoon at a Venture*, Four Square edition, page 177; see also page 58.

60 G. Maxwell, *Harpoon at a Venture*, Four Square edition, page 90.

61 G. Maxwell, *Harpoon at a Venture*, Four Square edition, page 185.

62 G. Maxwell, *Ring of Bright Water*, page 6.

63 There is every likelihood that, had Maxwell been able to keep himself afloat financially, his business would eventually have declined because of over-fishing. Since almost nothing is known about the basking shark's population size or breeding behaviour it would have been very difficult to assess an appropriate quota to ensure the sustainability

of his harvest. None the less, it seems that Maxwell never considered the need for such measures; his sole concern was maximising his catch. It is highly probable that his own efforts would have mirrored those of two other basking-shark fisheries – one operating off Achill Island in Ireland and one run by Norwegians in their national waters and those of Britain and Ireland. Both have followed the mindless boom-bust pattern so typical of European fisheries. The catch of the Achill operation declined in 1975 to only 38 sharks from the 1952 maximum of 1,808. The Norwegian total slumped by 1985 to almost a seventh of its 1960 total of 4,266. See Earll, B., 'The Basking Shark: Its fishery and conservation'. *British Wildlife*, Vol. 1 (1990), pages 121–9.

64 G. Maxwell, *Harpoon at a Venture*, Four Square edition, page 163–7.
65 *The Times*, pages 8, 28.5.1952.
66 G. Maxwell, *Harpoon at a Venture*, Four Square edition, page 163.
67 Memorandum, probably by Michael Longman, dated 24.11.1954, Longmans Green Archive, File no. 259/21, URL.
68 R. Frere, *Maxwell's Ghost*, page 71.
69 Interview with Douglas Botting, 23.5.1990.
70 Interview with Richard Frere, 29.7.1989.
71 G. Maxwell, *Harpoon at a Venture*, Four Square edition, page 26.
72 G. Maxwell, *The Rocks Remain*, page 96.
73 Letter from Maxwell to Mark Longman, dated 23.5.1955, Longmans Green Archive, File no. 267/10, URL.
74 R. Frere, *Maxwell's Ghost*, page 247.
75 G. Maxwell, *The Rocks Remain*, pages 111–14.
76 G. Maxwell, *Raven Seek Thy Brother*, pages 124–30.
77 G. Maxwell, *Harpoon at a Venture*, Four Square edition, page 23.
78 G. Maxwell, *Raven Seek Thy Brother*, page 34.
79 G. Maxwell, *Raven Seek Thy Brother*, page 167.
80 *Dictionary of National Biography 1961–1970* (Oxford, Oxford University Press, 1981), page 745.
81 G. Maxwell, *Raven Seek Thy Brother*, pages 2–3.
82 G. Maxwell, *The Rocks Remain*, pages 56.
83 Memorandum by John Guest, dated 18.3.1957, Longmans Green Archive, File no. 258/3, URL.
84 R. Frere, *Maxwell's Ghost*, pages 248–9.
85 G. Maxwell, *The Rocks Remain*, page 90.
86 G. Maxwell, *The Rocks Remain*, page 88.
87 G. Maxwell, *The Rocks Remain*, page 90.
88 G. Maxwell, *Raven Seek Thy Brother*, pages 13–14.
89 G. Maxwell, *Raven Seek Thy Brother*, page 13.
90 G. Maxwell, *Raven Seek Thy Brother*, page 3.
91 R. Frere, *Maxwell's Ghost*, page 29; also interview with Douglas Botting, 23.5.1990.
92 Interview with Richard Frere, 29.7.1989; also interview with Douglas Botting, 23.5.1990.
93 Memorandum by John Guest for Mark Longman, dated 7.4.1963, Longmans Green Archive, File no. 309/1, URL.
94 Interview with Richard Frere, 29.7.1989; also interview with Douglas Botting, 23.5.1990.
95 R. Adams, *The Adventures of Gavin Maxwell*, page 6.
96 G. Maxwell, *Raven Seek Thy Brother*, pages 45–6.
97 G. Maxwell, *Raven Seek Thy Brother*, page 5.
98 R. Frere, *Maxwell's Ghost*, page 21.

99   K. Raine, *The Lion's Mouth*, page 154.
100   G. Maxwell, *Raven Seek Thy Brother*, page 132.
101   E. Newby, *A Book of Travellers' Tales*, page 26.
102   Interview with John Hatt, 18.9.1989.

Chapter 7: The Purpose of the Traveller

1   Even this Tibetan form of pilgrimage seems mild compared with the exertions performed by the Nigerian Muslim Philby met in 1930, who claimed to be 120 years old, and who had been on the road for seventy years in his journey from Lagos to Jedda. By careful enquiry Philby established that the pilgrim had been in Khartoum at the time of General Gordon's murder in 1885. Philby also wrote of another man who had taken fourteen years to complete the round trip with his wife, and had a family of six en route. See H. St J. Philby, *A Pilgrim in Arabia*, pages 29–30.

2   G. Moorhouse, *The Fearful Void*, Paladin edition, pages 34–35.

3   Interview with Wilfred Thesiger, 17.5.1989.

4   For Byron's agnosticism see C. Sykes, *Four Studies in Loyalty*, page 91; for T. E. Lawrence see his *The Mint*, page 146; also J. Wilson, *Lawrence of Arabia*, page 713, and Lawrence James, *The Golden Warrior* (London, Weidenfeld & Nicolson, 1990), page 342; for Dervla Murphy see her *In Ethiopia With A Mule*, pages 156–7.

5   *The Evening Star*, review entitled 'Journey in Nyasaland', undated; see Hogarth Press reviews, album no. 2, pages 123–32, URL.

6   *Sunday Times*, review by Raymond Mortimer entitled 'Into Africa', 27.1.1952.

7   P. Fussell, *Abroad*, page 77.

8   *The Spectator*, review by Peter Fleming entitled 'African Close-ups', 22.2.1952.

9   *New Statesman*, review by V. S. Pritchett entitled 'Africa and her Prodigies', 26.1.1952.

10   *Daily Worker*, undated review entitled 'Mystery Journey'; see Hogarth Press reviews, album no. 2, pages 123–32, URL.

11   *Daily Herald*, review by Dudley Barker entitled 'A Poet in Search of Food', 29.1.1952.

12   *The Observer*, review by Harold Nicolson entitled 'Explorations', 27.1.1952.

13   P. Brent, *Far Arabia*, page 22.

14   H. M. Stanley, *How I Found Livingstone*, Time Life edition, page 411.

15   *Obituaries From The Times 1961–1970*, F. Roberts (Ed.), (London, Newspaper Archive Developments, 1975), page 43.

16   E. Newby, *A Short Walk in the Hindu Kush*, Picador edition, page 63.

17   W. Thesiger, *The Life of My Choice*, dustjacket blurb.

18   E. Newby, *A Short Walk in the Hindu Kush*, Picador edition, pages 246–247.

19   E. Newby, *A Short Walk in the Hindu Kush*, Picador edition, page 248.

20   G. Moorhouse, *To The Frontier*, page 239.

21   Interview with Geoffrey Moorhouse, 31.7.89.

22   G. Moorhouse, *The Fearful Void*, Paladin edition, page 99.

23   G. Maxwell, *A Reed Shaken by the Wind*, Four Square edition, page 83.

24   Harry Johnston, quoted in A. Moorehead, *The White Nile*, page 1.

25   A. Moorehead, *The White Nile*, page 72.

26   Viscount Strangford, quoted in F. McLynn, *Burton: Snow upon the Desert*, page 230.

27   F. McLynn, *Burton: Snow upon the Desert*, pages 233–5; also F. Brodie, *The Devil Drives*, Eland edition, pages 226–7.

28   A. Moorehead, *The White Nile*, page 97.

29   S. W. Baker, *The Albert N'Yanza*, Volume II, pages 88–90.

30   F. Brodie, *The Devil Drives*, Eland edition, pages 334–335.

31   F. Brodie, *The Devil Drives*, Eland edition, page 16.

32 F. Brodie, *The Devil Drives*, Eland edition, page 30.

33 F. Brodie, *The Devil Drives*, Eland edition, page 142.

34 F. McLynn, *Burton: Snow upon the Desert*, page 106.

35 F. Brodie, *The Devil Drives*, Eland edition, page 153.

36 M. Brown (Ed.), *The Letters of T. E. Lawrence* (London, Dent, 1988), page 325.

37 See L. Butler, *Robert Byron: Letters Home*, page 87.

38 F. McLynn, *Burton: Snow upon the Desert*, page 106.

39 L. Butler, *Robert Byron: Letters Home*, page 57. If not rebellious at school, both Gavin Maxwell and Wilfred Thesiger have written of their lack of achievement in boyhood. In *The House of Elrig* Maxwell wrote: 'I had been placed in a high form on my arrival at Stowe . . . I was soon indisputably last of the field. I slid, like a towel slipping sluggishly from a towel-horse, to the bottom of the form of twenty-eight boys, and there or thereabouts I remained during my two years at Stowe'. See the Penguin edition, pages 151–2. Thesiger has described himself as 'an unreceptive boy to teach, disinclined to concentrate on any subject that bored me. I certainly learnt next to nothing at St Aubyn's and when I took the Common Entrance examination for Eton I failed so ignominiously that the authorities wrote to my mother that it would be futile for me to try again'. See W. Thesiger, *The Life of My Choice*, page 68.

40 F. McLynn, *Burton: Snow upon the Desert*, page 373.

41 D. Garnett (Ed.), *The Letters of T. E. Lawrence* (London, Cape, 1938), page 559.

42 D. Garnett (Ed.), *The Letters of T. E. Lawrence*, page 551.

43 H. M. Stanley, *How I Found Livingstone*, Time Life edition, page 425.

44 H. M. Stanley, *How I Found Livingstone*, Time Life edition, page 430.

45 H. M. Stanley, *How I Found Livingstone*, Time Life edition, pages 430–45.

46 H. M. Stanley, *How I Found Livingstone*, Time Life edition, page 429.

47 Reginald Coupland, *Livingstone's Last Journey* (London, Collins, 1945), page 180.

48 F. McLynn, *Stanley: The Making of an African Explorer*, page 154.

49 J. H. Speke, *Journal of the Discovery of the Source of the Nile*, Dent edition, page 369.

50 F. Brodie, *The Devil Drives*, Eland edition, page 119 and 142. ˋ

51 L. van der Post, *Venture to the Interior*, page 12.

52 J. Raban, *Coasting*, Picador edition, page 18.

53 F. McLynn, *Burton: Snow upon the Desert*, page 367.

54 F. Brodie, *The Devil Drives*, Eland edition, page 16.

55 H. St J. Philby, *Forty Years in the Wilderness*, page 260.

56 H. St J. Philby, *Forty Years in the Wilderness*, pages 18–9.

57 H. St J. Philby, *Forty Years in the Wilderness*, page 76.

58 L. van der Post, *Jung and the Story of Our Time*, page 6.

59 L. van der Post, *Jung and the Story of Our Time*, page 42.

60 L. van der Post, *Venture to the Interior*, page 241.

61 L. van der Post, *The Heart of the Hunter*, page 10. If one accepts Frederick Carpenter's idea that van der Post has created in both his fiction and non-fiction 'a new kind of autobiographical hero, part history and part myth', and if one can view the fictional characters as a kind of avatar of the author himself, then van der Post's self-image as contemporary prophet reaches its apotheosis in one of his early novels *Flamingo Feather*.

The book, set in southern Africa in 1948, concerns a complex Soviet-backed plot to foment revolution throughout the continent. Operating under the cover of a major South African commercial company, the Russians have smuggled in large quantities of arms and also cigarette lighters containing odourless, colourless and tasteless organic poison, to be administered in every white household by black servants. The Soviets have also manipulated for their own ends an African tribal legend concerning a prophetic dream, whose occurrence will signal the moment for a final overthrow of the colonial powers.

Although the revolt is unfolding before their very eyes, the white administration is completely unaware. Having shunned the primitive element in themselves, 'the correct lovable island British' are unable to see 'the resurgent tide of neglected, hurt and dishonoured African darkness' that is about to overwhelm them. Singlehandedly, the book's hero, Pierre de Beauvilliers, a character extraordinarily similar to van der Post himself, sets out to foil the Soviet plot. In securing this end, van der Post's alter ego averts 'the biggest disaster Africa has ever seen'. He is thus the superman-like, world-saving hero, whose achievements go unnoticed by the English, as they 'sit sipping iced whiskies and sodas at tennis parties'.

It is interesting to note that van der Post's role as wise man and prophet is by no means exclusively self-proclaimed. Others have repeatedly expressed his exceptional qualities as a leader and interpreter of his age. Fellow officers in the Japanese prison in Java have written of him: 'Such a man in a P.O.W. camp is the equivalent of a host of angels, shedding light and strength upon all the sorts and conditions of men . . . Many lives were saved, tragedies averted and souls rescued by his activities'. Another wrote: 'If Christ ever comes back to earth it will be in the form of Colonel van der Post. He saved our sanity and our lives.' See F. I. Carpenter, *Laurens van der Post*, page 53.

Frank Debenham, the leader of one of van der Post's earlier journeys into the Kalahari and author of *Kalahari Sand*, has written:

> Waiting for me at the hotel was the man whom I rather suspect will be the dominant figure in this book. Just once or twice in a lifetime one meets a man whom one recognises instantly . . . as 'after one's own heart' . . . and for whom one falls almost at the first handshake . . . If I were the titular head of the Mission, it was Van who was the real head as far as organisation, planning and execution was [sic] concerned.

See *Kalahari Sand*, page 41.

Jean-Marc Pottiez, the interviewer in *A Walk with a White Bushman*, wrote: 'a man of all continents like him [van der Post] had to play the vital role of a bridge between individuals and nations torn apart by indifference, intolerance, war, hatred, ideologies, racism, nationalism, the black tide of all "isms".' See *A Walk with a White Bushman*, Penguin edition, page xx.

62 B. Allen, *The Proving Grounds*, dustjacket blurb.
63 B. Allen, *The Proving Grounds*, page 69.
64 N. Lewis, *A View of the World*, Eland edition, page 143.
65 Interview with Norman Lewis, 17.10.1990.
66 D. H. Lawrence, *Mornings in Mexico* (London, Heinemann 1975), page 1.
67 J. Raban, *Arabia Through the Looking Glass*, Flamingo edition, page 15.
68 P. Brent, *Far Arabia*, page 22.
69 The Collected Works of C. G. Jung, Volume 11, *Psychology and Religion: West and East*, H. Read, M. Fordham & G. Adler (Eds.), (London, Routledge & Kegan Paul, 1987), pages 308–309.
70 F. McLynn, *Burton: Snow upon the Desert*, page 367.
71 E. Newby, *A Short Walk in the Hindu Kush*, Picador edition, page 247.
72 Interview with Geoffrey Moorhouse, 31.7.89.
73 D. Murphy, *Where the Indus is Young*, Century edition, pages 261–2.
74 W. Thesiger, *Arabian Sands*, Penguin edition, page 80.
75 G. Maxwell, *Harpoon at a Venture*, Four Square edition, page 96.
76 J. Raban, *Coasting*, Picador edition, pages 46–7.
77 P. L. Fermor, *A Time of Gifts*, Penguin edition, pages 84–8.
78 P. L. Fermor, *The Traveller's Tree*, Penguin edition, page 329.

Notes

79 D. Murphy, *In Ethiopia With A Mule*, page 84.
80 Alexandra David-Neel (1868–1969). After an unhappy childhood, during which she ran away to England, David-Neel became *première chanteuse* at the Opéra-Comique. She also was a student of theosophy and Buddhism at the Sorbonne, visiting India, Ceylon and North Africa. In 1911 as a journalist she was commissioned to interview the Dalai Lama near Darjeeling, India. She stayed fourteen years, travelling to Tibet, Burma, Bhutan, Japan, Korea and across the Gobi Desert to Kumbum Monastery on the Tibetan border. In 1923 at the age of fifty-four she embarked on her journey to Lhasa reaching it the following year, the first European woman ever to do so. Typically, her claim to have travelled to and to have lived in Lhasa for two months was subsequently disputed. Her last travels, in China for a period of eight years, only came to a close when she was seventy-seven. David-Neel's books include *My Journey to Lhasa*, *Tibetan Journey* and *Magic and Mystery in Tibet*.

Chapter 8: Greece – The Dark Crystal

1 P. Fussell, *Abroad*, page 95.
2 P. Fussell, *Abroad*, page 79.
3 R. Byron, *The Road to Oxiana*, Picador edition, page 9.
4 R. Byron, *The Byzantine Achievement*, Routledge edition, pages xii–xiii.
5 Lecky's *History of European Morals*, quoted in *The Byzantine Achievement*, Routledge edition, page xxxxi.
6 C. Sykes, *Four Studies in Loyalty*, Century Hutchinson edition, page 107.
7 R. Byron, *The Byzantine Achievement*, Routledge edition, page 102.
8 R. Byron, *The Station*, Century edition, page 81.
9 R. Byron, *The Station*, Century edition, page 113.
10 R. Byron, *The Byzantine Achievement*, Routledge edition, page xvii.
11 R. Byron, *The Station*, Century edition, page 38.
12 R. Byron, *The Station*, Century edition, pages 37–8.
13 R. Byron, *The Byzantine Achievement*, Routledge edition, pages 199–200.
14 C. Sykes, *Four Studies in Loyalty*, Century Hutchinson edition, page 150.
15 C. Sykes, *Four Studies in Loyalty*, Century Hutchinson edition, page 107.
16 R. Byron, *The Station*, Century edition, page 13.
17 R. Byron, *The Byzantine Achievement*, Routledge edition, page 45.
18 R. Byron, *The Station*, Century edition, page 14.
19 C. Sykes, *Four Studies in Loyalty*, Century Hutchinson edition, page 104.
20 P. Fussell, *Abroad*, page 79.
21 R. Byron, *The Road to Oxiana*, Picador edition, page 56.
22 R. Byron, *The Road to Oxiana*, Picador edition, page 47.
23 R. Byron, *The Road to Oxiana*, Picador edition, page 37.
24 *The Independent*, 12.4.1991.
25 R. Byron, *The Station*, Century edition, page 195.
26 R. Byron, *The Byzantine Achievement*, Routledge edition, page 14.
27 *The Independent*, 12.4.1991.
28 R. Byron, *The Byzantine Achievement*, Routledge edition, page 18; see also F. Brodie, *The Devil Drives*, pages 42–3, and F. McLynn, *Burton: Snow upon the Desert*, page 19.
29 I. MacNiven (Ed.), *The Durrell-Miller Letters, 1935–1980*, page 51.
30 L. Durrell, *Prospero's Cell*, paperback edition, page 59.
31 P. Fussell, *Abroad*, page 95.
32 R. Aldington, 'A Note on Lawrence Durrell', *The World of Lawrence Durrell* (New York, Dutton, 1974), page 3.

33 L. Durrell, *Prospero's Cell*, paperback edition, page 12.
34 L. Durrell, *Prospero's Cell*, paperback edition, page 19.
35 L. Durrell, *Prospero's Cell*, paperback edition, page 96.
36 L. Durrell, *Spirit of Place*, paperback edition, pages 302–3.
37 L. Durrell, *Spirit of Place*, paperback edition, page 301.
38 L. Durrell, *Prospero's Cell*, paperback edition, page 42.
39 L. Durrell, *Prospero's Cell*, paperback edition, page 45.
40 L. Durrell, *Prospero's Cell*, paperback edition, page 126.
41 W. Manchester, *The Caged Lion: Winston Spencer Churchill, 1932–1940* (London, Michael Joseph, 1988), page 343.
42 L. Durrell, *Prospero's Cell*, paperback edition, page 114.
43 L. Durrell, *Reflections on a Marine Venus*, paperback edition, page 171.
44 L. Durrell, *Reflections on a Marine Venus*, paperback edition, pages 178–9.
45 L. Durrell, *Spirit of Place*, paperback edition, page 83.
46 L. Durrell, *Spirit of Place*, paperback edition, page 85.
47 H. Miller, *The Colossus of Maroussi*, Penguin edition, page 39.
48 I. MacNiven (Ed.), *The Durrell-Miller Letters, 1935–1980*, page 148.
49 I. MacNiven (Ed.), *The Durrell-Miller Letters, 1935–1980*, page 271.
50 H. Miller, *The Colossus of Maroussi*, Penguin edition, page 51.
51 P. L. Fermor, *The Traveller's Tree*, Penguin edition, page 75.
52 P. L. Fermor, *Mani*, Penguin edition, page 137.
53 R. Byron, *The Byzantine Achievement*, Routledge edition, page 22.
54 H. Miller, *The Colossus of Maroussi*, Penguin edition, page 51.
55 P. L. Fermor, *Mani*, Penguin edition, page 241.
56 I. MacNiven (Ed.), *The Durrell-Miller Letters, 1935–1980*, page 148.
57 P. L. Fermor, *Roumeli*, Penguin edition, page 172.
58 L. Durrell, *Bitter Lemons*, page 127.
59 L. Durrell, *Bitter Lemons*, page 209.
60 L. Durrell, *Bitter Lemons*, page 222.
61 L. Durrell, *Bitter Lemons*, page 224.
62 L. Durrell, *Bitter Lemons*, page 217.
63 L. Durrell, *Bitter Lemons*, page 223.
64 L. Durrell, *Bitter Lemons*, page 246.
65 L. Durrell, *Bitter Lemons*, page 192.
66 L. Durrell, *Bitter Lemons*, page 228.
67 I. MacNiven (Ed.), *The Durrell-Miller Letters, 1935–1980*, page 267.
68 I. MacNiven (Ed.), *The Durrell-Miller Letters, 1935–1980*, page 269.
69 L. Durrell, *Bitter Lemons*, page 156.
70 L. Durrell, *Prospero's Cell*, paperback edition, page 14.
71 L. Durrell, *Prospero's Cell*, paperback edition, page 15.
72 I. MacNiven (Ed.), *The Durrell-Miller Letters, 1935–1980*, page 186.
73 See P. L. Fermor, *Mani*, Penguin edition, page x.
74 O. Lancaster, *Classical Landscape with Figures* (1975 edition) pages 62–3.
75 I. MacNiven (Ed.), *The Durrell-Miller Letters, 1935–1980*, page 134.
76 P. L. Fermor, *Mani*, Penguin edition, pages 123–6.
77 I. MacNiven (Ed.), *The Durrell-Miller Letters, 1935–1980*, page 134.
78 P. L. Fermor, *Mani*, Penguin edition, page 228.
79 R. Byron, *The Station*, Century edition, page 39.
80 R. Byron, *The Byzantine Achievement*, Routledge edition, page 288.
81 P. L. Fermor, *Mani*, Penguin edition, page 63.
82 C. Sykes, *Four Studies in Loyalty*, Century Hutchinson edition, page 178. Sykes was

Notes

actually wrong. Byron's destination was not Greece, but Meshed in Persia: see R. Byron, *The Station*, Century edition, page 13.

83 D. Powell, *The Villa Ariadne*, page 166.
84 W. Stanley Moss, *Ill Met by Moonlight*, Efstathiadis edition, pages 93–107.
85 P. L. Fermor, *Mani*, Penguin edition, dustjacket blurb.
86 P. L. Fermor, *Mani*, Penguin edition, page 44.
87 P. L. Fermor, *Mani*, Penguin edition, page 241.
88 P. L. Fermor, *Roumeli*, Penguin edition, page 105.
89 P. L. Fermor, *Mani*, Penguin edition, page 161.
90 P. L. Fermor, *Mani*, Penguin edition, page 33.
91 P. L. Fermor, *Mani*, Penguin edition, pages 35–6.
92 P. L. Fermor, *Mani*, Penguin edition, page 38.
93 P. L. Fermor, *A Time of Gifts*, Penguin edition, page 41.
94 P. L. Fermor, *The Traveller's Tree*, Penguin edition, page 273.
95 W. Thesiger, *Arabian Sands*, Penguin edition, page 92.
96 P. Marsden-Smedley & J. Klinke, *Views From Abroad* (London, Paladin, 1989), page 29.
97 P. L. Fermor, *The Traveller's Tree*, Penguin edition, page 87. It is typical of Fermor's delight purely in the sounds of words that he has confessed to an early addiction to saying things backwards. See *A Time of Gifts*, Penguin edition, pages 273–4. Sometimes, however, his arrangement of sentences simply for their audible effect can be taken to excess: for example 'and the Austrian army, awfully arrayed, boldly, by battery, besieged Belgrade'. See *Between the Woods and the Water*, Penguin edition, page 51.
98 P. L. Fermor, *Mani*, Penguin edition, page 299.
99 P. L. Fermor, *A Time to Keep Silence*, Penguin edition, page 37.
100 H. Miller, *The Colossus of Maroussi*, Penguin edition, page 52.
101 P. L. Fermor, *Mani*, Penguin edition, pages 277–8.
102 L. Durrell, *The Greek Islands* (London, Faber & Faber, 1978; paperback 1980), page 18.
103 P. L. Fermor, *Mani*, Penguin edition, page 287.
104 H. Miller, *The Colossus of Maroussi*, Penguin edition, page 48.
105 L. Durrell, *Bitter Lemons*, page 127.

Chapter 9: The Real Tibet of my Imagination

1 P. L. Fermor, *Mani*, Penguin edition, pages 4–5.
2 J. MacGregor, *Tibet: A Chronicle of Exploration*, page 292.
3 The French traveller killed at Nagchuka in Tibet was Jules Dutreuil de Rhins, in 1894. Evidence was subsequently provided by one of his own employees that he had brought the attack upon himself by his own offensive behaviour. This version of affairs was disputed by Dutreuil de Rhins's companion, Fernand Grenard. See Peter Hopkirk's *Trespassers on the Roof of the World*, pages 102–4. The Englishman who was severely tortured was Henry Savage Landor, in 1897. The authenticity of Landor's account of his misadventures has also been disputed. Again, see Hopkirk's *Trespassers on the Roof of the World*, pages 114–36.
4 E. R. Huc & J. Gabet, *Travels in Tartary, Thibet and China, 1844–1846*, Dover edition, volume II, page 148.
5 F. M. Bailey, *No Passport to Tibet*, pages 18–22.
6 F. Kingdon Ward, *The Riddle of the Tsangpo Gorges*, page 205.
7 P. Fleming, *Bayonets to Lhasa*, Readers Union edition, pages 259–60.
8 P. Fleming, *Bayonets to Lhasa*, Readers Union edition, page 260.
9 L. A. Waddell, *Lhasa and Its Mysteries*, page 1.

10 L. A. Waddell, *Lhasa and Its Mysteries*, page 1.
11 F. Spencer Chapman, *Lhasa The Holy City*, Readers Union edition, pages 30–31.
    Frederick Spencer Chapman, 1907–71, was educated at Sedbergh School and St John's College, Cambridge. During his years at university he befriended the explorer, Gino Watkins, who invited him on an expedition to Greenland. Chapman's record of his experiences on the British Arctic Air Route Expedition was published in 1932 in his first travel book, *Northern Lights*. This was followed two years later by *Watkins' Last Expedition*, an account of a second Greenland journey during which its leader, Watkins, was killed. While teaching at Aysgarth School in north Yorkshire Chapman was asked to accompany a Himalayan expedition in 1935. His period in Asia culminated in his climbing of the 7,000-metre Tibetan peak, Chomo Lhari, and his invitation to join the Gould mission to Lhasa in 1938, the subject of his third book, *Lhasa The Holy City*. During the war Chapman distinguished himself as an expert on Asian jungle warfare, earning the DSO in 1944. These experiences were recorded in his most successful book *The Jungle is Neutral*. During the post-war period Chapman occupied a range of educational posts, but was increasingly frustrated by a sense of failure, and finally shot himself in Reading on 8 August 1971. He received a string of awards for his travels, including the Gill Memorial from the Royal Geographical Society (1941) and the Lawrence of Arabia memorial medal from the Royal Central Asian Society (1950).
12 H. Harrer, *Seven Years in Tibet*, page vii.
13 P. Fleming, *Bayonets to Lhasa*, Readers Union edition, page 151.
14 F. Younghusband, *India and Tibet*, page 178.
15 C. Allen, *A Mountain In Tibet*, page 16.
16 F. O'Connor, *Things Mortal*, page 55.
17 J. Hanbury-Tracy, *Black River of Tibet*, page 33.
18 R. Kaulback, *Tibetan Trek*, pages 67–8.
19 F. Kingdon Ward, *The Land of the Blue Poppy*, page 48.
20 M. C. Goldstein & C. M. Beall, *Nomads of Western Tibet*, page 22.
21 P. Fleming, *Bayonets to Lhasa*, Readers Union edition, pages 240–41.
22 P. Fleming, *Bayonets to Lhasa*, Readers Union edition, page 102.
23 L. A. Waddell, *Lhasa and Its Mysteries*, page 101.
24 L. A. Waddell, *Lhasa and Its Mysteries*, page 1.
25 L. A. Waddell, *Lhasa and Its Mysteries*, page 41.
26 L. A. Waddell, *Lhasa and Its Mysteries*, page 160.
27 Ostensibly the Indian government justified the mission to Lhasa as an attempt to resolve long-standing legal disputes, in which they had been the injured party. These included: the grazing of Tibetan livestock in British-claimed territory; the overturning of British boundary posts by Tibetans; their obstructive behaviour over British trade facilities in Tibet. In reality, however, the mission was a simple exercise in imperial domination. Its real motive was to pre-empt Russian diplomatic activity in Lhasa, and to establish Tibet as a buffer state within the Anglo-Indian political hegemony. The Anglo-Tibetan Convention signed by Younghusband in the Potala in 1904 guaranteed that the Tibetans would not cede, lease or sell any part of their territories without prior British consent; that they would not allow any foreign power to intervene in Tibetan affairs without prior British consent; nor give any railway, road or mining concessions nor even dispose of their own revenues without agreement from their southern neighbours. They were obliged to open up three trade marts to the British and destroy all fortifications between British India and Gyantse and Lhasa. The Tibetans were obliged to pay an indemnity of £500,000 to cover the cost of the British military invasion and to hand some territory (the strategically important Chumbi Valley) over to British control for seventy-five years until the debt was paid. The last two clauses were later abandoned by the British Conservative government.

The more sinister nature of Britain's purpose in Tibet, which had been presented to the world as the rectification of years of Tibetan intransigence, was fully revealed in a letter from the Prime Minister of the day, Arthur Balfour, to Edward VII. In it he discussed the steps that might be taken if the Tibetans refused to conclude a signed agreement:

> We cannot retire without striking some blow at an enemy, which will neither keeps its old engagements nor discuss new ones. The Cabinet decided that, if the [Dalai] Lama refuses even to consider our very reasonable and moderate offers, we have no choice but to turn the expedition from a peaceful into a punitive one: and with every regard to the religious feelings of the Tibetans, to destroy such buildings as the walls and the gates of the city, and to carry [off] some of the leading citizens as hostages.

This classic piece of Balfourian casuistry disguised a policy that had a much less high-sounding title amongst Indian army circles – 'butcher and bolt'. Peter Fleming, a commentator highly sympathetic to the agents and sponsors of the British mission, called Balfour's proposed course of action 'petulant, barbarous and sterile'. See *Bayonets to Lhasa*, Readers Union edition, pages 237–8.

28 L. A. Waddell, *Lhasa and Its Mysteries*, page 39.

29 F. Spencer Chapman, *Lhasa The Holy City*, Readers Union edition, page 316.

30 F. Spencer Chapman, *Lhasa The Holy City*, Readers Union edition, page 44.

31 E. R. Huc & J. Gabet, *Travels in Tartary, Thibet and China, 1844–1846*, Dover edition, volume II, page 191.

32 F. Spencer Chapman, *Lhasa The Holy City*, Readers Union edition, page 158.

33 S. & R. Gelder, *The Timely Rain*, page 113.

34 Another example of the deep, almost obsessive fear that could be aroused in Protestant Britain towards religious personnel who also wielded political power was the general response at the turn of the century to a personality in the Lhasan government called Dorjieff. This monk was a Buryat Mongol from the region of Lake Baikal and thus a Russian citizen by birth. However, he had studied in Tibet for many years and, by virtue of his talents and the patronage of the Dalai Lama, had risen to a position of some influence in the Lhasan government. It was his journeys to western Russia, to raise funds to finance the studies of other Buryat Buddhist monks and to act as a quasi-official diplomat on behalf of Tibet, that first aroused British suspicions. Peter Fleming has argued that, although Dorjieff's contacts with Russian court members were probably without any real political significance, it was with his appearance that 'The Tibetan problem, for so long a petty administrative-diplomatic imbroglio, began to assume a strategic significance' (*Bayonets to Lhasa*, page 45).

In an atmosphere of ignorance and conjecture, Dorjieff loomed large in the British imagination, and loomed larger, perhaps, for being a monk. One of the interesting things about Dorjieff was his characterisation by Britons, who so often portrayed him as a mysterious, sinister, creepy, Fu Manchu-like *éminence grise*. Typically Waddell called him an 'evil genius', and asserted without any concrete evidence that 'On getting the ear of the young Dalai Lama he poisoned his mind against the English' (*Lhasa and Its Mysteries*, pages 387 and 38 respectively). Although there were additional ingredients to arouse public interest in the case of Rasputin, there seem to be some parallels between the fascination with Dorjieff and with the later Russian holy man.

35 L. Thomas Jr., *Out Of This World* (London, Travel Book Club, 1952), page 135.

36 L. A. Waddell, *Lhasa and Its Mysteries*, page 410.

37 L. A. Waddell, *Lhasa and Its Mysteries*, page 446.

38 L. A. Waddell, *Lhasa and Its Mysteries*, page 228.

39 L. A. Waddell, *Lhasa and Its Mysteries*, pages 238–9.
40 L. A. Waddell, *Lhasa and Its Mysteries*, page 241.
41 F. Spencer Chapman, *Lhasa The Holy City*, Readers Union edition, page 54.
42 L. A. Waddell, *Lhasa and Its Mysteries*, pages 192 and 199.
43 L. A. Waddell, *Lhasa and Its Mysteries*, page 446.
44 F. Mariani, *Secret Tibet*, page 82.
45 F. Younghusband, *India and Tibet*, page 124.
46 E. R. Huc & J. Gabet, *Travels in Tartary, Thibet and China, 1844–1846*, Dover edition, volume II, page 32.
47 F. Kingdon Ward, *The Land of the Blue Poppy*, pages 60–61.
48 *Geographical Journal*, volume 108, page 233.
49 J. Hanbury-Tracy, *Black River of Tibet*, pages 159–60.
50 J. Hanbury-Tracy, *Black River of Tibet*, page 42.
51 F. Younghusband, *India and Tibet*, page 124.
52 F. Spencer Chapman, *Lhasa The Holy City*, Readers Union edition, page 244.
53 P. Fleming, *Bayonets to Lhasa*, Readers Union edition, page 221.
54 S. & R. Gelder, *The Timely Rain*, page 22.
55 J. Hanbury-Tracy, *Black River of Tibet*, page 35.
56 L. Thomas Jr., *Out Of This World*, page 132.
57 R. Kaulback, *Tibetan Trek*, page 214.
58 J. Hanbury-Tracy, *Black River of Tibet*, page 221.
59 R. Kaulback, *Tibetan Trek*, page 148.
60 R. Kaulback, *Tibetan Trek*, page 265.
61 R. Kaulback, *Tibetan Trek*, page 187.
62 R. Kaulback, *Tibetan Trek*, page 103.
63 R. Kaulback, *Tibetan Trek*, page 255.
64 R. Kaulback, *Tibetan Trek*, page 230.
65 R. Kaulback, *Tibetan Trek*, page 231.
66 R. Kaulback, *Tibetan Trek*, page 277.
67 F. Kingdon Ward, *The Land of the Blue Poppy*, page 57.
68 J. Hanbury-Tracy, *Black River of Tibet*, page 160.
69 J. Hanbury-Tracy, *Black River of Tibet*, page 229.
70 F. Spencer Chapman, *Lhasa The Holy City*, Readers Union edition, pages 287–8.
71 J. Hanbury-Tracy, *Black River of Tibet*, page 160.
72 H. Harrer, *Seven Years in Tibet*, page x.
73 P. Theroux, *Riding the Iron Rooster*, Penguin edition, page 472.
74 R. Kaulback, *Tibetan Trek*, page 68.
75 J. Hanbury-Tracy, *Black River of Tibet*, page 74.
76 J. Hanbury-Tracy, *Black River of Tibet*, page 159.
77 J. Hanbury-Tracy, *Black River of Tibet*, pages 57–8.
78 S. & R. Gelder, *The Timely Rain*, page 71.
79 J. Hanbury-Tracy, *Black River of Tibet*, page 28.
80 J. Hanbury-Tracy, *Black River of Tibet*, page 86.
81 J. Hanbury-Tracy, *Black River of Tibet*, page 69.
82 L. Thomas Jr., *Out Of This World*, page 25.
83 Sven Hedin, *To The Forbidden Land*, pages 96–9.
84 C. Allen, *A Mountain In Tibet*, page 201.
85 F. Kingdon Ward, *The Riddle of The Tsangpo Gorges*, page 205.
86 H. Harrer, *Return to Tibet*, Penguin edition, page 173.
87 A. David-Neel, *My Journey to Lhasa*, Virago edition, page 17.
88 A. David-Neel, *My Journey to Lhasa*, Virago edition, page 76.

Notes

89 A. David-Neel, *My Journey to Lhasa*, Virago edition, pages 40 and 141.

90 A. David-Neel, *My Journey to Lhasa*, Virago edition, page 79.

91 J. Hanbury-Tracy, *Black River of Tibet*, page 29.

92 J. Hanbury-Tracy, *Black River of Tibet*, page 52.

93 F. Spencer Chapman, *Lhasa The Holy City*, Readers Union edition, page 32.

94 L. Thomas Jr., *Out Of This World*, page 33.

95 L. Thomas Jr., *Out Of This World*, page 131.

96 L. A. Waddell, *Lhasa and Its Mysteries*, pages 292–3.

97 L. A. Waddell, *Lhasa and Its Mysteries*, page 329.

98 V. Kewley, *Tibet: Behind the Ice Curtain*, page 19.

99 V. Kewley, *Tibet: Behind the Ice Curtain*, page 103.

100 *Tibet and the Chinese People's Republic*: A Report to the International Commission of Jurists by Its Legal Inquiry Committee on Tibet (Geneva: International Commission of Jurists, 1960), page 278.

101 V. Kewley, *Tibet: Behind the Ice Curtain*, pages 121–5.

102 V. Kewley, *Tibet: Behind the Ice Curtain*, page 91.

103 J. Hanbury-Tracy, *Black River of Tibet*, page 57.

104 S. & R. Gelder, *The Timely Rain*, page 127.

Chapter 10: The Coca-Cola Age

1 N. Lewis, *A Dragon Apparent*, Eland edition, page 17.

2 N. Lewis, *A Dragon Apparent*, Eland edition, page 8.

3 N. Lewis, *A Dragon Apparent*, Eland edition, page 12.

4 W. Thesiger, *Arabian Sands*, Penguin edition, page 11.

5 W. Thesiger, *Arabian Sands*, Penguin edition, page 9.

6 E. Newby, *A Traveller's Life*, pages 301–2.

7 L. Durrell, *Spirit of Place*, paperback edition, page 156.

8 L. Durrell, *Spirit of Place*, paperback edition, page 158.

9 L. Durrell, *Spirit of Place*, paperback edition, page 94.

10 P. L. Fermor, *Mani*, Penguin edition, pages x–xi.

11 P. L. Fermor, *The Traveller's Tree*, Penguin edition, pages 58–9.

12 P. L. Fermor, *The Traveller's Tree*, Penguin edition, page 59.

13 C. Thubron, *Jerusalem*, Century edition, page 148.

14 D. Murphy, *In Ethiopia With A Mule*, page 40.

15 R. Byron, *The Road to Oxiana*, Picador edition, page 74.

16 R. Byron, *The Road to Oxiana*, Picador edition, pages 74–7.

17 J. Gunther, *Inside Africa*, page ix.

18 J. Gunther, *Inside Africa*, pages 56 and 75.

19 J. Gunther, *Inside Africa*, page 186.

20 J. Gunther, *Inside Africa*, page 103.

21 J. Gunther, *Inside Africa*, page 101.

22 J. Gunther, *Inside Africa*, pages 48, 50 and 187.

23 D. Murphy, *Where the Indus is Young*, Century edition, page 15.

24 L. Durrell, *Spirit of Place*, paperback edition, pages 296–8.

25 W. Thesiger, *Arabian Sands*, Penguin edition, page 82.

26 W. Thesiger, *The Life of My Choice*, page 443.

27 W. Thesiger, *Arabian Sands*, Penguin edition, page 11.

28 Interview with Wilfred Thesiger, 17.5.1989.

29 H. St J. Philby, *Arabia of the Wahhabis*, page 6.

30 R. Byron, *The Station*, Century edition, page 206.

31 P. L. Fermor, *Roumeli*, Penguin edition, page 116.
32 P. Fussell, *Abroad*, page 215.
33 E. Newby, *A Short Walk in the Hindu Kush*, Harvill edition, page 12.
34 E. Newby, *A Traveller's Life*, page 301.
35 A. Moorehead, *No Room in the Ark*, Penguin edition, page 92.
36 P. Fussell, *Abroad*, page 210.
37 F. Spencer Chapman, *Lhasa The Holy City*, Readers Union edition, page 42.
38 H. M. Stanley, *How I Met Livingstone*, Time Life edition, page 338.
39 See F. McLynn, *Stanley: The Making of an African Explorer*, pages 54, 117, 134–5; also F. McLynn, *Stanley: Sorcerer's Apprentice*, page 396.
40 P. L. Fermor, *Mani*, Penguin edition, page 30.
41 P. L. Fermor, *Mani*, Penguin edition, pages 31–2.

Bibliography

Unpublished Sources

Papers of Lieutenant-Colonel Frederick Marshman Bailey, 1900–67 (MSS. EUR. F. 157),
    India Office Library and Records, London (IOR).
Colonial Office Files, CO 1015/479, Public Record Office, London (PRO).
Hogarth Press Archive, University of Reading Library, Reading (URL)
Longmans Archive, University of Reading Library, Reading (URL).
Papers of Richard Meinertzhagen, Rhodes House Library, Oxford (RHL).

Published Sources

Adams, R., *The Adventures of Gavin Maxwell*, London, Ward Lock, undated.
Alexander, P. F., *William Plomer, A Biography*, Oxford, Oxford University Press, 1989.
Allen, B., *The Proving Grounds*, London, HarperCollins, 1991.
Allen, C., *A Mountain In Tibet*, London, André Deutsch, 1982.
Bailey, F. M., *China–Tibet–Assam*, London, Jonathan Cape, 1945.
———. *Mission to Tashkent*, London, Jonathan Cape, 1946.
———. *No Passport to Tibet*, London, Rupert Hart-Davis, 1957.
Baker, S. W., *The Albert N'Yanza, Great Basin of the Nile*, London, Macmillan, 1866.
Balfour, P., *The Orphaned Realm*, London, Percival Marshall, 1951.
Bass, C., *Inside the Treasure House: A Time in Tibet*, London, Gollancz, 1990.
Bedford, S., *A Visit to Don Octavio*, London, Collins, 1960.
Bordewich, F. M., *Cathay: A Journey in Search of Old China*, London, Grafton, 1991.
Brent, P., *Far Arabia: Explorers of the Myth*, London, Weidenfeld & Nicolson, 1977.
Brodie, F. M., *The Devil Drives: a Life of Sir Richard Burton*, London, Eyre & Spottiswoode,
    1967 (London, Eland Books, 1986).
Burton, R., *First Footsteps in East Africa*, London, Tylston & Edwards, 1894.
———. *The Lake Regions of Central Africa*, London, Longmans Green, 1860.
Butler, L., *Robert Byron: Letters Home*, London, John Murray, 1991.
Byron, R., *Europe in the Looking Glass*, London, Routledge, 1926.
———. *The Station*, London, Duckworth, 1928 (Century, London, 1984).
———. *The Byzantine Achievement*, London, Routledge, 1929 (Routledge & Kegan Paul,
    London, 1987).
———. *First Russia, Then Tibet*, London, Macmillan, 1933 (Harmondsworth, Penguin,
    1985).

————. *The Road to Oxiana*, London, Macmillan, 1937 (London, Picador, 1981).

Cameron, J., *An Indian Summer*, London, Macmillan, 1974.

Cameron, K. M., *Into Africa: The Story of the East African Safari*, London, Constable, 1990.

Campbell, J., *The Hero with a Thousand Faces*, Princeton, Princeton University Press, 1949 (St Albans, Paladin, 1988).

————. *Oriental Mythology: The Masks of God*, Harmondsworth, Penguin, 1982.

Carpenter, F. I., *Laurens van der Post*, New York, Twayne, 1969.

Chatwin, B., *In Patagonia*, London, Jonathan Cape, 1977.

————. *The Songlines*, London, Jonathan Cape, 1988.

————. *Utz*, London, Jonathan Cape, 1988.

————. *What Am I Doing Here*, London, Jonathan Cape, 1989.

David-Neel, A., *My Journey to Lhasa*, London, Heinemann, 1927 (London, Virago, 1983).

Debenham, F., *Kalahari Sand*, London, G. Bell, 1953.

Douglas, N., *Siren Land*, London, Dent, 1911.

————. *Old Calabria*, London, Secker & Warburg, 1915.

————. *South Wind*, London, Secker & Warburg, 1917.

Durrell, L., *Prospero's Cell*, London, Faber & Faber, 1945 (Faber paperback, 1952).

————. *Reflections on a Marine Venus*, London, Faber & Faber, 1953 (Faber paperback, 1960).

————. *Bitter Lemons*, London, Faber & Faber, 1957.

————. *Spirit of Place*, London, Faber & Faber, 1969 (Faber paperback, 1988).

————. *Sicilian Carousel*, London, Faber & Faber, 1976.

————. *The Greek Islands*, London, Faber & Faber, 1978 (Faber paperback, 1980).

————. *Caesar's Vast Ghost*, London, Faber & Faber, 1990.

Farson, N., *Behind God's Back*, London, Victor Gollancz, 1940.

Fermor, P. L., *The Traveller's Tree*, London, John Murray, 1950 (Harmondsworth, Penguin, 1984).

————. *The Violins of Saint-Jacques*, John Murray and André Deutsch, 1953.

————. *A Time to Keep Silence*, London, John Murray, 1957 (Harmondsworth, Penguin, 1988)

————. *Mani*, London, John Murray, 1958 (Harmondsworth, Penguin, 1984).

————. *Roumeli*, London, John Murray, 1966 (Harmondsworth, Penguin, 1983).

————. *A Time of Gifts*, London, John Murray, 1977 (Harmondsworth, Penguin, 1979).

————. *Between the Woods and the Water*, London, John Murray, 1986 (Harmondsworth, Penguin, 1988).

Fleming, P., *Brazilian Adventure*, London, Jonathan Cape, 1933.

————. *News from Tartary*, London, Jonathan Cape, 1936.

————. *Bayonets to Lhasa*, London, Rupert Hart-Davis, 1961 (London, Readers Union, 1962).

Frater, A., *Chasing the Monsoon*, London, Viking, 1990.

Frere, R., *Maxwell's Ghost*, London, Victor Gollancz, 1976.

Freeth, Z. & Winstone, V., *Explorers of Arabia – from the Renaissance to the Victorian Era*, London, George Allen & Unwin, 1978.

Fussell, P., *Abroad: British Literary Travelling Between the Wars*, Oxford, Oxford University Press, 1980.

Gavet-Imbert, M., (Ed.), *The Guinness Book of Explorers and Exploration*, London, Guinness, 1991.

Gelder, S. & R., *The Timely Rain*, London, Hutchinson, 1964.

Goldstein, M. C. & Beall, C. M., *Nomads of Western Tibet*, London, Serindia, 1990.

Gunther, J., *Inside Africa*, London, Hamish Hamilton, 1955.

Hanbury-Tracy, J., *Black River of Tibet*, London, Frederick Muller, 1938.

Bibliography

Harrer, H., *Seven Years in Tibet*, London, Rupert Hart-Davis, 1953.
————. *Return to Tibet*, London, Weidenfeld & Nicolson, 1984 (Harmondsworth, Penguin, 1985).
Holt, P., *In Clive's Footsteps*, London, Hutchinson, 1990.
————. *The Big Muddy*, London, Hutchinson, 1991.
Homer, *The Odyssey*, Harmondsworth, Penguin, 1976.
Hopkirk, P., *Trespassers on the Roof of the World*, London, John Murray, 1982.
Huc, E. R. & Gabet, J., *Travels in Tartary, Thibet and China, 1844–1846*, London, Routledge, 1928 (London, Dover, 1987).
Hudson, M., *Our Grandmother's Drums*, London, Secker & Warburg, 1989.
Hudson, W. H., *Far Away and Long Ago*, London, Dent, 1918.
Huxley, E., *Red Strangers*, London, Chatto & Windus, 1939.
————. *The Sorcerer's Apprentice*, London, Chatto & Windus, 1948.
————. *A Thing to Love*, London, Chatto & Windus, 1954.
————. *Four Guineas*, London, Chatto & Windus, 1954.
————. *The Red Rock Wilderness*, London, Chatto & Windus, 1957.
————. *The Flame Trees of Thika*, London, Chatto & Windus, 1959.
————. *The Mottled Lizard*, London, Chatto & Windus, 1962.
————. *Their Shining Eldorado*, London, Chatto & Windus, 1967.
————. *Nellie: Letters from Africa*, London, Weidenfeld & Nicolson, 1980.
————. *Out in the Midday Sun*, London, Chatto & Windus, 1985.
Kaulback, R., *Tibetan Trek*, London, Hodder & Stoughton, 1934.
Keay, J., *When Men and Mountains Meet*, London, John Murray, 1977.
————. (Ed.). *The Royal Geographical Society History of World Exploration*, London, Hamlyn, 1991.
Kewley, V., *Tibet: Behind the Ice Curtain*, London, Grafton, 1990.
Kingdon Ward, F., *The Land of the Blue Poppy*, Cambridge, Cambridge University Press, 1913.
————. *The Riddle of the Tsangpo Gorges*, London, Edward Arnold, 1926.
————. *Modern Exploration*, London, Jonathan Cape, 1945.
Kinglake, A. W., *Eothen*, London, 1844.
Lancaster, O., *Classical Landscape with Figures*, London, John Murray, 1947, 1975.
Lawrence, T. E., *Seven Pillars of Wisdom*, London, Jonathan Cape, 1935.
————. *The Mint*, London, Jonathan Cape, 1955.
Lewis, N., *A Dragon Apparent*, London, Jonathan Cape, 1951 (Eland, London, 1982).
————. *Golden Earth*, London, Jonathan Cape, 1954.
————. *Naples '44*, London, Collins, 1978.
————. *Voices of the Old Sea*, London, Hamish Hamilton, 1984 (Harmondsworth, Penguin, 1985).
————. *A View of the World*, London, Eland, 1986.
————. *The Missionaries*, London, Secker & Warburg, 1988.
————. *A Goddess in The Stones*, London, Jonathan Cape, 1991.
Liddell, R., *Aegean Greece*, London, Jonathan Cape, 1954.
Lister, C., *Between Two Seas*, London, Secker & Warburg, 1991.
Livingstone, D., *Missionary Travels and Researches in South Africa*, London, John Murray, 1857.
MacGregor, J., *Tibet: A Chronicle of Exploration*, London, Routledge & Kegan Paul, 1970.
MacNiven, I., (Ed.). *The Durrell-Miller Letters, 1935–1980*, London, Faber & Faber, 1988.
Marco Polo, *The Travels*, Harmondsworth, Penguin, 1979.
Mariani, F., *Secret Tibet*, London, Hutchinson, 1954.
Maxwell, G., *Harpoon at a Venture*, London, Rupert Hart-Davis, 1952 (London, Four Square, 1966).

————. *God Protect me from my Friends*, London, Longmans Green, 1956 (London, Readers Union, 1957).

————. *A Reed Shaken by the Wind*, London, Longmans Green, 1957 (London, Four Square, 1959).

————. *The Ten Pains of Death*, London, Longmans Green, 1959.

————. *Ring of Bright Water*, London, Longmans Green, 1960.

————. *The Rocks Remain*, London, Longmans Green, 1963.

————. *Lords of the Atlas*, London, Longmans Green, 1965 (London, Century, 1983).

————. *The House of Elrig*, London, Longmans Green, 1965 (Harmondsworth, Penguin, 1974).

————. *Raven Seek Thy Brother*, London, Longmans Green, 1968.

Mazrui, A., *The Africans*, London, BBC Publications, 1986.

McLynn, F., *Stanley: The Making of an African Explorer*, London, Constable, 1989.

————. *Burton: Snow upon the Desert*, London, John Murray, 1990.

————. *Stanley: Sorcerer's Apprentice*, London, Constable, 1991.

Meinertzhagen, R., *Kenya Diary*, Edinburgh, Oliver & Boyd, 1957.

Melchett, S., *Passionate Quests*, London, Heinemann, 1991.

Migot, A., *Tibetan Marches*, London, Rupert Hart-Davis, 1955.

Miller, H., *The Colossus of Maroussi*, London, Secker & Warburg, 1942 (Harmondsworth, Penguin, 1985).

Millman, L., *Last Places*, London, André Deutsch, 1990.

Monroe, E., *Philby of Arabia*, London, Faber & Faber, 1973.

Moorehead, A., *No Room in the Ark*, London, Hamish Hamilton, 1959 (Harmondsworth, Penguin, 1962).

————. *The White Nile*, London, Hamish Hamilton, 1960.

Moorhouse, G., *Calcutta*, London, Weidenfeld & Nicolson, 1971.

————. *The Fearful Void*, London, Hodder & Stoughton, 1974 (St Albans, Paladin, 1975).

————. *India Britannica*, London, Collins Harvill, 1983.

————. *To the Frontier*, London, Hodder & Stoughton, 1984.

————. *Imperial City*, London, Hodder & Stoughton, 1988.

Murphy, D., *In Ethiopia With A Mule*, London, John Murray, 1968.

————. *Where the Indus is Young*, London, John Murray, 1977 (London, Century, 1983).

Newby, E., *A Short Walk in the Hindu Kush*, London, Secker & Warburg, 1958 (London, Picador, 1981).

————. *Slowly Down The Ganges*, London, Hodder & Stoughton, 1966.

————. *A Traveller's Life*, London, Collins, 1982 (London, Picador, 1983).

————. *On the Shores of the Mediterranean*, London, Collins Harvill, 1984.

————. *A Book of Travellers' Tales*, London, Collins, 1985.

O'Connor, F., *Things Mortal*, London, Hodder & Stoughton, 1940.

Philby, H. St J., *The Heart of Arabia*, London, Constable, 1922.

————. *Arabia of the Wahhabis*, London, Constable, 1928.

————. *The Empty Quarter*, London, Constable, 1933 (London, Century, 1986).

————. *Arabian Days*, London, Robert Hale, 1948.

————. *A Pilgrim in Arabia*, London, Robert Hale, 1948.

————. *Arabian Highlands*, New York, Cornell University Press, 1952.

————. *Forty Years in the Wilderness*, London, Robert Hale, 1957.

Powell, D., *The Villa Ariadne*, London, Hodder & Stoughton, 1973.

Psychoundakis, G., *The Cretan Runner*, Athens, John Murray, 1955.

Raban, J., *Arabia Through the Looking Glass*, London, Collins, 1979 (London, Fontana, 1983).

————. *Old Glory*, London, Collins, 1981.

————. *Coasting*, London, Collins Harvill, 1986 (London, Picador, 1987).

Bibliography

Raine, K., *The Lion's Mouth*, London, Hamish Hamilton, 1977.

Robinson, J., *Wayward Women*, Oxford, Oxford University Press, 1990.

Said, E. W., *Orientalism*, London, Routledge & Kegan Paul, 1978.

Schapera, I. (Ed.). *Livingstone's Missionary Correspondence 1841–1856*, London, Chatto & Windus, 1961.

Seth, V., *From Heaven's Lake*, London, Chatto & Windus, 1983.

Somerville, C., *The Other British Isles*, London, Grafton, 1990.

Somerville-Large, P., *A Shaggy Yak Story*, London, Sinclair-Stevenson, 1991.

Speke, J. H., *Journal of the Discovery of the Source of the Nile*, London, Blackwood, 1863 (London, Dent, 1906).

Spencer Chapman, F., *Lhasa The Holy City*, London, Chatto & Windus, 1940 (London, Readers Union, 1940).

Stanley, H. M., *How I Found Livingstone*, London, Sampson Low, 1872 (Amsterdam, Time Life, 1972).

————. *Through The Dark Continent*, London, Sampson Low, 1878.

————. *In Darkest Africa*, London, Sampson Low, 1890.

Stanley Moss, W., *Ill Met By Moonlight*, London, George Harrap, 1950.

Stark, F., *The Valley of the Assassins*, London, John Murray, 1936.

————. *The Southern Gates of Arabia*, London, John Murray, 1936.

————. *Perseus in the Wind*, London, John Murray, 1948.

————. *Traveller's Prelude*, London, John Murray, 1950.

————. *Beyond Euphrates*, London, John Murray, 1951 (London, Century, 1983).

————. *The Coast of Incense*, London, John Murray, 1953.

————. *Riding to the Tigris*, London, John Murray, 1959.

————. *Dust in the Lion's Paw*, London, John Murray, 1961.

Stevens, S., *Malaria Dreams: An African Adventure*, London, Simon & Schuster, 1990.

Swinson, A., *Beyond the Frontiers: The Biography of Colonel F. M. Bailey – Explorer and Secret Agent*, London, Hutchinson, 1971.

Sykes, C., *Four Studies in Loyalty*, London, Collins, 1946 (London, Century Hutchinson, 1986).

Taylor, S., *The Mighty Nimrod: A Life of Frederick Courteney Selous*, London, Collins, 1989.

Theroux, P., *The Great Railway Bazaar*, London, Hamish Hamilton, 1975.

————. *The Old Patagonian Express*, London, Hamish Hamilton, 1979.

————. *The Kingdom by the Sea*, London, Hamish Hamilton, 1983.

————. *Riding the Iron Rooster*, London, Hamish Hamilton, 1988 (Harmondsworth, Penguin, 1989).

————. *Travelling The World*, London, Sinclair-Stevenson, 1990.

Thesiger, W., *Arabian Sands*, London, Longmans Green, 1959 (Harmondsworth, Penguin, 1984).

————. *The Marsh Arabs*, London, Longmans Green, 1964 (Harmondsworth, Penguin, 1985).

————. *Desert, Marsh and Mountain*, London, Collins, 1979.

————. *The Life of My Choice*, London, Collins, 1987.

————. *Visions of a Nomad*, London, Collins, 1987.

Thomas, B., *Arabia Felix*, London, Jonathan Cape, 1932.

Thubron, C., *Mirror to Damascus*, London, Heinemann, 1967.

————. *The Hills of Adonis*, London, Heinemann, 1968.

————. *Jerusalem*, London, Heinemann, 1969 (London, Century, 1986).

————. *Journey Into Cyprus*, London, Heinemann, 1975.

————. *Behind the Wall*, London, Heinemann, 1987.

Turnbull, C., *The Forest People*, London, Jonathan Cape, 1961.

van der Post, L., *Venture to the Interior*, London, Hogarth Press, 1952.

————. *Flamingo Feather*, London, Hogarth Press, 1955.

————. *The Dark Eye in Africa*, London, Hogarth Press, 1955.

————. *The Lost World of the Kalahari*, London, Hogarth Press, 1958.

————. *The Heart of the Hunter*, London, Hogarth Press, 1961.

————. *The Seed and the Sower*, London, Hogarth Press, 1963.

————. *Journey Into Russia*, London, Hogarth Press, 1964.

————. *Jung and the Story of Our Time*, London, Hogarth Press, 1976.

————. *Yet Being Someone Other*, London, Hogarth Press, 1982.

————. *A Walk with a White Bushman*, London, Chatto & Windus, 1986 (Harmondsworth, Penguin, 1987).

Vaurie, C., *Tibet and Its Birds*, London, Witherby, 1972.

Waddell, L. A., *Lhasa and Its Mysteries*, London, John Murray, 1905.

Wilson, J., *Lawrence of Arabia*, London, Heinemann, 1989.

Young, G., *Return to the Marshes*, London, Collins, 1977.

————. *Worlds Apart: Travels in War and Peace*, London, Hutchinson, 1987 (Harmondsworth, Penguin, undated).

————. *Beyond Lion Rock*, London, Hutchinson, 1988.

Younghusband, F., *India and Tibet*, London, John Murray, 1910.

Index

Index

Index

Liberia, 81
Libya, 81
Liddell, Robert, 175
Livingstone, David, 3, 45, 50, 71, 139, 144, 165, 210
  Missionary Travels, 6–7
  Stanley encounters, 152–3
Lloyd, Lord, 155
Lloyd George, David, 186
Lohit River, 21, 22
Longman, Mark, 103
Luke, Sir Harry, 190

Macaulay, Rose, 190
Macdonald, David, *Twenty Years in Tibet*, 219
Mackenzie, Compton, 175
McLynn, Frank, 151–2, 162, 258
Madani el Glaoui, 102
Maghreb, 100
Malawi, 75
Manasarowar, Lake, 213, 238
Manchester Courier, 24
Manchuria, 23
Mariani, Fosco, *Secret Tibet*, 231
Manning, Thomas, 219
Marrakesh, 4
Mauritania, 143
Maxwell, Gavin, 17, 54, 58–9, 74, 135, 149, 165, 202, 248, 269 n.16, 270 n.52
  books, 163
  character, 98–9, 115–17
  God Protect me from my Friends, 101–2, 103, 108, 112–13, 116, 121, 123, 126, 128, 130
  Harpoon at a Venture, 107–8, 109, 110–11, 114, 117–21, 123–4, 163
  The Haywire Winter, 125
  The House of Elrig, 129
  Lords of the Atlas, 102–3, 112, 113, 116, 128, 129, 130
  mechanical equipment, 122–4
  physical frailty, 99–100
  Raven Seek Thy Brother, 101, 108, 111, 123, 129, 130
  A Reed Shaken by the Wind, 65–6, 74, 101, 103–4, 106, 108, 112, 130
  Ring of Bright Water, 101, 108, 109, 111, 115, 121, 122, 125, 127
  The Rocks Remain, 101, 108, 111, 123, 126, 127–8
  shark-fishing, 96–8, 106–8, 110–11, 117–21, 270 n.52, 270 n.63
  The Ten Pains of Death, 103, 108, 130, 179
  The Tunnel, 126
Mecca, 40, 46, 47, 132
Meinertzhagen, Richard, 166
Mekong, 213
Meru, Mount, 213
Mesopotamia, 41, 42, 263 n.6
Milarepa, 229
Miller, Henry, 175, 177, 184, 185, 193, 205
  The Colossus of Maroussi, 192–3
Mir Samir, 140, 141, 142, 143
Miriam bint Abdullah al Hasan, 46
Missouri River, 148
Mlanje, Mount, 71, 75–6, 78, 79, 93–4

Monemvasia, 176
Monroe, Elizabeth, 53
Moorehead, Alan, 71, 252
  The White Nile, 146
Moorhouse, Geoffrey, 5, 104, 162–3
  Against All Reason, 134
  Calcutta, 106
  The Fearful Void, 134–5, 142–4
Morocco, 17, 53, 55, 69, 100, 102, 111, 248
Morris, Jan, 5, 176
Morshead, Henry, 3, 22, 26–7, 29, 35
Mortimer, Raymond, 75, 136
Moscow, 21
Moss, William Stanley, 195
Mount Athos, 171, 175
Mountbatten, Lord, 162
Mourtzinos, Strati, 198–200
Mozambique, 81
Muhammad al Auf, 64, 68
Murphy, Dervla, 5, 71, 74, 135, 164–5, 247
  Full Tilt, 158, 248
  A Place Apart, 165
  Where the Indus is Young, 163

Naipaul, V. S., 5
Namibia, 81, 82
National Review, 75
Navarino, battle of, 185–6
Nepal, 10, 32, 35, 36, 209
Newby, Eric, 5, 244–5, 249, 251, 252
  A Short Walk in the Hindu Kush, 140–2, 143, 158, 250–1
News Chronicle, 8
Nicolson, Harold, 75, 137, 138, 181
Nicosia, 190
Niebuhr, Carsten, 250
Niger River, 147, 210
Nile, 153, 165, 210
  source, 3, 144–9
Nimiec, Max, 191
North Africa, 125
North Yemen, 71
Northern Plateau, Tibet, 210
Norwich, John Julius, 173, 174
Nuristan, 140
Nyasaland, 75, 80, 82, 135
Nyika, 75, 79–80, 157

The Observer, 8
O'Connor, Frederick, 221
Okovango Swamp, 87
Oman, 55
  Imam of, 56
Omdurman, 57
Oxford Companion to English Literature, 5

Palestine, 41, 43, 263 n.6
Palgrave, W. P., 2
Panos, 188–9, 190
Papua New Guinea, 157, 251
Park, Mungo, 147, 165
Pasha el Atrish, Sultan, 57
Pax Romana, 173–4
Philby, Dora, 40, 46, 67

292

Index

Index